WITHDRAWN

COGNITIVE BEHAVIOURAL TREATMENT
OF SEXUAL OFFENDERS

WITHDRAWN

WILEY SERIES IN
FORENSIC CLINICAL PSYCHOLOGY

Edited by

Clive R. Hollin

Centre for Applied Psychology, The University of Leicester, UK

and

Mary McMurran

East Midlands Centre for Forensic Mental Health, Leicester, UK

COGNITIVE BEHAVIOURAL TREATMENT OF SEXUAL
OFFENDERS
William L. Marshall, Dana Anderson and Yolanda Fernandez

Further titles in preparation

VIOLENCE, CRIME AND MENTALLY DISORDERED
OFFENDERS: Concepts and methods for effective treatment and
prevention
Sheilagh Hodgins and Rüdiger Müller-Isberner (*Editors*)

COGNITIVE BEHAVIOURAL TREATMENT OF SEXUAL OFFENDERS

William L. Marshall
Dana Anderson
and
Yolanda Fernandez

Queen's University, Kingston, Ontario, and
Bath Institution Sexual Offenders' Program, Ontario, Canada

With contributions from

Rachel Mulloy
Queen's University, Kingston, Ontario, Canada
and
Anthony Eccles
Eccles, Hodkinson & Associates, Forensic Behaviour Services, Ontario, Canada

JOHN WILEY & SONS, LTD
Chichester · New York · Weinheim · Brisbane · Singapore · Toronto

Other Wiley Editorial Offices

John Wiley & Sons, Inc., 605 Third Avenue,
New York, NY 10158-0012, USA

WILEY-VCH Verlag GmbH, Pappelallee 3,
D-69469 Weinheim, Germany

Jacaranda Wiley Ltd, 33 Park Road, Milton,
Queensland 4064, Australia

John Wiley & Sons (Asia) Pte Ltd, 2 Clementi Loop #02-01,
Jin Xing Distripark, Singapore 129809

John Wiley & Sons (Canada) Ltd, 22 Worcester Road,
Rexdale, Ontario M9W 1L1, Canada

Library of Congress Cataloging-in-Publication Data

Marshall, William L.
   Cognitive behavioural treatment of sexual offenders / W.L.
Marshall, Dana Anderson, and Yolanda Fernandez.
      p.   cm. — (Wiley series in forensic clinical psychology)
   Includes bibliographical references and index.
   ISBN 0-471-97566-4 (pbk.)
   1. Sex offenders—Rehabilitation.   2. Cognitive therapy.
I. Anderson, Dana, 1968–   . II. Fernandez, Yolanda.   III. Title.
IV. Series.
RC560.S47M37   1999
616.85'830651—dc21   99–40981
                                                                              CIP

£24·95

British Library Cataloguing in Publication Data

A catalogue record for this book is available from the British Library

ISBN 0-471-97566-4

Typeset in 10/12pt Palatino by Dorwyn Ltd, Rowlands Castle, Hants
Printed and bound in Great Britain by Bookcraft (Bath) Ltd, Midsomer Norton, Somerset
This book is printed on acid-free paper responsibly manufactured from sustainable forestry,
in which at least two trees are planted for each one used for paper production.

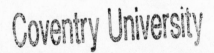

We hate the criminal, and deal with him severely, because we view in his deed, as in a distorting mirror, our own criminal instincts.

Sigmund Freud, 1856–1939

CONTENTS

LIST OF TABLES AND FIGURES

TABLES

FIGURES

ABOUT THE AUTHORS

William L. Marshall, Ph.D.

William L. Marshall, Ph.D., is a Professor of Psychology and Psychiatry at Queen's University in Kingston, Canada. Bill is an active clinician and researcher, and has over 200 publications including five books, most of which concern sexual offending. He is currently President-elect of the Association for the Treatment of Sexual Offenders and is a past recipient of that Association's Lifetime Achievement Award. Bill is also the 1999 recipient of the Queen Sophia Centre's Santiago Grisolia Chair.

Yolanda Fernandez, M.A.

Yolanda Fernandez has an M.A. from Queen's University. She is currently in the third year of a Ph.D. at Queen's. In addition to her studies, Yolanda is a therapist for the Sexual Offender Program at Bath Institution (a medium security federal penitentiary). She is an active researcher whose 15 publications include one co-authored book and one co-edited book.

Dana Anderson, M.A.

Dana Anderson has an M.A. from Queen's University. Dana is working on her Ph.D. at Queen's, and is the Clinical Director of the Sexual Offenders' Treatment Program at Kingston Penitentiary (a maximum security federal penitentiary). She is an active researcher and, among her publications, she has co-authored one book on the treatment of sexual offenders.

CONTRIBUTORS

Rachel Mulloy

Rachel Mulloy is a graduate student at Queen's University. Her interest in attachment theory began as an undergraduate at Simon Fraser University in British Columbia. Since then, she has used this theoretical framework in several different research areas, including romantic relationships, juvenile delinquency, and adult offending.

Anthony Eccles, Ph.D.

Dr Tony Eccles received his doctorate from Queen's University. He currently runs a community-based forensic clinic that provides assessment and treatment services to sexual offenders. His research interests include denial and minimization in sexual offenders and phallometric assessment methodology.

SERIES EDITORS' PREFACE

ABOUT THE SERIES

At the time of writing it is clear that we live in a time, certainly in the UK and other parts of Europe, if perhaps less so in other parts of the world, when there is renewed enthusiasm for constructive approaches to working with offenders to prevent crime. What do we mean by this statement and what basis do we have for making it?

First, by "constructive approaches to working with offenders" we mean bringing the use of effective methods and techniques of behaviour change into work with offenders. Indeed, this might pass as a definition of forensic clinical psychology. Thus, our focus is application of theory and research in order to develop practice aimed at bringing about a change in the offender's functioning. The word *constructive* is important and can be set against approaches to behaviour change that seek to operate by destructive means. Such destructive approaches are typically based on the principles of deterrence and punishment, seeking to suppress the offender's actions through fear and intimidation. A constructive approach, on the other hand, seeks to bring about changes in an offender's functioning that will produce, say, enhanced possibilities of employment, greater levels of self-control, better family functioning, or increased awareness of the pain of victims.

A constructive approach faces the criticism of being a "soft" response to damage caused by offenders, neither inflicting pain and punishment nor delivering retribution. This point raises a serious question for those involved in working with offenders. Should advocates of constructive approaches oppose retribution as a goal of the criminal justice system as incompatible with treatment and rehabilitation? Alternatively, should constructive work with offenders take place within a system given to retribution? We believe that this issue merits serious debate.

However, to return to our starting point, history shows that criminal justice systems are littered with many attempts at constructive work with offenders, not all of which have been successful. In raising the spectre of success, the second part of our opening sentence now merits attention: that is, "constructive approaches to working with offenders *to prevent crime*". In order to achieve the goal of preventing crime, interventions must focus on the right targets for behaviour change. In addressing this crucial point, Andrews and Bonta (1994) have formulated the *need principle*:

> Many offenders, especially high-risk offenders, have a variety of needs. They need places to live and work and/or they need to stop taking drugs. Some have poor self-esteem, chronic headaches or cavities in their teeth. These are all "needs". The need principle draws our attention to the distinction between *criminogenic* and *noncriminogenic* needs. Criminogenic needs are a subset of an offender's risk level. They are dynamic attributes of an offender that, when changed, are associated with changes in the probability of recidivism. Non-criminogenic needs are also dynamic and changeable, but these changes are not necessarily associated with the probability of recidivism. (p. 176)

Thus, successful work with offenders can be judged in terms of bringing about change in noncriminogenic need *or* in terms of bringing about change in criminogenic need. While the former is important and, indeed, may be a necessary precursor to offence-focused work, it is changing criminogenic need that, we argue, should be the touchstone of working with offenders.

While, as noted above, the history of work with offenders is not replete with success, the research base developed since the early 1990s, particularly the meta-analyses (e.g. Lösel, 1995), now strongly supports the position that effective work with offenders to prevent further offending is possible. The parameters of such evidence-based practice have become well established and widely disseminated under the banner of "What Works" (McGuire, 1995).

It is important to state that we are not advocating that there is only one approach to preventing crime. Clearly there are many approaches, with different theoretical underpinnings, that can be applied. Nonetheless, a tangible momentum has grown in the wake of the "What Works" movement as academics, practitioners, and policy makers seek to capitalise on the possibilities that this research raises for preventing crime. The task now facing many service agencies lies in turning the research into effective practice.

Our aim in developing this Series in Forensic Clinical Psychology is to produce texts that review research and draw on clinical expertise to advance effective work with offenders. We are both committed to the ideal of evidence-based practice and we will encourage contributors to the Series to follow this approach. Thus, the books published in the Series will not be practice manuals or "cook books": they will offer readers authoritative and critical information through which forensic clinical practice can develop. We are both enthusiastic about the contribution to effective practice that this Series can make and look forward to it developing in the years to come.

ABOUT THIS BOOK

There are many different types of crime but it is difficult to imagine, with the exception of murder, that any crime has the same destructive impact as sex offences. It is clear that the physical and psychological effects of sexual attacks can scar both individuals and their friends and families for life. The prevention of sexual crime is therefore one that rightly demands much public attention and concern: communities wish to be safe from all crime, but there is a particular anxiety that adults and children are safe from sexual attack.

Acknowledging that many sex offences remain hidden from public view, the issue remains of how the criminal justice system should manage known sex offenders. Professor Marshall is a leading advocate of the view that forensic clinical psychology has a role to play in preventing recidivism with this type of offender. In this book Professor Marshall and his colleagues offer a frank description and appraisal of many of the issues related to working with sexual offenders. The interplay between research and practice is writ large throughout the text, honestly highlighting the weaknesses as well as the strengths of the field.

In our view this is an excellent book that will richly inform researchers and practitioners. We are delighted to have it as the first book in our new Series.

August 1999

Clive Hollin and Mary McMurran

References

Andrews, D.A., & Bonta, J. (1994). *The Psychology of Criminal Conduct*. Cincinnati, OH: Anderson Publishing Co.

Lösel, F. (1995). Increasing consensus in the evaluation of offender rehabilitation? Lessons from recent research syntheses. *Psychology, Crime & Law*, **2**, 19–39.

McGuire, J. (Ed.). (1995). *What Works: Reducing Reoffending*. Chichester: John Wiley.

PREFACE

Despite the fact that we have had a clinical program for the assessment and treatment of sexual offenders in a community setting for 29 years, and in various prison settings for 26 years, this book represents our first attempt at comprehensively describing our work. Part of the impetus to write this book came in the form of a request by Clive Hollin for us to consider contributing to the series he is editing for John Wiley & Sons. In addition, we have increasingly had requests for details of our program that were not addressed in sufficient detail in our journal articles or book chapters; writing a book describing our program seemed like a reasonable response to these requests. We also teach a course on the assessment and treatment of sexual offenders for which there is no currently available book that covers the issues addressed in this course. Finally, we believe, rightly or wrongly, that there are some unique features to our approach in which others may be interested. John Wiley & Sons were, fortunately, persuaded that the publication of our manuscript was worthwhile. We hope this faith will be justified.

Sexual offending, as we will make clear in this book, is an extensive problem in our societies causing untold harm to many innocent victims. It, therefore, behooves us to take whatever actions we can to reduce its frequency and alleviate the suffering of those so abused. However, sexual offenders also typically have a personal history of abuse of various kinds and it seems obvious to us that most of them would prefer to live offence-free lives. It takes courage, however, for them to face their own problems and to deal with the consequences of their actions on their victims, the victims' families, and their own families and friends. Our treatment program presses these offenders into facing the facts and taking responsibility for their actions, but we attempt to do so in a firm but supportive manner.

We believe this is not only a humane approach, but also the most effective way to engage the offenders in the process of change toward a better, more satisfying, and less damaging lifestyle.

Many people, including numerous colleagues and ex-students, have helped us along the way. Without their very significant contributions, this book could not have been conceived in its present form. In particular, our erstwhile colleague and continuing friend, Howard Barbaree, has made an immeasurable and direct contribution to our thinking about sexual offenders. Similarly, Gene Abel, Richard Laws, Bill Murphy, Janice Marques, Bill Pithers and Vern Quinsey have indirectly contributed to, or challenged, our thinking over the years, and we are grateful to them.

In the process of producing this book, several people at John Wiley, namely Michael Coombs, Wendy Hudlass and Lesley Valerio, have been inexhaustibly patient in waiting for our manuscript, whose generation was held up by a seemingly endless series of unexpected delays. Clive Hollin has been his usual helpful self, and we thank him.

Our colleague, Liam Marshall, has offered support and challenges, and our partners, Jean, Steve, and Gord gave us encouragement when we needed it most. Most of all, we would like to thank Val Angus, who not only typed the manuscript, but also offered very constructive feedback. Val's patience and energy seem unlimited, and we are extremely grateful to her.

Finally, we thank our clients whose challenges and courage to change have made our work so rewarding.

WILLIAM L. MARSHALL
DANA ANDERSON
YOLANDA FERNANDEZ

Chapter 1

INTRODUCTION

> *Homo sum: humani nil a me alienum puto* (I am a man, and nothing
> pertaining to man is alien to me).
>
> Terence 190–159BC

Sexual offending constitutes a very serious problem in western societies.
While there are problems in providing an estimate of the incidence and
prevalence of sexual abuse, the available data strongly suggest that many
lives are damaged by these offenders. It is characteristically assumed that
the damage that results from sexual abuse is limited to the victim and,
indeed, the evidence reveals that in most cases the consequences to the
victim are extensive and traumatizing (Ageton, 1983; Beitchman et al., 1992;
Conte, 1988; Finkelhor & Browne, 1985; Koss & Harvey, 1991). However, the
victim's family (both present and future) is also profoundly affected and so
too are the members of the offender's family.

Official data, derived from police and court records, appear to be an
underestimate of the actual incidence. Many people indicate they have been
the victim of sexual abuse but have not reported the offence to the authorities, and this is true of child molestation (Russell, 1986) and rape (Russell,
1984). Although similar systematic studies of exhibitionism, voyeurism and
frotteurism have not been reported, it seems safe to assume that these crimes
are also markedly underreported. As a result, researchers have turned to
surveys of the general population to estimate the frequency of sexual crimes.

The Committee on Sexual Offenses against Children and Youth (1984)
reported the results of national surveys of Canadians. These data revealed
that one-half of the female and one-third of the male respondents had been
sexually victimized, with 70% of the male victims and 62% of the females
victims indicating that the assaults occurred when they were prepubescent.

Surveys in other countries have revealed similar figures (Katz, in press). In an examination of the rape of adult women, Marshall and Barrett (1990) estimated that, every seven minutes, a Canadian woman is sexually assaulted. Koss, Gidycz and Wisniewski (1987) found that 15% of a United States national sample of college women reported that they had been raped as an adult and a further 12% said a male had attempted to rape them. The results of an international survey (van Dijk & Mayhew, 1992) revealed somewhat different figures for rape across various European, Asian, and North and South Pacific nations, but in all cases the rates were sufficiently high to cause concern.

Rooth (1973) examined the convictions for exhibitionism in several countries. He concluded that it was by far the most commonly prosecuted sexual offence, accounting for over one-third of all convictions and as many as 50% of adult women report having been the victim of an exhibitionist (Di Vasto et al., 1984). Although there are no studies that have attempted to estimate the frequency of incidents of voyeurism and frotteurism, Abel (personal communication, 1996), who has considerable experience working with frotteurs, suggests that the rate is extremely high in persistently crowded places such as on rush-hour subway trains.

This high incidence of sexual offences calls for a systematic, sustained and rational approach. Unfortunately, such a response has been lacking, although there has been a marked increase in attention to the problem in recent years. Research examining the frequency of sexual offences and studies examining both victims and offenders has been modestly supported by public funding over the past two decades. However, our societies still rely heavily on the energy and goodwill of researchers and clinicians, and characteristically underfund their work. There are at least three areas toward which we should allocate resources and direct our energies: prevention, assistance for victims, and treatment for offenders.

The development of preventative programs would seem to be an obvious way to attempt to reduce the incidence of these damaging behaviours. To illustrate that a relatively simple program can have significant effects, we will describe the efforts made by a local child protection agency in Ontario, Canada. Selecting five schools to target, this agency introduced a simple educational component indicating that sexual abuse of children was reasonably common, and typically committed by a man the child thought they could trust. The children were instructed that, if they were to report such abuse, they would be believed and supported. Within two years, the number of reports of sexual abuse made by children in these schools, that were subsequently confirmed by police investigations, increased by almost 300%. In comparison, the schools that did not receive the educational component showed no increase in reports over the same period. No doubt there are other preventative approaches. Keith Kaufman and his colleagues at the

Columbus Children's Hospital in Ohio, for example, are attempting to discern the typical tactics that child molesters use to gain sexual assess to children (Kaufman et al., 1996). Their hope is that this will arm parents and agencies working with children in a way that will permit them to recognize potential offenders. Similarly, William O'Donohue and his colleagues at the University of Nevada in Reno are in the process of developing a program to sensitize college males to the issue of sexual assault and harassment. Hopefully there will be an expansion of prevention programs in the near future.

Perhaps the area of greatest neglect in society's current approach to sexual offending is the allocation of resources to assist victims. There have been some developments in providing help for victims through the criminal investigation and prosecution process, but these services remain rare and, where they do occur, they are often rather limited. All too often help is provided by women volunteers who, unfortunately, tend to burn out as a result of lack of support. Treatment of the victims and counselling for their families in Canada has been expected to be provided by current service agencies such as child protection agencies and mental health services, but rarely have additional funds been made available. The same seems to be true worldwide. Services for victims are all too often overloaded, so once again, workers in some agencies, particularly women's refuges and child protection services, have taken on the extra work in their own unpaid time. These inadequate responses to victims and their families by our societies should be a source of shame. Victims of sexual assault are, after all, innocent of any wrongdoing. Were adult males the primary victims of sexual assault, rather than women and children, this sorry state of affairs would almost certainly not exist.

Finally, interventions aimed at reducing the future risk to reoffend of sexual offenders will, if effective, serve to reduce the number of people victimized by these men. It is our view that such interventions should sensibly combine treatment with incarceration. These men knowingly engage in behaviours that are unlawful, as evidenced by the fact that they take great care to avoid detection and by the fact that most attempt to prevent their victims from reporting the offence. Thus, they are as culpable, and should be held equally responsible, for their crimes as are nonsex offenders. These men do not have a disease, nor indeed, any type of disorder, that places their aberrant behaviour beyond their control. An examination of their *modus operandi* reveals very clearly that their offensive actions are very much under their control; they often engage in quite complex manipulations of others and develop intricate strategies and plans for gaining access to victims. This is deliberate, well-controlled behaviour. Clear feedback from society, by way of a prison sentence, makes it apparent to these men, as it does to all other offenders, that their abusive actions are not acceptable. However, for the purpose of rehabilitation (and for that concern only) a period of 3–5 years seems to be sufficient to secure the leverage and time needed to effectively engage these men in treatment.

This line of reasoning is not the product of a vindictive sentiment as seems to be true of more draconian proposals such as castration (chemical or physical), life sentences, lifetime parole, most community notification proposals, and in its most extreme form, execution. It is difficult when dealing with an emotionally laden topic such as sexual offending to set aside our desire for vengeance to be wreaked upon these men, particularly when the media seem desperate to portray sexual offenders as evil and devoid of any possibility of redemption. However, society's decisions should be based on the following simple principle: What can we expect will maximally reduce the future risk that sexual offenders present? If this meant no time in prison, we would advocate such a strategy, but we do not believe this would effectively achieve the goal. If it meant treating these men with unqualified positive regard, as the early Rogerians might have suggested, we would advocate that, but again, we do not believe this would be effective. What we should do is follow what the data tell us, not what we think is best. In this book, we hope to persuade our readers that there is a reasonable, cost-effective, way to deal with sexual offenders that achieves the goal of significantly reducing the number of these men who reoffend.

AN APPROACH TO THE OFFENDER

Within the field of sexual offender research and therapy, there are those who take a punitive attitude toward these men and there are those who believe that treatment is a waste of time. Such views play into the current approach of the media and the rather inflammatory views of some members of society. However, it is important to note that there is little or no evidence to support these views.

To illustrate this, let us take the recommendation made by Quinsey (Quinsey, Khanna & Malcolm, 1996) that treatment efforts should be abandoned with sexual offenders. Instead, so Quinsey suggests, when they are finally returned to the community, sexual offenders should be intensively supervised for at least 10 years. Quinsey bases the former part of this proposal on his view that treatment with these men does not work. This view, in turn, derives from one of his own failed treatment efforts and his mistaken belief that data he had collected on a treatment program operated by Correctional Services of Canada's Regional Treatment Centre (Ontario) demonstrated that this program was also ineffective (Quinsey et al., 1996). When appropriate comparison data were provided (T. Nicholaichuk, personal communication, January, 1998) for this Corrections program, however, it was clear that treatment had been very effective (52% recidivism in the untreated comparison group, 27% in the treated group). As for Quinsey's own failed program, Marshall and Pithers (1994) provided a critical appraisal of this and essentially concluded that the treatment that was provided had been quite inadequate for what was an extremely dangerous group of offenders. While the issue of treatment effectiveness may be still somewhat uncertain, the balance of evidence so far can reasonably be interpreted as at least providing grounds for optimism.

Setting aside concerns about treatment effectiveness, what is the value of prolonged, intense supervision once a sexual offender is back in the community? Such intense supervision over a ten-year period would certainly be very expensive and there should, therefore, be some empirical or theoretical grounds for thinking that it would work before we implement such a program. First, let us note that there is no direct evidence at all in support of the value of such supervision. This is not to imply that all supervision should be abandoned. Short-term supervision is sensible, practical, economically feasible, and can be made quite effective (Hanson et al., 1997). However, the sort of supervision Quinsey is suggesting not only lacks data, there are good reasons to suppose it will not be effective. For example, work with children has shown that strict supervision by others prevents the development of the meta-cognitions necessary for self-control (Meichenbaum, 1977) and it has been found that, when children learn on their own, they not only do better, they also take greater responsibility for their learning (Ladouceur, 1995). Similarly, within token economies, it has been shown that once the monitoring of behaviours necessary to produce contingent rewards are withdrawn, the behaviours are no longer maintained (Kazdin, 1975). Finally, Lipper and Green's (1978) analysis of the "overjustification effect" makes it clear that there can be serious negative consequences of rewarding behaviours. Such behaviours can very easily come to be emitted only when the person dispensing the rewards (i.e., monitoring the behaviours) is present. These data appear to us to make a strong case against extended supervision of sexual offenders. We believe these data suggest that once supervision is withdrawn the abusive behaviour may re-emerge because the sexual offender will not only not have developed self-control, he will have come to accept that he needs supervision to avoid reoffending. +rewards.

In any case, those who advocate these various excessively punitive measures appear to be unaware of the evidence that casts doubts on their proposed strategy. Perhaps, as the philosopher, Barrows Dunham, suggested, ". . .the doctrine that you can't change human nature has a larger purpose: defence of the existing social arrangements" (p. 51, Dunham, 1947). We offer the following as an alternative view of sexual offenders, that is in keeping with not only a more humane view of these men, but is also consistent with the ethical guidelines of the professions involved in managing and treating sexual offenders.

Teratology (i.e., the study of monsters) is a legitimate and respected bio-logical discipline. The examination of physical deformities in development, it is expected, can lead to a better understanding of normative processes. As Stephen J. Gould (1983) points out, "The laws of normal growth are best formulated and understood when the causes of their exceptions can be established" (p. 187). Such accidents of physical development, when they occur in other humans, are characteristically regarded with repulsion and are seen as ugly and frightening, largely because we do not understand them and we fear what we do not comprehend. But is this appropriate, or should we at least try to be more compassionate? In fact, once we are privy to the details of even a bizarrely, physically deformed person's life (e.g., the gentle Joseph Merrick, the so-called Elephant Man), our discomfort and intrusive curiosity are replaced with an overwhelming concern, Sexual offenders can be construed as having a personal history that has psychologically deformed them, or rather, deformed a limited aspect of their behaviour.

It is important to note, however, that it is inappropriate to consider sexual offenders to be monsters. As Marshall (1996a) has pointed out, the actual offending behaviour of these men occupies a small proportion of their lives. Even if we add the time they spend on preoffence planning, grooming and manipulation, the total percentage of their time spent on sexual offending still falls well below 10%. For many, it is much lower. If readers find this hard to accept, we suggest you calculate for a real offender the time spent in planning and offending, and weigh it against his waking hours spent in mundane or prosocial behaviour. Everyone gets up in the morning, cleans his/her teeth, eats breakfast, goes to work, or searches for a job, and so on. We conducted such an analysis with a chronic predatory child molester who had offended against over 400 boys during a 20-year period, by relying on the very detailed (even obsessive) diaries that he kept prior to his arrest. As a result, we concluded that the time he spent on the whole process of seeking a victim and offending over that 20-year span amounted to no more than 8% of his time. The offences he committed had, not surprisingly, very damaging effects on most of his victims, and no doubt they and their families saw him as a monster. But does it make sense to completely define someone in terms of less than 8% of their behaviour? Every Sunday, this man volunteered his whole day to helping the infirm female residents of an old folks' home with no evidence (upon very thorough police interviews) of any untoward behaviour. These activities occupied more than 8% of his time, yet no one thought to define him entirely in terms of his caring and compassion for elderly women. He had been an accountant all his working life, but does the descriptor "accountant" any better convey the complex-ities, strengths, and weaknesses of this man than the descriptors monster, child molester, or helper of old people? We suggest not. Indeed, we believe that therapists spend far too much time focussing on clients' deficiencies, and not enough time encouraging them to believe in their strengths and capacities to change. The need most people, including therapists, have to pigeonhole others has not been particularly valuable in the history of humankind, or in psychological research, and has no place in treatment.

None of us has much control over our history and it is easy for those of us with comfortable lives to view with contempt people who fail to overcome their background. However, with privilege comes responsibility. It behooves us to do our best to display compassion, along with our concern to prevent further harm to innocent people, when we address the problem of sexual offending within our societies. Those of us who work with sexual offenders not only need to show respect for our clients, in order that they can come to believe they have the potential to change, we also should accept responsibility for educating the public toward a more tolerant attitude to these offenders, particularly those who seek to rehabilitate themselves. Not tolerance toward their offence behaviour, let us be clear, but acceptance of these offenders as part of the human spectrum to whom we all owe responsibility, and we should see them as potentially responsive to our efforts at rehabilitation.

In the course of our work with sexual offenders, we constantly have to make inferences about their motivation, thoughts, feelings and behaviours that are all too often obscure to the offender himself. How are we to do this? Perhaps the best way, and likely the way we usually do it, is to base our guesses on our understanding of our own processes and on the ways we often keep these processes opaque to ourselves. Each of us makes endless inferences each day about the meaning of and motives behind the behaviour of almost everyone with whom we come in contact. To do this with sexual offenders, however, we must consider them to be like ourselves, at least in terms of the processes that govern their behaviour. So long as we demonize sexual offenders, we will continue to struggle to understand them. Seeing them as more like us than different gives us a window into their world that would otherwise remain closed. Unless we accept that except for their offending behaviour sexual offenders do not differ from other people, we will never generate insights that will help these clients understand and change their behaviour. Even the worst of sexual offenders, the sadists and murderers are, in the course of their daily lives, hardly different from the rest of us. We want them to be different in order to distance ourselves from their behaviours, but we do so at a cost to our capacity to understand and treat them.

Sexual offending can be construed as behavioural teratology and, just as we can learn from physical deformities about normative developmental processes, so also can we learn from deformities of action about the etiology of normative human behaviour. In this sense, it is essential that our work with sexual offenders be embedded within a theoretical framework that can be fleshed out as we accumulate evidence from research and clinical endeavours. Insofar as we understand the etiology and maintenance of sexual offending, we will come to understand better how normal human behaviour evolves through each person's life. If we are open to it, each group session we spend with sexual offenders can teach us much about ourselves, about our own history and its meaning, and most of all, about our capacity for tolerance toward people while not necessarily tolerating some aspects of their behaviour.

Chapter 2

THE DEVELOPMENT OF COGNITIVE BEHAVIOURAL APPROACHES

That men do not learn very much from the lessons of history is the most important of all lessons of history.

Aldous Huxley, 1894–1963

Although from the time of John B. Watson (1924) behavioural analyses of human problems, and treatment procedures derived from these analyses, have been described in the literature, it was only during the 1960s that behaviour therapy emerged as an organized approach offering a unique way of conceptualizing and treating human problems. The applications of Watson's views by Mary Cover Jones (1924a), Knight Dunlap (1932), Edwin Guthrie (1935), and others, might have led to a far earlier development of behaviour therapy but, for a variety of reasons, Freudian approaches came to dominate psychological speculations about human behaviour.

The predominant philosophy of science during the 1920s and 1930s was logical positivism as exemplified by the so-called Vienna Circle (comprising, among others, Moritz Schlick, Rudolph Carnap and Otto Neurath). The verificationist perspective of this school essentially declared that the only meaningful propositions were those that could, at least in theory, be empirically tested. All propositions that eluded the possibility of confirmation or disconfirmation were to be disregarded as essentially metaphysical and unprovable statements. It is perhaps no surprise to note that Karl Popper, given his later definition of the task of science (Popper, 1959), was a younger and somewhat peripheral member of the Vienna Circle. Had this verificationist principal been rigorously applied to psychology at that time, behaviourism would have held a distinct advantage over theories that posited unconscious (and therefore, unobservable) processes governing human be-haviour. Indeed, Popper and other logical positivists condemned psycho-analysis as the very epitome of pseudoscience since its notion of the inexhaustible interpretability of the unconscious does not permit empirical analysis.

Unfortunately for behaviourism, Freud's (1933) theories proved very at-tractive to many philosophers who were influenced by Ludwig Wittgen-stein's remarkable lectures and discussions during the 1930s at Cambridge, and which were published posthumously in *Philosophical Investigations* (Wittgenstein, 1953). These followers of Wittgenstein saw a parallel between his view of the philosopher as the analyst of words whose aim was to clarify and resolve conceptual problems, and that of Freud as the analyst of the psyche whose goal was to clarify and resolve emotional problems. In philosophy, Wittgenstein's followers won the day and Freud's theories, ac-cordingly, gained in respectability. Freud's theories were embraced by pop-ular culture influencing writers, dramatists and movie-makers. For the therapists of the day, psychoanalysis found a welcoming audience eager to have a theoretical framework that relied on creative thought, thereby reliev-ing them of the painstaking and laborious task of doing research and being guided by its results. Behaviourism was denigrated as resting on mindless stimulus–response analysis which, it was said, missed the real wonder and complexity of human functioning. Psychoanalytic views seemed to raise the human mind to a richness and drama that fitted the view of themselves that people apparently wished to embrace.

Thus, although logical positivism permeated the thought of researchers and theorists in the physical and biological sciences, both experimental and clinical psychology, for the most part, turned their backs on behaviourism. Not only did Watson's (1919) revolt against mentalism have little impact on the practice of clinical psychology, its influence within experimental psychology was also rather limited until Hull began his pioneering work at Yale in the mid-1930s. Even then, it is important to note, the research at Yale began as an attempt to examine the possibility that experimental and observational data could be obtained in support of Freud's theory (Samuelson, 1981, 1985). Other researchers at Yale during this period included Neal Miller, John Dollard, O. Hobart Mowrer, and R.R. Sears. These five attempted to integrate Pavlovian conditioning theory and Freud's psychoanalysis (Dollard, Doob, Miller, Mowrer & Sears, 1939; Dollard & Miller, 1950), while ignoring Watson's radical behaviourism. It was only later, when Sears was asked by the New York based Social Science Research Council to survey the evidence for and against psychoanalysis, that it be-came clear that psychoanalytic approaches to therapy were seriously want-ing (Sears, 1943). Hans Eysenck's (1952) dramatic, and widely publicized, subsequent attack on psychoanalysis occurred at a time when at least some clinical psychologists were eagerly seeking an experimentally based approach to treatment. Eysenck's very influential paper, combined with Monte Shapiro's (1961; Shapiro & Nelson, 1955) advocacy of the single-case experimental analysis of clients' problems, paved the way for the emergence of behaviour therapy in Britain. At about the same time in North America, the influence of B.F. Skinner and his students was beginning to transform the approach of clinical psychologists dealing with a whole range of problems. Skinner's students saw these problems as amenable to an operant conditioning analysis within experimental single-case designs.

However, this emergence of behaviour therapy during the late 1950s and throughout the 1960s was certainly not the first time these approaches had been employed with clinical patients. Descriptions of psychological treatment procedures that were either explicitly behavioural, or that matched modern behavioural techniques, first appeared in the literature toward the end of the last century and in the early part of this century, although the Roman scholar, Pliny the Elder (23–79 AD) had far earlier advocated the use of aversive procedures to treat alcoholism. Some of these quasi-behavioural procedures described around the turn of the 20th century were aimed specifically at aberrant sexual behaviour. Charcot and Magnan (1882) directed a homosexual male to substitute images of women instead of men whenever he became sexually excited, and Schrenk-Notzing (1895) employed a similar procedure. Using what he called association therapy, Moll (1911) had men who were attracted to boys develop sexual interests in boyish women in order to move them toward more acceptable behaviour. These examples illustrate early attempts to apply what are now described as aversion therapy (Pliny the Elder), masturbatory reconditioning (Charcot & Magnan and Schrenk-Notzing), and a variant of what Barlow and Agras (1973) identified as shaping (Moll). It is as well to keep in mind that some developments in our field are not always as new as they seem and we might profit from an historical awareness of developments.

However, it was not just in the development of treatment procedures that there were important, but today all but lost, innovations. Alfred Binet, the French psychologist best known for developing intelligence tests for school children, articulated a theory of sexual deviations in the early 1900s that declared them to be learned responses. This learning was, according to Binet, often the result of accidental experiences with the deviant act. A theory that is even more akin to modern conceptualizations of the acquisition of deviant sexuality was advanced by Norman (1892). He declared that a sexual desire for unacceptable acts was formed by repeated masturbation to sexual fantasies involving specific deviant behaviours. In the 1960s, largely as a result of a growing acceptance at that time that sexual expressions were learned (Ford & Beach, 1952; Kinsey, Pomeroy, Martin & Gebhard, 1953), several authors outlined theories of sexual deviations that were remarkably similar to these early conceptualizations (e.g., Evans, 1968; McGuire, Carlisle & Young, 1965). Again, we are reminded that much of what we take to be recent advances are, in fact, older ideas in modern dress.

These early attempts, however, were isolated from each other so that a unified approach was not developed. Furthermore, these attempts remained remote from experimental research into psychological functioning. It was only with the articulation of behaviourism as a psychological and philosophical theory that it became obvious that the appropriate approach would be to systematically extrapolate laboratory observations to the remediation of human problems.

Watson's behaviourism grew out of his work at the University of Chicago and then at Johns Hopkins University, which he joined in 1908. Among Watson's colleagues were some like-minded individuals (e.g., Knight Dunlap, Herbert Jennings, and Karl Lashley) who influenced his thinking and encouraged his rejection of the structuralist and functionalist schools of psychology, both of which employed introspection in their search for the elements and processes of thought. Behaviour, declared Watson (1913), is the proper focus of the science of psychology, and, in his subsequent book (Watson, 1914) he outlined the relevant experimental applications of this principle to the analysis of animal behaviour. In 1919, Watson's second book extended these principles to human behaviour and laid the foundations for the development of behaviour therapy which sputtered into life intermittently over the next 40 years to finally blossom in the 1960s.

From Watson's early beginnings, several applications of a behavioural approach were reported or defined over the following four decades. However, because psychoanalysis had such a firm grip on the consciousness not only of mental health workers, but also of the intelligentsia and the general public, these sporadic endeavours by behaviourally oriented clinicians had little impact. Watson's doctoral student, Mary Cover Jones (1924a; 1924b) provided excellent demonstrations of the value of the direct application of conditioning procedures to the treatment of children's fears, and her work might otherwise have initiated a burst of behavioural treatments for various problems had the intellectual and socio-political climate been right. Unfortunately, Watson's affair with his student (later his wife), Rosalie Raynor, led to his public denunciation and withdrawal from academic and public life. As a result, behaviourism lost its dynamic leader and was, for the next several years, without a unifying base. Efforts to apply behaviour therapy became sporadic and isolated, although once the connection had been made between behavioural theory and animal learning studies on the one hand, and practical applications on the other, a slow but inexorable course of development was begun.

Over the next four decades (1920s to 1950s), studies of animal learning became increasingly detailed and complex, and theoretical interpretations were, correspondingly, increasingly sophisticated. Many students of animal learning recognized the relevance of their observations for human behaviour, and an increasing number devised treatment procedures based on knowledge derived from animal experimentation. Knight Dunlap (1932) described what he called "negative practice" which required clients to repeatedly engage in their undesirable behaviour. Dunlap recognized that simple repetition was not enough; certain conditions had to be obtained, otherwise repetition might increase rather than decrease the behaviour in question. In particular, repetition in the absence of reinforcement was thought to be necessary in order to produce extinction of the target behaviour. Many years later, Yates (1958) reformulated Dunlap's procedure in terms of Clark Hull's (1943) hypothetico-deductive theory, and effectively applied it to the problems of a ticquer.

Edwin Guthrie's (1935) associationism, or contiguity learning, also provided a basis for linking animal research and theory with the treatment of human problems. Guthrie believed that consequences did nothing to strengthen behaviour, but rather, by serving to remove the evoking stimulus (e.g., if you eat, you remove the stimulus of hunger), consequences ensure that unlearning will not occur; that is, the stimulus–response connection will not be disrupted by subsequent responses in the presence of the eliciting stimulus. Thus, in treatment aimed at eliminating undesirable responses, the therapist must ensure that alternative, preferably incompatible, responses occur in the presence of the eliciting stimulus. One way in which Guthrie suggested this could be achieved was by repeatedly presenting the stimulus at full strength, thereby continuously evoking the undesirable response. This, Guthrie said, would lead to the exhaustion of the undesirable response such that an alternative response (e.g., fatigue or boredom) would then come to be associated with the stimulus. Guthrie's procedure, then, foreshadowed the use of flooding therapy with phobic patients (Marshall, Gauthier & Gordon, 1979). In the late 1970s, Marshall (1979; Marshall & Lippens, 1977) utilized a variant of this procedure, which he called "satiation", to extinguish the provocative value of deviant sexual stimuli.

Prior to the revival of behavioural approaches in the late 1950s, several theorists either proposed learning-based accounts of human behaviour problems, or offered conditioning translations of psychodynamic formulations (Cameron & Margaret, 1951; Dollard & Miller, 1950; Mowrer, 1950; Shaffer, 1936). Similarly, a few practitioners described treatment procedures that were behaviourally based (Herzberg, 1945; Salter, 1949), and traditional forms of psychotherapy were construed as effective only insofar as conditioning or learning opportunities were fortuitously provided (French, 1933; Margaret, 1950; Shaffer, 1947). In a clear statement of this position, Shoben (1949) declared that "psychotherapy is essentially a learning process and should be subject to study as such." (p. 367).

THE BEGINNING OF THE MODERN ERA

After Eysenck's (1952) condemnation of traditional psychotherapy, as having failed to demonstrate any utility, the climate was finally ripe for a revolution in approach to psychological treatment. On the North American continent, and in Britain and South Africa, experimentally trained clinicians, dissatisfied with the failure of current treatment methods, began to look to psychological research for answers to the problems presented to them in their daily work. In 1958, Joseph Wolpe, a South African psychiatrist, published a landmark book, *Psychotherapy by Reciprocal Inhibition*, which served as a catalyst, particularly in Britain, for the development of behaviour therapy. In the 1950s, at the Institute of Psychiatry in London, a group of clinical psychologists (e.g., H. Gwynn Jones, Victor Meyer, Aubrey Yates) encouraged by the clinical director, Monte Shapiro, derived learning procedures to treat a variety of conditions. The subsequent arrival of one of Wolpe's students, Stanley Rachman, and the appointment of psychiatrists Michael Gelder and Isaac Marks, led to an expansion of the application of behaviour therapy to include the treatment of sexual deviations (Marks & Gelder, 1967; Marks, Gelder & Bancroft, 1970; Marks, Rachman & Gelder, 1965).

The British clinicians, for the most part, based their treatment techniques on Pavlovian conditioning, whereas North Americans were initially influenced most markedly by Skinner's (1938, 1953) operant analyses. In North America during this period, operant analyses were directly applied to modifying the behaviours of psychotics (Lindsley, 1960; 1963), retarded children (Bijou & Orlando, 1961), stutterers (Goldiamond, 1962) and autistic children (Ferster & DeMyer, 1962), to cite just a few of the legion of human problems addressed by manipulating the consequences of behaviour.

The treatment of sexual variants

In Britain, Skinner's views also generated some degree of interest. For example, Quinn, Harbison and McAllister (1970) employed a shaping technique, derived from Skinner's approach, to increase penile responses. They deprived a homosexual male of fluids for 18 hours and then used drinks as a reinforcer for increased erectile responses to images of females. Over 20 sessions of gradually increasing the required value of erectile responding before giving access to a drink, this patient displayed a changed gender orientation. Bancroft (1971) also used shaping to change the sexual desires of a masochist. Prior to treatment, this man generated full erections to the thought of a male beating him. The first step in Bancroft's procedure was to have the patient imagine that the male who was beating him was completely naked. Once the patient could do this and generate a full erection, he was required to imagine a naked female beating him. When he could achieve a full erection to this scene, the woman's whip was gradually reduced in size until it disappeared. Scenes were gradually changed in this way as a function of erection responses until the patient could imagine having intercourse with the woman. Two North American researchers, Barlow and Agras (1973), used a similar shaping procedure, except that they employed pictures which gradually faded from the deviant stimulus to an appropriate stimulus.

Initially these early articles, describing behavioural approaches to the treatment of aberrant sexual behaviours, involved primarily case reports with the majority utilizing some form of aversion therapy. In these procedures, an aversive event was paired with either images of the behaviour to be eliminated (classical conditioning), or with the enactment of some aspect of the aberrant behaviour (punishment). For example, the injection of apomorphine (or some other nausea-inducing substance) was associated with the sexual activities (or images of them) of homosexuals (Freund, 1960; James, 1962), transvestites (Blakemore, Thorpe, Barker, Conway & Lavin, 1963; Glynn & Harper, 1961) and fetishists (Raymond, 1956). Faradic aversion, where an uncomfortable electric shock to the arm or leg was associated with aberrant sexual images or acts, rapidly replaced apomorphine partly because the use of emetics was distressful to staff and patients, but also because the timing of the unpleasant event (nausea) was difficult to predict. Electric aversion therapy became the treatment of choice for homosexuals (Bancroft, 1969; McGuire & Vallance, 1964), transvestites and fetishists (Marks & Gelder, 1967; McGuire & Vallance, 1964) and for various sexual offenders (Abel, Levis & Clancy, 1970; Bancroft & Marks, 1968; Evans, 1968, 1970; Fookes, 1969; Marshall, 1971, 1973). The use of various other aversive events was also investigated, including foul odours (Colson, 1972; Laws, Meyer & Holmen, 1978), covert aversive images (Callahan & Leitenberg, 1973; Cautela, 1967) and the induction of shame or embarrassment (Serber, 1970, 1972; Wickramasekera, 1976). Overall, however, it must be said that aversion therapy, in any form, has not been convincingly demonstrated to be effective in producing long-lasting changes in sexual behaviour (Quinsey & Earls, 1990; Quinsey & Marshall, 1983).

The fact that aversive procedures were so readily utilized in the treatment of socially unacceptable sexual expressions reflects two things: (1) behaviourist views of the acquisition and modification of unusual sexual behaviours; and (2) a socially condoned negative view of those who displayed such behaviours. Behaviourist conceptualizations of eccentric and offensive sexuality was expressed most clearly by McGuire et al. (1965) in their seminal account of the conditioning bases of these behaviours. For them, early sexual experiences were of greatest importance because, to an inexperienced child or youth, these experiences provided the "fantasy which invariably accompanied later masturbation" (p. 185). It was this association, of masturbatory-linked sexual arousal and fantasy images, that McGuire et al. believed entrenched the aberrant sexual preferences. If these early experiences were with, for example, a young child, then sex with children would become established, by thereafter masturbating to such images, as the person's primary sexual preference. This hypothesis, although neither then nor now supported by more than anecdotal evidence (see O'Donohue & Plaud (1994) and Marshall & Eccles (1993) for reviews of the relevant literature), proved to be so appealing that it quickly came to be accepted as doctrine and persists to this day. Acceptance of this theory demands that we direct treatment at eliminating deviant sexual preferences.

This "sexual motivational" account of the acquisition of deviant sexual behaviour, and the corresponding targeting of deviant arousal as the prime focus of treatment, may, in part, have been so readily accepted because there was available a sophisticated measurement procedure that evaluated sexual preferences. Kurt Freund had developed the phallometric assessment technology in his native Czechoslovakia in 1957 and introduced the procedure to the neophyte behaviour therapists at the Institute of Psychiatry in London. Subsequently, Bancroft, Jones and Pullan (1966) and Barlow, Becker, Leitenberg and Agras (1970) developed somewhat simpler apparatuses to measure erectile responses. Having available objective measurement procedures that seemed to be less influenced by attempts at faking than were patients' self-reports, may have encouraged a predominant focus in treatment and theorizing on sexual motivation. These measures of erectile responding quickly became the standard in evaluating behavioural treatments of aberrant sexual behaviours and the influence on the field of Freund's innovative approach cannot be overestimated.

Because early behaviour therapists attempted to derive their procedures from laboratory studies of animal and human learning, it was quite logical to choose aversion therapy since it was clearly established that such procedures readily induced in animals an aversion to previously preferred stimuli or behaviours (Church, 1963; Franks, 1963; Solomon & Brush, 1956). Regardless of the laboratory evidence, it was also true that people who had difficulties controlling their appetitive behaviour (e.g., alcoholics, compulsive eaters, and sexual eccentrics) were regarded by many with scorn, if not contempt. This made it easy for both therapists and patients alike to accept punitive or aversive procedures as necessary treatment components for these problems.

These societal attitudes were essentially negative and had a strong punitive flavour, as exemplified in the various laws enacted against victimless sexual behaviours, simply because they were not the dominant form of sexual expression. Homosexuality took the brunt of this hostility, and it is no surprise that most of the early applications of a behavioural approach to supposedly deviant sexual expressions were unfortunately employed to alter the gender preferences of these adult males (Bancroft, 1969; Feldman & McCulloch, 1971). A long line of behavioural studies failed to address the ethical issues involved in such treatment. Finally, however, Davison (1974) made explicit the ethical problems and denounced attempts to change the orientation of homosexuals. Soon thereafter, the treatment of homosexuals was essentially abandoned by the majority of behaviourists, although some (e.g., McConaghy, 1993) continue to consider this an appropriate clinical service. Other behavioural interventions from this early era were aimed at changing the preferences of similarly nonoffensive, if eccentric, forms of sexual expression, such as fetishism and transvestism (Marks & Gelder, 1967).

These early applications contributed to the prevailing notion at the time (which still endures in some people) that behaviour therapists were insensitive and ethically naive. The truth is, many were. However, behaviour therapy, or at least its evolved form, cognitive behavioural therapy, now represents an ethically conscious, sophisticated approach that is capable of embodying all of the supposedly necessary features of good therapy (e.g., warmth, support, nonjudgmental). Unfortunately, negative societal views of sexual offenders are, if anything, stronger today than they were in the past, and it seems that some therapists share these popular views. Marshall (1996a) and Kear-Colwell and Pollack (1997) have argued that the use of severely confrontational approaches reflects an underlying abhorrence of these offenders by their therapists since the early evidence (Beech & Fordham, 1997) indicates that such approaches are ineffective compared with more compassionate and less judgmental ways of addressing these problems.

In addition to these ethical objections to the use of aversion therapy with homosexuals, its use may create other problems. Rachman and Teasdale (1969), for example, noted numerous possible undesirable consequences to the use of aversive procedures, including likely failures to generalize outside of the therapy office, broader suppression of appetitive responses, and the elicitation of aggression. In addition, aversion therapy may damage the client–therapist relationship and adversely affect other targets of treatment. As we will see in the chapter on treatment processes, one aspect of the job of the therapist is to instill in sexual offenders a sufficient sense of self-worth so they can rebuild their lives in a constructive and prosocial manner. Using aversion therapy may be counterproductive, not just because these procedures are punitive, but perhaps more importantly, because of the attitude that the use of such procedures may induce in both therapist and client. As it is, too many therapists seem to have problems in balancing the need to challenge sexual offenders with the need to maintain good relations with clients, without entrenching within treatment procedures the understandable animosity toward these men that most people feel.

As is evident from the preceding discussion, the earliest behavioural approaches to the modification of sexual offending reflected an assumption that such behaviours were distorted or deviant manifestations of sexual desire. This view lives on and is expressed, even if indirectly, by a number of current researchers and clinicians. Indeed, the view that deviant sexual preferences form the motivation for aberrant sexually related behaviours such as child molestation, rape, exhibitionism, voyeurism, and frotteurism, is typically identified as the *sine qua non* of the behavioural approach to these problems. In fact, the evidence supporting the view that the paraphilias are the manifestations of persistent sexual preferences is, at best, rather sparse. Reviews of the literature by Marshall and his colleagues (in press; Marshall & Eccles, 1991, 1993; Marshall & Fernandez, 1998), and O'Donohue and Plaud (1994), found little support for these claims or for the claim that such preferences result from conditioning processes. These issues will be taken up in more detail in the chapter on the modification of deviant preferences.

The treatment implications of this rather crude assumption (that the problem for sexual deviates is simply a distortion in the direction of their sexual desire) were made clear by Bond and Evans (1967). They declared that "if they (sexual deviants) can abstain from their deviant behaviour for a sufficient period of time, normal outlets for the control of sexual arousal will develop." (p. 1162). Bond and Evans saw this thesis as indicating that the optimal treatment for sexual deviates would simply involve reducing their deviant sexual responses. While this view is nowadays considered naive or overly simplistic, the notion that deviant sexual preferences are central to the motivational forces that drive deviant sexual behaviour remains an important aspect in most behavioural views of the etiology and treatment of sexual offending.

While cognitive behavioural approaches with sexual offenders have evolved into quite comprehensive programs, some still adhere to the sexual motivation account and advocate the use of some procedure to reduce deviant arousal (Quinsey & Earls, 1990). Quinsey and Earls (1990) note that, although electric aversion therapy has gone out of fashion, this was "certainly not on empirical grounds" (p. 285). This, unfortunately, could be read as suggesting that there is extensive research supporting the use of electric aversion with sexual offenders. This, however, is not true. The only report demonstrating, in a controlled comparative study, the clear efficacy of aversion therapy is one of Quinsey's own studies (Quinsey, Chaplin & Carrigan, 1980). McConaghy, for example, found not only that aversion therapy did not modify sexual preferences (McConaghy, 1975), but that it did not produce any signs of a conditioned aversive response (McConaghy, 1969). Despite these findings, Quinsey and his colleagues continued, at least until recently, to employ electric aversion as a significant component in their treatment of sexual offenders. For example, in a report by Rice, Quinsey and

Harris (1991), aversion therapy aimed at reducing deviant arousal was the primary focus in their description of their treatment of child molesters. These clients, housed in the Oak Ridge Mental Health Centre, were all chronic and quite dangerous offenders, and yet the program involved little more than the procedures aimed at reducing deviant arousal. No attempt was made to enhance appropriate sexual interests, although some of the participants also received limited social skills training and some were given sex education. Not surprisingly, this limited treatment with these very dangerous and chronic offenders was ineffective. A point that is often overlooked when considering the value of the Rice et al. report is that the program they evaluated originated in the 1970s. Consequently, the report can be seen as documenting the poverty of early programs based on the sexual motivation hypothesis.

Most clinicians who express a behavioural view would today consider the Rice et al. program to be a less than complete treatment for these very difficult clients, as, indeed, does the group from Oak Ridge themselves (see Quinsey, Chaplin, Maguire & Upfold, 1987). Nevertheless, so long as it is claimed that these offences are primarily sexually motivated, Rice et al.'s treatment program seems justified. If other components are to be added to treatment, then additional hypotheses regarding the etiology and maintenance of sexual offending must be added to the sexual motivation theory or an alternative or additional motivational theory must be proposed. Certainly, additional treatment targets have been added to most programs, but these targets have only rarely been derived from an explicit theory. As late as 1982, Kelly observed that 75% of behavioural treatment reports dealing with child molesters had as a major focus the suppression of deviant arousal.

The move to comprehensive programs

Marquis (1970) suggested that enhancing alternative, more acceptable sexual interests would constitute a satisfactory treatment for males who engaged in aberrant sexual behaviours. He provided numerous case illustrations of the effectiveness of what he called "orgasmic reconditioning", which was aimed solely at increasing the arousal elicited by normative sexual acts. Apparently it was assumed that making these acts attractive would eliminate the need to engage in deviant behaviours or would lead to an extinction of the sexual valence of such acts. Marquis, however, did not demonstrate that this happened, nor has there been any compelling evidence provided since to suggest that orgasmic reconditioning serves on its own as an effective treatment (Laws & Marshall, 1991). However, Marquis' technique did provide a means by which sexual offenders could enhance their attraction to socially acceptable sexual expressions, and it quickly came to be incorporated into many treatment programs.

Marshall (1971) proposed that modifying sexual preferences (i.e., reducing deviant arousal and increasing appropriate sexual interests) constituted an incomplete treatment program for sexual offenders. He suggested that many sexual offenders also lacked the social skills necessary to function effectively with adult partners, so that changing their sexual preferences alone would not guarantee they could act appropriately on these changed desires. Similar suggestions were later made by other authors (e.g., Barlow, 1974; Crawford, 1981). However, these recommendations took some time to be expressed in actual programs. Adams and Sturgis (1977) found that only 5% of treatment reports attempted to change more than two features of sexual offenders' problems. Barlow (1974) drew attention to the potential value of other behavioural interventions, and his article, although largely concerned with a review of studies of male homosexuals, encouraged the expansion of treatment targets in behavioural approaches with sexual offenders. These expansions directly followed the emerging trend in behaviour therapy at that time (Kazdin, 1978) to conceive of all psychological problems as multi-faceted and as requiring a component treatment approach rather than a single-technique intervention.

In a treatment report that involved clients with various sexual disorders, Marshall (1973) reported the first phallometric assessment of rapists and the first behavioural treatment of these offenders. In this program, Marshall used orgasmic reconditioning techniques to enhance appropriate sexual interests together with a form of electric aversion therapy, derived from Abel, Levis and Clancy (1970), to reduce deviant arousal. In addition, these clients were provided social skills training as part of their more general therapeutic treatment (Marshall & McKnight, 1975). This program proved to be effective in eliminating subsequent offensive acts and provided the basis for Marshall's later development of behavioural treatment programs for rapists and child molesters. However, these later developments involved a considerable expansion of the range of treatment techniques and were aimed at a much broader range of problems (Marshall, Earls, Segal & Darke, 1983).

A symposium held in San Francisco, at the 1975 meeting of the Association for the Advancement of Behaviour Therapy, brought together for the first time a group of behaviour therapists whose interests concerned the assessment and treatment of sexual offenders. Gene Abel and his colleagues, Edward Blanchard and Judith Becker, organized the symposium and invited Richard Laws and Bill Marshall to join them in presenting their tentative first steps toward a behavioural analysis of these offenders. This initial meeting led to subsequent larger gatherings of clinicians and researchers interested in this field, and these meetings ultimately led to the formation of the Association for the Behavioral Treatment of Sexual Abusers (the term,

Behavioral, has now been dropped from this title to more accurately reflect the breadth of orientations of the members and to indicate that strict behaviourism no longer adequately describes most of the work in the field).

Abel's own series of excellent studies (Abel, 1976; Abel, Barlow, Blanchard & Guild, 1977; Abel, Becker, Blanchard & Flanagan, 1981; Abel, Becker, Murphy & Flanagan, 1981) resulted in a considerable expansion of our knowledge of sexual offenders and his reports have inspired other researchers throughout the world. Abel and his colleagues described the development of their treatment program in a series of papers (Abel, Becker & Skinner, 1983; Abel, Blanchard & Becker, 1978; Abel, Osborn, Anthony & Gardos, 1992), and the evolution of his approach was matched by an expansion in the targets of other treatment programs for sexual offenders (Knopp, 1984; Marshall & Williams, 1975; Perkins, 1977). Indeed, Abel is correctly identified as the early leader in the development of the cognitive behavioural treatment for sexual offenders.

As noted, these changes in behavioural treatment programs reflected corresponding changes in behaviour therapy more generally. For instance, cognitive issues were directly brought into mainstream behaviour therapy in the mid-1970s by Donald Meichenbaum (1974) and Michael Mahoney (1974), and by co-opting elements in the treatment packages of the leading cognitive therapists, such as Aron Beck (1970) and Albert Ellis (1962). Earlier, Tolman (1948; 1952) and Guthrie (1959) had argued that mediating processes were essential to an understanding of both human and animal learning, and Miller, Galanter and Pribram (1960) had detailed a complex model that reconciled stimulus–response learning and cognition. Lloyd Homme's (1965) seminal article on coverants (i.e., the operants of the mind) applied operant conditioning analyses to mental functioning and provided the basis for Joseph Cautela's (1967) covert conditioning procedures. More recently, therapists have added to these elaborate programs components derived from Alan Marlatt's (Marlatt & Gordon, 1985) relapse prevention approach to the treatment of addictions. Janice Marques (1982, 1984) was the first to articulate the possible application of relapse prevention to the treatment of sexual offenders, and she and Bill Pithers (Pithers, Marques, Gibat & Marlatt, 1983) have been the foremost advocates of this approach. In this reformulation, relapse prevention forms the framework and justification for all the treatment components, and involves specific components that identify risk factors in order to develop strategies for avoiding or dealing with future risks.

Despite these complex changes, and their ready acceptance by the majority of practitioners in the field (Knopp, 1984), very little was done until recently to provide empirical evaluations of treatment. Since treatment outcome evaluations must wait for enough treated offenders to be discharged for sufficient time (with four years at risk being the minimum requirement), it is perhaps not surprising that few recidivism studies of treated offenders were conducted until the late 1980s. However, these considerations are not relevant to an evaluation of the efficacy of the various components of treatment, and yet only a handful of studies have examined whether or not specific treatment techniques achieve their stated goal. In one of the few early exceptions to this rule, Quinsey's (Quinsey, Chaplin & Carrigan, 1980) study of aversion therapy and biofeedback explored the utility of these procedures in reducing deviant sexual interests. On the other hand, despite their widespread popularity, few studies have examined the value of masturbatory techniques aimed at changing deviant arousal patterns (Laws & Marshall, 1991). For the various other components of comprehensive cognitive behavioural programs (e.g., social skills training, cognitive restructuring, empathy enhancement), little or no efforts were made until recently to determine their effectiveness in producing the changes deemed necessary. Clearly, one of the main tasks before us is to empirically justify the use of each of the components in our comprehensive treatment programs. However, if we are to be seen as scientists, we not only need empirical data to back our use of particular procedures, we also need a comprehensive theory to underpin our overall approach. It is to the development of such theories that we now turn.

COGNITIVE BEHAVIOURAL THEORIES

Conditioning theories

Given the early popularity of procedures aimed at modifying deviant sexual interests (e.g., Max, 1935; Raymond, 1956), it is perhaps not surprising that the earliest behavioural theories of sexual offending were cast in conditioning terms. In fact, the majority of these early conditioning theories attempted to explain the acquisition and maintenance of all aspects of deviant sexual behaviours in terms of classical conditioning processes with no acknowledgment of the influence of even operant conditioning, never mind social learning. Furthermore, these accounts focussed exclusively on sexual motivation and neglected to consider that conditioning might act on other arousal factors such as aggression-induced arousal, excitement elicited by control and power, and risk-taking excitement.

Essentially, Pavlovian theories of sexual offending (Abel & Blanchard, 1974; McGuire et al., 1965) claim that a previously neutral stimulus (the conditional stimulus or CS) will come to elicit arousal on its own when repeatedly paired with masturbation (the unconditioned stimulus or UCS) that automatically elicits sexual arousal (the unconditioned response or UCR). Thus, if a male repeatedly imagines female children (the CS) while masturbating (the UCS), he will eventually be sexually aroused by the thought (or sight) of female children (the conditioned response or CR). Conditioning theorists maintain that deviant sexual interests acquired in this way are the underlying bases that induce men to act deviantly. Although some conditioning theorists are not always clear on the specifics, McGuire et al. (1965) suggested that an actual experience (most likely, fortuitous) provides the basis for the subsequent repeated masturbatory fantasies that entrench a strong attraction to the deviant act. One of their illustrations of this process depicted a young man urinating in a secluded wooded area, only to be surprised in the act by an attractive woman. Afterward, the idea of this woman seeing him in this compromising act aroused the young man and he masturbated to the image of her looking at his exposed penis. Repeated masturbatory practices involving this fantasy established deliberate exposure as a sexually attractive behaviour, and this was ultimately enacted.

Abel and Blanchard (1974), on the other hand, seem to suggest that fantasies need no such fortuitous overt experience. They appear not so much concerned with what initially prompts the fantasies, but rather with the notion that repeated fantasizing, in conjunction with masturbation, builds a dominant sexual preference for deviant acts. In their view, and in McGuire et al.'s theory, deviant sexual preferences are established *prior* to the deliberate enactment of clearly deviant behaviour. However, Abel's own data (Abel et al., 1987) do not confirm these suggestions. In Abel et al.'s study, only 50% of nonfamilial child molesters who abused boys, 40% of those who molested girls, and only 25% of incest offenders said they had developed deviant sexual preferences prior to offending. In Marshall, Barbaree and Eccles' (1991) study of this issue, the figures were even lower: just over 20% of these three groups of child molesters reported having deviant sexual fantasies prior to their first offence. Of course sexual offenders do not always tell the truth so these two reports may provide an underestimate, although both researchers attempted to establish conditions that might be expected to increase honesty. Thus, exactly what role deviant fantasies play in prompting deviant sexual acts is not clear and the presently available data do not offer unequivocal support for conditioning theories as they have currently been explicated.

Marshall and Eccles (1993) reviewed Pavlovian conditioning theories of sexual offending and found little in the way of empirical support for them. Animal research has certainly demonstrated that nonsexual stimuli can, through Pavlovian pairings, affect sexual responding (Cutmore & Zamble, 1988; Farris, 1967; Graham & Desjardins, 1980; Zamble, Hadad, Mitchell & Cutmore, 1985; Zamble, Mitchell & Findley, 1986), but the observed changes are not the sort expected by conditioning theories of human deviant sexual behaviour. In these animal studies, the CS was not demonstrated to have become sexually attractive to the animals (i.e., the animals did not attempt to copulate with the stimulus itself) but rather, the CS was shown to increase attempts at copulation with a female (i.e., conditioning simply facilitated an increase in normative sexual behaviour).

A number of studies have attempted to evaluate more directly the implications of conditioning theories. However, many of these studies did not follow the procedures claimed by McGuire et al. to induce deviant sexuality. These less than appropriate appraisals used as the UCS a visual stimulus that was previously shown to elicit sexual arousal. According to McGuire et al.'s theory, however, the power of these visual stimuli to elicit sexual arousal is the result of prior conditioning processes; that is, these stimuli are acquired CSs. Acquired CSs can function as UCSs in higher order conditioning, but generally they are not as effective as an original UCS (in this case, masturbation). As we will see, studies using these second order UCSs (i.e., visual stimuli) did not reliably produce conditioned sexual arousal to previously neutral stimuli. Some studies with human subjects have shown that pairing a CS with a nontactile UCS (e.g., a coloured slide of a naked female) has resulted in some degree of subsequent arousal being displayed to the CS (Beech, Watts & Poole, 1971; McConaghy, 1970; Rachman, 1966; Rachman & Hodgson, 1968). In two of these reports, however, the degree of post-training arousal to the CS was not made clear (Rachman, 1966; Rachman & Hodgson, 1968), while in another (Beech et al., 1971), alternative explanations seem equally plausible (see Marshall, 1974, for these alternative explanations). In McConaghy's (1970) study, the CSs were red circles and green triangles. Stimuli such as these would not be expected, from a preparedness view of conditioning (Seligman, 1970), to be good candidates for acquiring conditioned sexual arousal properties. In fact, as long ago as 1929, English demonstrated that such stimuli do not serve as effective CSs and, more recently, Öhman, Erixon and Lofberg (1975) have produced similar findings. Later studies with sexual deviates (Herman, Barlow & Agras, 1974; Marshall, 1974) have also failed to find consistent evidence of conditioning, even after extensive (300 plus) pairings of the CS–UCS (Marshall, 1974). Also, as we have seen, aversion therapy does not appear to produce consistently beneficial changes and, when it does, there is no evidence that these are the result of a conditioned aversion (McConaghy, 1969, 1975).

Studies pairing a CS with masturbatory-induced sexual arousal should provide a more accurate evaluation of Pavlovian theories, but the only reported research using such procedures has consisted of treatment studies of masturbatory conditioning. Laws and Marshall (1991) did an exhaustive review of such studies and found little in the way of support for the value of these techniques. That is to say, these presumptively conditioning procedures did not reliably change sexual preferences. Indeed, in the only satisfactorily controlled study of Marquis' (1970) "orgasmic reconditioning", which requires deviant subjects to pair thoughts of appropriate sex with masturbatory-induced arousal, the procedure proved ineffective (Conrad & Wincze, 1976). While there is some, but very limited, support for alternative strategies pairing nonarousing stimuli with masturbation, the evidence doe not support the idea that these, or any other, procedures aimed at changing sexual preferences achieve their goal (when they do) by conditioning processes (Laws & Marshall, 1991; Quinsey & Earls, 1990).

If, of course, deviant sexual interests are acquired in the way conditioning theorists suggest, then those men who act deviantly should manifest sexual preferences at assessment. We will review the literature on the phallometric assessment of sexual preferences in a later chapter, but it is sufficient to point our here that far less than 100% of sexual offenders display deviant interests at these evaluations. Assuming that phallometry is an appropriate procedure for evaluating sexual preferences, these findings indicate, at the very least, that other explanations for deviant sexual behaviour must be invoked to account for those offenders who do not show deviance at assessment.

A somewhat more elaborate conditioning theory has been proposed by Laws and Marshall (1990). In this account, operant processes (i.e., the effects of consequences on the future probability of behaviour) are given at least as much emphasis as is Pavlovian conditioning. In addition, the role of social learning in the acquisition of deviant behaviour is emphasized by Laws and Marshall (1990). Despite the more detailed and comprehensive perspective of Laws and Marshall's theory, the conditioning aspects cannot be said to be any better supported by the evidence.

Insofar as we accept that conditioning processes are involved in the acquisition and maintenance of deviant sexuality, we suggest that, in those limited number of sexual offenders who display deviant preferences, the acquisition of these preferences do not always (if at all) result from entertaining deviant thoughts while masturbating as the earlier conditioning theorists maintained. Marshall and Eccles (1993) presented evidence suggesting that repeated actual experiences of deviant sex are more likely to provide the conditioning basis for the development of deviant sexual acts, than is prior masturbation paired with fantasies. This, of course, would still imply a conditioning basis, but of a different nature, and would, therefore, entail different implications for treatment.

More specifically, the conditioning of deviant sexual behaviour does not necessarily demand that the excitement associated with the deviant acts must be exclusively sexual. The nature of the excited state could easily differ across offenders and across occasions within the same offender. From a conditioning point of view the nature of the excitation generated by a stimulus does not matter. Thus, so long as excitement is generated, deviant images or acts may acquire excitatory properties. No doubt acting in a sexually deviant manner generates excitement, but is this only sexual?

According to many offenders, the risk-taking element of offending is excit-
ing and this, plus the arousal generated by control, domination and the
expression of aggression, is at least as likely as sexual arousal to function as
an element in the compound response that enhances the attractiveness of
deviant sexual acts. In fact, there is evidence that the enactment of aggression is in itself rewarding (Leon, 1969; Storr, 1972) and this consequence
should, therefore, serve to increase the frequency of those acts that involve
aggressive behaviour. No doubt the thought of, and the act of, humiliating
and degrading a victim of sexual assault also generates excitation that serves
to reinforce these acts.

In this view, it is not necessary at all that sexual offenders display deviant
sexual arousal at laboratory assessment. If deviant sexual behaviours become entrenched because the generation of nonsexual excitement serves as a
UCS for these behaviours, then we would not expect to see sexual arousal in
response to deviant stimuli. Indeed, it would be expected that only a limited
number of sexual offenders should display deviant sexual preferences, and
this is exactly what has been found. In the sexual assault of adult females,
where there is clear evidence (Darke, 1990) that the humiliation and degra-
dation of the victim are the pre-eminent motives of the offender (expressing,
of course, power and control over the victim), and where gratuitous aggression is the norm (Christie, Marshall & Lanthier, 1979), we would expect
these elements to generate nonsexual excitement. This nonsexual excitement
is very likely to make offending attractive. If this is true, then among rapists
(who seem primarily concerned with power, control and the expression of
aggression) few should show deviant sexual preferences and this appears to
be true (Marshall, in press, a). For child molesters, on the other hand, where
these other sources of excitation appear to be somewhat less prominent, and
where sexual excitement seems to be somewhat more primary, we would
expect to find more evidence of deviant sexual preferences among these
men than among rapists, and we do (Barbaree & Marshall, 1989). However,
even in child molesters, and particularly among incest offenders where
power and control seem to be more prominent features of the relationships,
we would still expect nonsexual pleasure to be important. Consequently,
many of these offenders, particularly the incest offenders, should also fail to
display deviant sexual preferences.

Conditioning processes may very well play an important role in the development, maintenance, and enhancement of sexual offending, but it seems
unlikely to us that sexual excitement is the sole, and perhaps not even the
primary, factor that enhances the attractiveness of such acts. Even so, conditioning processes alone do not adequately explain the development of sexual offending. Why is it that deviant thoughts occur to some males and not
to others (or at least are not experienced as frequently and as strongly in
others)? Why is it that when these thoughts occur, some males can readily

dismiss them, while others find them irresistibly attractive? Why is it that some young males and some adult males can have a single deviant sexual experience and never again succumb to such temptations? Obviously, there are numerous other factors that shape the thinking and behaviour that lead to sexual offending.

Comprehensive theories

Over the past two decades Marshall and his colleagues have attempted to elaborate a general theory (Marshall, 1984, Marshall & Fernandez, in press, b; Marshall & Barbaree, 1984, 1990) that attempts to account for the development and maintenance of sexual offending. Of course, Marshall has not been alone in these endeavours. David Finkelhor (Finkelhor, 1984, 1986; Williams & Finkelhor, 1990), Neil Malamuth (Malamuth, 1984; Malamuth, Heavey & Linz, 1993), Gordon Hall (Hall & Hirschman, 1991) and Diana Russell (1984) have elaborated similar theories of sexual offending. Readers could as readily turn to those accounts as to the one that is to follow. In particular, Finkelhor's account is helpful in providing a framework for treating sexual offenders. He suggests there are four preconditions that must be met for sexual abuse to occur: (1) the offender must be motivated to offend; (2) he must overcome his internal inhibitions; (3) he must overcome external obstacles to offending; and (4) he must overcome the victim's resistance. Treatment providers can utilize these preconditions to establish with each offender the ways in which he managed to be able to offend.

Earlier, Marshall (1982) argued that an all-encompassing account of any complex human behaviour may not be able to achieve the status of a true scientific theory in the sense that it could serve to reasonably precisely predict the behaviour in question. The best we can hope for is to link by speculative connections those factors that the evidence suggests are present in either the history or current status of sexual offenders. Accordingly, Marshall and his colleagues have attempted to elucidate the influence of specific factors, including: sexual arousal (Barbaree & Marshall, 1991), conditioning (Laws & Marshall, 1990), attachments, intimacy and loneliness (Marshall, 1989a, 1993a, 1994a; Marshall, Hudson & Hodkinson, 1993; Ward, Hudson, Marshall & Siegert, 1995a), pornography (Marshall, 1989b), empathy (Marshall, Hudson, Jones & Fernandez, 1995), self-esteem (Marshall, Anderson & Champagne, 1996), cognitions (Marshall & Langton, 1997; Ward, Hudson, Johnston & Marshall, 1997; Ward, Hudson & Marshall, 1995), and shame and guilt (Bumby, Langton & Marshall, in press). Hopefully, these attempts to integrate knowledge will not only prove satisfying and provide a perspective for informing or guiding others (including clients), but will also encourage research. These theoretical attempts have already generated data that have not always been entirely supportive, but have always served to shape our thinking.

The unifying thread in Marshall et al.'s theory concerns the notion of vulnerability. Vulnerability lies on a dimension with strong resilience at one end, and extreme weakness at the other. Vulnerability or resilience develop over the life-span and can be reversed (momentarily or more fixedly) by circumstances or by transitory internal states. Resilience describes a set of personal features that provides a resistance to possible temptations or chances to offend, and may be understood as involving various attitudes, beliefs, cognitive and behavioural skills, and emotional dispositions, all of which are learned. The degree to which there is a failure to learn any or all of these skills, attitudes, and emotional capacities results in a corresponding degree of vulnerability. Such an individual would, therefore, be more likely to create, recognize, or give in to, opportunities to sexually offend. The main initial source of acquired resilience (or vulnerability) is the person's childhood experiences, particularly with their parents.

Marshall et al. (1993) have described in some detail the importance for the development of sexual offending of attachment bonds between children and their parents. Secure attachment bonds are characterized by a sensitive caregiver (Ainsworth, Blehar, Waters & Walls, 1978). When children feel insecure with their parents, they do not have the opportunity to use those relationships to gain self-confidence and to practice the skills necessary for subsequent interactions with peers, particularly for relationships that allow the effective fulfilment of sexual and intimacy needs. Indeed, insecure parent/child attachments cause the child to develop either fearful or avoidant attitudes toward closeness with another person (Lamb, Gaensbauer, Malkin & Schultz, 1985). Insecure children are unfriendly, dependent, moody, lacking in warmth, low in self-esteem, and socially ill-at-ease or incompetent (Grossman & Grossman, 1990). These features tend to persist into adolescence and adulthood (Feeney & Noller, 1990) and are the features we consider to make the person vulnerable to becoming a sexual offender. Of course, parents who reject their children also provide poor models for intimacy and, all too frequently, provide models of aggression.

Children from these unhappy homes have been found to be at greater risk to be sexually abused (Finkelhor, Hotaling, Lewis & Smith, 1990), presumably because they are vulnerable to the attention and rewards offered by an adult abuser, and because their parents offer poor supervision. Certainly, sexual offenders appear to have more frequently been abused as children both physically (Rada, 1978) and sexually (Dhawan & Marshall, 1996; Hanson & Slater, 1988) than nonoffenders. Furthermore, the presence of such childhood abuse is predictive of general antisocial behaviour (Loeber, 1990; Loeber & Dision, 1983) and sexual offenders frequently also have a history of nonsexual crimes (Weinrott & Saylor, 1991). In their examination of both incarcerated sexual offenders and university students, Smallbone and Dadds (in press) found that insecure maternal attachments predicted a general adult antisocial disposition, whereas poor attachments to their father was specifically predictive of adult coercive sexual behaviour. Finally, Prentky et al. (1989) found that the disruptive childhood experiences of sexual offenders predicted the severity of their sexual aggression.

These findings suggest both a modelling effect and also a distortion of the internal working model that is said to guide the person's approach to all relationships (Bowlby, 1969). According to Bowlby and others (e.g., Main, Kaplan & Cassidy, 1985), experiences with relationships in childhood provide the basis for developing interpersonal schema about relationships in general. The content, nature and outcome of childhood relationships determines not only the child's desire for, and anxiety about, intimacy, but also the manner in which it is sought (Bowlby, 1969). When a vulnerable child is sexually abused by an adult, particularly in the context of an otherwise rewarding relationship, this experience may provide a template for the unskilled child to later seek intimacy as an adult through an abusive sexual relationship.

When a boy who has experienced insecure relationships with his parents reaches puberty, he is ill-equipped to deal with the stresses and changes that his sudden growth spurt, and remarkable hormonal changes, presents. Testosterone levels increase at least fourfold during a two-year period at puberty (Sizonenko, 1978) and this, together with other dramatic physical, personal, and social changes, make the transition from childhood to adolescence a difficult process. A vulnerable young male will seek ways of thinking and behaving that confer on him an otherwise absent sense of power, control and prestige, and that allow him to realize his sexual needs despite his lack of confidence and poor social skills. Both pornography, which lies about sexual relations and about the sexuality of males, females and children (Zillman, 1989), and acts of forced sex or sex with children, meet these requirements and will, accordingly, appeal to such a vulnerable youth. In the context of masturbatory-induced sexual arousal (or the nonsexual excitement generated by feelings of power and control) the acts depicted in pornography or simply fantasized (rape or child molestation), and the associated attitudes, will come to be accepted and be seen as attractive by these vulnerable boys. Similarly, from among the various social messages our culture proffers, these vulnerable boys will more likely select those beliefs that confer upon them a sense of masculinity and power. Among the various social attitudes prevalent in our society are those that have been demonstrated to characterize sexual offending: an acceptance of interpersonal violence, negative views of women and children, male dominance, and a tolerance toward rape and the sexual molestation of children (Burt, 1980; Marshall & Barrett, 1990; Otterbein, 1979; Russell, 1984; Sanday, 1981). These are just the sort of attitudes that will appeal to vulnerable adolescents. Unfortunately, these attitudes are not displayed in pornography alone, although in that context they may be exaggerated; advertising and the entertainment media also contain clear messages that are derogatory toward women and depict children as possessions. Women and children are all too often sexualized in advertising and men are portrayed as the powerful and dominant figures.

If the vulnerable adolescent boy either seizes an opportunity to offend, or actively creates the chance to do so, or is persistently excited by thoughts of offending, then he may have begun a process that will lead to an entrenchment of sexual deviance. We have already described how we believe the conditioning processes associated with deviance unfold, but it is important to remember that the elements that become endowed with offence-eliciting properties can include any stimuli (internal or external) that elevate arousal (both sexual and nonsexual). Entertaining thoughts of power and control, or of aggressing against someone, generate arousal that may be as readily conditioned as is sexual excitement, although these other sources of arousal are unlikely to be apparent in the evaluation of sexual preferences.

Associating particular antisocial beliefs (e.g., an acceptance of myths about rape and child sexual abuse, the dominance of males, and contemptuous attitudes toward women and children) with a complex of excitation generated by actually sexually abusing someone or by repeatedly fantasizing enacting such abuse, will so strongly entrench these beliefs that they will be very difficult to change. Ordinarily, males overtly express, or covertly entertain, attitudes and beliefs (either positive or negative) about these matters primarily when they are engaged in discussion or argument on the issues. This is generally rather infrequent and so we would not expect these attitudes and beliefs to be as well-entrenched in nonoffenders as they are in offenders who, according to our perspective, rehearse their antisocial views far more frequently (whenever they offend or masturbate) and in the context of a pleasing state of arousal (not just sexual in nature).

In addition to these developmental and sociocultural influences, the role of transitory situational or personal factors has long been recognized as part of the causative chain in sexual offending. Cohen, Seghorn and Calmus (1969), in describing their typology, claimed that "regressed" offenders engage in child sexual abuse in response to short-term stress. Similarly, alcohol intoxication was recognized quite early as a disinhibitor of whatever social constraints sexual offenders have (Swanson, 1968), and momentary anger was said by Rada (1978) to motivate rape. We have shown that alcohol intoxication markedly enhances the sexual arousal that nonoffender males display to rape (Barbaree, Marshall, Yates & Lightfoot, 1983) and anger evoked by a female has similar, somewhat more profound effects (Yates, Barbaree & Marshall, 1984). Research by Pithers and his colleagues (Long,

Pithers et al

Wuesthoff & Pithers, 1989; Pithers, Beal, Armstrong & Petty, 1989; Pithers, Buell, Kashima, Cumming & Beal, 1987) has identified a number of other transitory features that appear to trigger offending in these men. They found, for example, that anxiety, depression, boredom, resentment, feelings of deprivation, and a temporary aimlessness, were among the factors that put their subjects at risk to sexually offend.

Of course, opportunity (that is, being in a situation where offending can readily occur) is the most important risk factor; however, the question is why do some men respond to this opportunity, while others do not? Indeed, why do nonoffenders, in situations that sexual offenders see as provocative, rarely even recognize the potential to sexually offend? Similarly, we need to ask why it is that sexual offenders can sometimes abstain when presented with the opportunity to offend? Our theory, we believe, provides an approximate answer to these questions. When in a potential situation, only those men who are chronically vulnerable (as a result of their developmental, social, and conditioning histories) will recognize this as an opportunity to offend and, depending on their momentary vulnerability (the effect of transitory factors), they may or may not seize the chance to sexually abuse a woman or a child. Clearly, the goal of treatment is to build resilience and the description of our treatment program will indicate how we go about achieving this goal.

Chapter 3

THE STRUCTURE, CONTEXT AND FORMAT OF TREATMENT

Words are healers of the sick tempered.

Aeschylus, 525–456 BC

STRUCTURE

Sexual offenders are a heterogeneous group. On almost all measures that have been used with these men, the variability of their responses is more evident than their conformity. This heterogeneity presents problems for research, theory, and for some aspects of clinical practice, not the least of which concerns the problem of fitting such a variable group within the same treatment program. There have been attempts to reduce variability by classifying these offenders according to their offence type (i.e., rapists, child molesters, etc.), or according to DSM-IV diagnostic criteria, or according to one or another alternative systems of classification (e.g., Gebhard, Gagnon, Pomeroy & Christenson, 1965; Groth, 1979; Knight & Prentky, 1990; Seghorn & Cohen, 1980). However, these various attempts at classifying sexual offenders have not proved to be of much value in allocating sexual offenders to treatment. Indeed, there may be an advantage to mixing different types of sexual offenders in treatment groups. Rapists, for example, typically present themselves as somehow morally superior to child molesters, and non-familial child molesters occasionally claim the high ground over incest offenders because they did not abuse their own children. Given that sexual offenders are treated with disgust by most other members of society, it is no surprise that they engage in their own hierarchical absurdities. It is, however, good for them to learn in treatment that they all share in common the fact that they have caused their victims distress and that this is the central issue with which they must deal.

In terms of the most effective delivery of treatment, particularly when dealing with reasonably large numbers of offenders, as is typically the case in prison settings, the extent of treatment needs is the most salient feature on which the appropriate allocation of offenders to treatment should be based. As an example of how this might be done, we will describe the system operating within the Canadian penitentiaries where we do our treatment and research.

In the Ontario Region of the Correctional Services of Canada, all incoming offenders are thoroughly assessed to determine their security requirements, their future risk to reoffend, and the extent of their treatment needs. More often than not, these three features correspond; that is, those with extensive treatment needs are typically the ones whose risk to reoffend is greatest and who require the most restrictive security. Penitentiaries run by the Correctional Services of Canada are classified as maximum, medium or minimum, according to their peripheral and internal security systems. Within medium security prisons, some are deemed to be "soft" because the internal security is more relaxed.

As a result of the assessments completed at the Millhaven Assessment Unit, sexual offenders are then sent to one of several possible treatment programs within different institutions. Figure 3.1 outlines the typical allocation of sexual offenders to the various institutions. There is also a system for cascading offenders. For example, after treatment at Warkworth Institution, a sexual offender may move to Bath Institution (where internal security is somewhat more relaxed) for further treatment, and then move to Pittsburgh Institution prior to release. A system of escorted or unescorted temporary

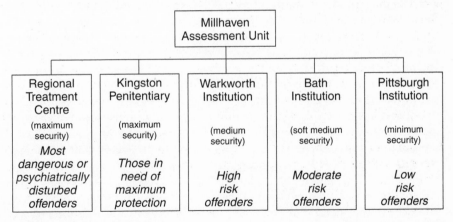

Figure 3.1 Allocation to treatment programs in the Ontario Region of Correctional Services of Canada

absences may be part of a graduated release program, or an offender may be placed in a community-based halfway house before being given full parole. The intensity of supervision for paroled sexual offenders depends upon their risk status and it is eased off as they demonstrate an ability to effectively readjust and as post-release assessments or treatment indicate that they are ready for greater independence.

CONTEXT

Each of Canada's federal institutions, where treatment is available for sexual offenders, offers a full range of programs. For example, at Bath Institution, where our treatment program is located, there are 16 programs in addition to the sexual offender program, as well as high quality educational upgrading and vocational training. These additional programs include, for example, cognitive skills, anger management, and substance abuse, which are obviously relevant to the proper treatment of sexual offenders. Thus the specialized sexual offender programs do not have to extensively address issues other than those that are common to all sexual offenders. The following chapters will describe each of these common issues (which we call "offence-specific" issues) and will outline the treatment approach we take to each of these problems. However, the reader should bear in mind that all our clients receive, in addition, treatment aimed at various other aspects of their functioning (which we call "offence-related" features).

At Bath Institution, where our program operates, the administration, program and case management staff, as well as security staff, are all supportive of our efforts, and they offer encouragement to the offenders. While we do our best to maintain this support by being respectful and friendly to all staff, the institution functions effectively because, from the Commissioner of Penitentiaries down to the prison wardens, all administrative staff are dedicated to the rehabilitation of all prisoners. In addition to this on-line support and encouragement, Bath Institution permits inmates at least three face-to-face visits each week. These visits occur during the evenings so that the inmate's daily routine of work and program participation is not interrupted, and so that it is easier for working family members to attend visits. In addition, all inmates are eligible for conjugal visits (two full days with their spouse or family) once every three months. These visits (both evening and conjugal) provide offenders with the opportunity to enact the skills they are learning in treatment, consolidate their relationships, and rebuild their lives in a way that will hopefully reduce stress after release. The effect of these visits (in addition to the therapeutic benefits) seems to be to calm the inmates and make them more tractable to programming. Alec Spencer (the former Governor of Peterhead Prison in Scotland) has clearly described the best way to establish such a supportive environment that is conducive to effective sexual offender treatment (Spencer, 1998).

FORMAT

The format of our treatment is group therapy. We do not engage in any individual therapy because we believe that it is both less efficient and less effective. In particular, when it comes to challenging the clients' views, other offenders play an essential role. They are often seen as more credible than the therapist who, after all, has no personal experience with being an offender. In addition, when the offenders challenge each other, they often illustrate their point with their own experience which not only helps the person being challenged, but also the challenger. By using their own experience as a basis for challenging others, the offenders come to a better understanding of their own crimes. Furthermore, groups necessarily provide extensive opportunities for vicarious learning. When one client is challenged, the other participants have a chance to recognize their own inappropriate thinking or behavioural strategies, and adjust them accordingly. Also, within a prison setting the group participants know about, and observe, a good deal of each other's behaviours outside the group setting, and this often provides a basis for challenging one another. This information would rarely be available to a therapist working one-to-one with an offender.

Camp and Thyer (1993) reviewed treatment outcome studies with adolescent sexual offenders. The studies they discussed reported sexual recidivism rates of their treated sample ranging from 5% to 14%. One exception was a comparison of multi-systemic therapy and individual one-to-one treatment (Borduin, Henggeler, Blaske & Stein, 1990). This evaluation randomly assigned participants to one of the two treatment conditions and followed the participants for an average of 37 months. Borduin et al. found that the sexual recidivism rate among those in the multi-systemic therapy condition was 12.5%, whereas the sexual recidivism rate for those in the individual therapy condition was a stunning 75%. Given that some programs are exclusively group therapy and others utilize an individual treatment component, the findings of Borduin et al. suggest the need for further examination of differences in effects of these two methods of intervention, but do not provide encouraging news for the use of individual therapy.

Working in groups also allows us to encourage mutual support and assistance among the clients not only within therapy sessions, but also in the rest of their time. For instance, when we encounter an offender who cannot read or write, and yet is intellectually capable of participating in a group, we can have one of his colleagues act as his reader and scribe for homework assignments. Similarly, since the group process encourages cohesion among its members, they often carry on the supportive challenging beyond the therapy hours. Not only are these supportive efforts helpful to the client being supported, they also provide an opportunity for the supporter to be nurturant – not an experience with which these men are usually familiar. The ability to be nurturant is related to effective social and intimacy skills, and to the capacity for empathy, all of which are goals of therapy. In addition, being nurturant enhances the offender's sense of self-worth. Finally, the group context allows the therapists to model appropriate ways of relating to others, particularly concerning racial, ethnic, and gender issues.

We attempt to have female and male co-therapists in each of our groups, although when resources are limited, we adjust accordingly with no obvious loss of effectiveness. It is simply easier on therapists to have a co-facilitator, particularly someone of the opposite gender, but it does not appear to be essential. It does, however, reduce the risk of therapist burnout, which can be a problem in this field, and we cannot really afford to lose good therapists. On this point, it is worth noting some of the things that may reduce the probability of burnout. Certainly minimizing the workload is important. We consider it unwise to run more than two or three treatment sessions per week for each group. When we have done more, we have found that both the therapists and the clients are emotionally exhausted and not particularly resourceful in the fourth and fifth sessions. Furthermore, clients seem less enthusiastic about homework when there are four or five sessions per week, because they look forward to their time off treatment. Running two to three sessions weekly seems to circumvent this problem. In addition to workload considerations and their effect on burnout, we find it useful to schedule the opportunity to discuss among the therapists issues concerning our clients, particularly those that produce emotional distress in the therapist. Accordingly we spend one full morning each week discussing cases, but we are also readily available to support each other at a moment's notice.

Therapists also need to have other fulfilling activities both at work and in the rest of their lives. This is one reason why all staff in our program participate in the design, implementation and publication of research, and contribute on an ongoing basis to the format, process, and content of treatment. It is critical that therapists do research, because they are the ones (rather than researchers who are removed from the clinical frontline) most likely to recognize the problems in need of attention, and also because it provides stimulation essential to continued enthusiasm for this very demanding work. We also do training for other prison staff which not only facilitates their cooperation with our treatment efforts, but also provides additional stimulation for our staff.

All our groups have approximately 10 offenders teamed with one or two therapists and run for 2.5 hours per session with a 10 minute break in the middle. Each group member is required to actively participate in all sessions; that is, they are not permitted to remain simply observers, nor are they allowed to give one-word responses. Active participation is viewed by us as essential, not only because evidence indicates that participation facilitates the acquisition of new skills and attitudes (Bandura, 1986), but also because it appears to promote self-awareness and self-confidence. Active participation also provides opportunities for the therapist to judge how deeply felt are the offender's expressions of prosocial views.

Therapists working with sexual offenders in the Correctional Services of Canada are automatically provided with detailed victim statements and police reports of what is said to have happened in the offence(s). In addition, court transcripts are accessible if necessary, as is the offender's complete criminal history. These official documents provide an excellent basis for the therapists to challenge the offender's disclosure of his offence(s), which almost invariably contains elements of denial, distortions, and minimization. Without this information, it would be more difficult, although not impossible on the basis of reasonable guesses, to challenge an offender's exculpatory position.

Sexual offenders within federal prisons, where the majority in Canada are incarcerated, are under several constraints that encourage their participation in treatment. If they refuse treatment, sexual offenders are likely to be placed in an institutional setting that is not program-oriented, that is more secure and restrictive than are program-based prisons, and that also holds more hostile nonsex offenders. This placement is not meant to be punitive (although it certainly functions that way) but is simply necessary in order to accommodate within program-based institutions those offenders who seek treatment. In addition, sexual offenders who refuse treatment will almost certainly be refused parole, whereas effective participation markedly increases their chances of early release. For the most part the Parole Board is responsive to the recommendations and conclusions of treatment providers. This is because treatment providers in Canadian penitentiaries tend to generate recommendations based on actuarial estimates of risk (see Quinsey, Lalumière, Rice & Harris, 1995) modified by an objectively based estimate of treatment change. Thus, recommendations are not always seen by the offender as reflections of unqualified support, but are viewed by the Parole Board as soundly based. The effect of these contingencies is to elevate the level of "voluntary" participation in treatment. Somewhat more than 80% of sexual offenders in Canadian penitentiaries agree to become involved in treatment and this is far higher than would be expected without this leverage. This is at least one significant reason why we advocate incarceration as part of the effective response to sexual offenders.

We specifically address the following issues in treatment: self-esteem, cognitive distortions, empathy, intimacy/loneliness and attachment styles, sexual and nonsexual fantasies or preferences, and relapse prevention. In fact, we rarely address sexual preferences, although we will consider these issues in one of our subsequent chapters because it is believed by most therapists and researchers to be an essential component of treatment for sexual offenders. We will not discuss the adjunct programs to which our clients are referred, because we do not provide that treatment. Correctional Services of Canada hires the services of specialists in anger management, living without violence (which addresses many gender issues), substance abuse, parenting skills, and cognitive skills (including problem-solving), to name some of the more relevant programs to which our clients are referred. As noted, we describe these programs as addressing "offence-related" targets (Barbaree & Marshall, 1998; Marshall, in press b; Marshall & Eccles, 1995). The components of our specialized program are referred to as "offence-specific".

The following chapters will describe the evidence demonstrating that these offence-specific features do, indeed, characterize sexual offenders. That will be followed in each chapter by a description of our treatment procedures addressing each of these targets and, where available, the evidence on the effects of each component in producing the hoped-for changes. Finally, the closing chapter will review the issues involved in conducting an outcome evaluation of treatment, the evidence supporting or denying the value of treatment, and a cost–benefit analysis of treatment.

Chapter 4

THERAPEUTIC PROCESSES AND CLIENT SELF-ESTEEM

Hate the sin and love the sinner.
                    Mohandes Karamchard Gandhi, 1869–1948

Research examining therapeutic process variables has not received as much attention by those who advocate a behavioural or cognitive behavioural perspective compared to clinicians of other orientations (Schaap, Bennun, Schindler & Hoogduin, 1993). Nonbehavioural therapists were, if anything, preoccupied with therapeutic process, almost to the exclusion of procedure (e.g., Fiedler, 1950; Rogers, 1951; Storr, 1980; Truax & Carkuff, 1967). Indeed, among the early objections of behaviour therapists toward their more traditional colleagues was that procedures were never specified, whereas the processes involved in engaging clients were discussed at length. Not surprisingly, behaviour therapists and their successors have placed inordinate emphasis on the description of procedures. These procedures have been demonstrated to be effective across a broad range of problems, and this effectiveness seems to have discouraged most behavioural researchers from bothering to examine the contribution of therapist characteristics and style to treatment outcome. Some behaviour therapists, however, showed an early interest in these processes (De Voge & Beck, 1978; Sweet, 1984; Wilson & Evans, 1976), and it is now clear that features of treatment having to do with the therapist's style and the client–therapist relationship contribute to the variance in outcome (Schaap et al., 1993). As Mahoney and Norcross (1993) put it, "therapeutic techniques and therapeutic relationships are not (and cannot be) mutually exclusive: they are inherently interrelated and interdependent" (p. 423).

Apparently, behaviour therapists themselves consider these processes to be important (Swan & McDonald, 1978) and their clients certainly do (Staples, Sloane, Whipple, Cristol & Yorkson, 1975). Studies have also examined the influence of therapeutic processes on outcome in behaviour therapy. Features such as warmth, sincerity, support and empathy appear to characterize behaviour therapists at least as much as they do therapists from other schools (Brunink & Schroeder, 1979; O'Dell & Bahmer, 1981; Sloane, Staples, Cristol, Yorkson & Whipple, 1975) although behaviour therapists tend to be more directive and active (Greenwald, Kornblith, Hersen, Bellack & Himmelhoch, 1981; Sloane et al., 1975). So, while behaviour therapists have not shown the same interest in these variables as have therapists from other schools, their therapeutic behaviour, nevertheless, appears to be characterized by these presumably advantageous features.

Despite the clear findings across all schools of psychotherapy that therapist style, and the client–therapist relationship thereby engendered, effectively contributes to beneficial outcome (Frank, 1971, 1973; Hartley & Strupp, 1982; Schaap et al., 1993), there are few studies of the influence of these processes in behavioural and cognitive behavioural therapies. More specifically, there has only been one such study in the field of sexual offender treatment (Beech & Fordham, 1997) and this study was not planned, but rather, emerged from an evaluation of several community-based programs. While Beech and Fordham's study represents a beginning, it cannot be said to have provided any more than tentative suggestions. However, this study, and other commentaries, suggest that sexual offender therapists are beginning to recognize the relevance of the way in which they conduct treatment.

Kear-Colwell and Pollack (1997) make a strong case for their claim that a confrontational style can be expected to produce limited benefits or, at worst, negative effects on sexual offenders. They point out that, because the confrontational approach involves a series of negative assumptions about sexual offenders (e.g., that they have committed more offences than have been identified, and that they will stubbornly deny all aspects of even known offences), the advocates of such an approach consider it necessary to behave in an authoritarian, even aggressive, manner toward their clients. This makes the clients vulnerable and powerless, and forces them to accept the label of sexual offender. This approach, according to Kear-Colwell and Pollack, lacks empathy and leads self-confident or assertive offenders to become resistant and argumentative. Responses of this kind will likely result in the offender being removed from treatment or, if not, he will be unlikely to profit from remaining in the program. Other confident clients might develop a manipulative response style, thereby seeming to cooperate in order to placate the therapist but, again, not profiting from treatment. Clients who lack self-confidence are likely to be bullied into submission by this approach, with their self-esteem being eroded even further. As we will see, enhancing clients' self-confidence should be a goal of therapy if benefits are to be derived from treatment.

Given these rather obvious consequences to the use of a confrontational approach, we might wonder why anyone would adopt such a style. Garland and Dougher (1991) claim to have an answer to that question. They suggested that therapists who take a confrontational approach do so to meet their own needs rather than the needs of their clients. A confrontational style, Garland and Dougher suggested, "can often (reflect) disguised, rationalized therapist hostility" (p. 306). Marshall (1996a) has made a case, similar to that offered by Kear-Colwell and Pollack, for adopting what he calls "a positive approach to treatment". This approach precludes a confrontational style and emphasizes those features of a therapist's behaviour that has been shown to maximize treatment benefits (see Table 4.1).

Mann (1998) has suggested that the relapse prevention movement has essentially a negative focus in that it concentrates almost exclusively on what she calls "avoidance goals". Sexual offenders in relapse prevention programs are required to identify obstacles to their future possibility of maintaining an offence-free life. While there is some sense to this, Mann has pointed out that evidence from other bodies of literature indicate that approach goals are more readily attained than are avoidance goals. She therefore suggests that treatment providers focus on the strengths of their clients

Table 4.1 Therapist features

Reliably identifiable	Not reliably identified
Empathic	Trustworthy
Respectful	Accepting
Warm and friendly	Supportive
Sincere and genuine	Flexible
Rewarding and encouraging	Emotionally responsive
Directive vs. reflective	Enhances clients' self-esteem
Confident	Creates favourable expectancies
Interested	
Nonconfrontational challenging	
Noncollusive	
Appropriately self-disclosing	
Appropriate use of humour	
Communicates clearly	
Encourages active participation	
Encourages prosocial attitudes	
Asks open-ended questions	
Deals appropriately with frustration/difficulties	
Spends appropriate time on issues	

From Marshall, Mulloy & Serran (1998).

and on building skills that would allow their clients to meet their needs in prosocial ways, rather than constructing avoidance strategies. In addition, it is clear that sexual offenders typically have many opportunities to offend, but in most instances, they abstain. We suggest that perhaps an exploration of why they did not offend when the chance arose might be as valuable in understanding these men, and their offence proclivities, as would the typical analyses, focussing as they do on what steps they took to be able to offend. Indeed, we suggest that focussing only on our clients' deficits, while charac- teristic of the more general approach to mental health problems, is a mis- taken strategy. This strategy not only involves the problematic approach that Mann has identified, it also conveys to our clients that we believe they are broadly dysfunctional. Inadvertently communicating this message to our clients may convince them that they do not have the strengths necessary to meet their needs in prosocial ways which may persuade them they are unable to avoid future offending.

Consistent with both Marshall's (1996a) view and that of Kear-Colwell and Pollock (1997), Beech and Fordham (1997) found that a confrontational approach to treating sexual offenders failed to produce the hoped-for im- provements on various measures of treatment change. Beech and Fordham used Moos' (1986) Group Environment Scale to describe the overall climate of 12 sexual offender treatment groups run at seven community centres in Britain. To illustrate their findings, Beech and Fordham compared the two groups that diverged most clearly on their measures of group climate and leadership. Group D had the most positive ratings and scored higher than all other groups on cohesion, independence, order and organization, and leader support. Group C, on the other hand, had the most negative ratings on cohesion, independence, and leader support, and they produced the highest ratings on leader control. The style of Group D approximately matched what Marshall called the "positive approach to treatment", while Group C dis- played features of the confrontational therapist style described by both Kear-Colwell and Pollack (1997), and Marshall (1996a). In terms of changes on a variety of within-treatment measures (e.g., increases in clients' self- esteem, empathy, cognitive distortions, assertiveness, identification of of- fence chain, and development of relapse prevention strategies), Group D did significantly better than Group C, strongly suggesting that the more positive therapeutic climate maximizes the benefits to be gained from the procedures employed in sexual offender therapy programs.

Studies conducted with other treatment clients have also demonstrated that a confrontational style is counter-therapeutic. Lieberman, Yalom and Miles (1973), for example, showed that such a style led to harmful rather than beneficial effects, and Annis and Chan (1983) found such a style to be particularly damaging to low self-esteem clients. W.R. Miller and Sovereign (1989) randomly assigned problem drinkers to confrontational treatments or to a challenging but supportive style of treatment. They found higher levels of resistance and greater empathic denial among the clients in the confrontational group. Moreover, confrontation produced increased levels of drinking one year later, while the supportive approach yielded greater client change. For our sexual offenders, perhaps the most important implications of these findings concern our efforts to increase their self-esteem and to instill empathy. Engaging in a confrontational style, or a style that is devoid of warmth, seems certain to damage self-esteem and seems guaranteed to fail to inculcate empathy. If we wish to increase our clients' self-esteem, it seems obvious that we must treat them respectfully, and the evidence indicates that this is essential to effective treatment (Schaap et al., 1993). Similarly, if we want our clients to display greater empathy for their victims and others, we should model empathy ourselves. Again, the evidence overwhelmingly indicates that empathy is an essential feature of an effective therapist, whether the therapist adopts a behavioural approach (W.R. Miller & Bacca, 1983; Morris & Suckerman, 1974) or another perspective (Batchelor, 1988).

What then are these positive therapeutic features? Table 4.1 outlines some of the demonstrably effective characteristics of the therapist's behaviours that lead to the creation of a positive therapeutic climate. In addition, this table indicates those features that we have been able to reliably identify and those we have been unable to reliably identify in a study we presently have under way (Marshall, Mulloy & Serran, 1998).

Most of these features will not be discussed here as they have a long history of being accepted as aspects of the necessary features of a good therapist. For example, therapists from all schools accept that empathy, warmth and acceptance by the therapist are critical to effective treatment, and the research literature emphatically supports these views. In fact, in one behavioural study, Alexander, Barton, Schiavo and Parsons (1976) found that therapist features explained 60% of the variance on outcome measures.

Behaviour therapists have characteristically distinguished the client from his/her behaviour, and this is particularly relevant to dealing with sexual offenders. We believe it is essential to indicate acceptance of our clients but to clearly indicate that we do not accept their offensive behaviours. As part of our attempt to achieve this goal, we do not permit our clients to describe themselves as sexual offenders, rapists, child molesters, exhibitionists, etc. Nor do we allow them to adopt any of the multitude of derogatory colloquial descriptors (e.g., "diddler", or "rape-hound" in Canada, "beast" in Scotland). We ask them to think and speak of themselves as someone who has committed a sexual offence rather than as someone who is a sexual offender. Seeing oneself as an offender can be expected to engender shame, which implies an inability to change (see Bumby, Langton & Marshall, in press). On the other hand, construing oneself as someone who has engaged in offending behaviour engenders guilt which facilitates a belief in potential for change. Thus, acceptance in the treatment of sexual offenders should distinguish them as persons with strengths as well as problems, from their behaviours, some of which display their strengths, while others are problematic behaviours. It is the problematic behaviours that need to be changed, not the whole person. As Fisher and Ury (1981) once said, "Be soft on the person, hard on the problem".

From the client's perspective, these features of the therapist translate into a number of characteristics. Clients do best in treatment when they feel supported and are comfortable discussing personal problems without feeling attacked, and they do better when they perceive the therapist as sympathetic, warm, understanding, empathic, and confident (Schaap et al., 1993). In most studies, clients report that they desire advice and direction from their therapists (see Proctor & Rosen, 1983, for a review). Some studies have indicated that giving advice and direction is related to positive therapeutic outcomes in both behaviour therapy (Alexander et al., 1976; Schindler, Revenstorf, Hahlweg & Brengelman, 1983) and more traditional treatment approaches (Beutler, Crago & Arizmendi, 1986; Mintz, Luborsky & Auerbach, 1971). However, Ashby, Ford, Guerny and Guerny (1957) observed that a reflective style was more effective with aggressive and defensive clients, while a directive approach increased levels of aggression and defensiveness. Since many sexual offenders, particularly in their early stages of treatment, tend to be defensive and some display aggressive responses to challenging, it appears best to be flexible by being reflective when appropriate and directive at other times.

It is neither possible nor necessary to discuss in detail all the features outlined in Table 4.1. For the interested reader, the excellent book by Schaap et al. (1993) provides a detailed analysis of therapeutic processes in behaviour therapy. Suffice to say here, we attempt to produce a therapist style that generates all the features outlined in Table 4.1. From our perspective, the issue of the client's self-esteem seems to illustrate, as well as any other issue, the importance of the therapist's style.

SELF-ESTEEM

People's thoughts about themselves have been, and still are, viewed by many theorists and researchers as the crux of adaptive functioning (e.g., Beck, 1967; Freud, 1940; Harter, 1993; Higgins, 1987; James, 1890). Campbell and Lavallee (1993) defined the self-concept as the knowledge or beliefs people have about their attributes, while self-esteem is seen as the evaluative component of the self (that is, the attitude an individual forms toward him/herself after evaluating his/her attributes). This evaluative component, self-esteem, is considered to be the central aspect of the self-concept (Greenwald,

Bellezza & Banaji, 1988) because it influences the way self-thoughts are organized and what aspects of the self will be most salient in particular circumstances.

Self-esteem has been considered by some (Coopersmith, 1967; Rosenberg, 1965) to be a stable, global, overall evaluation of the self that is highly resistant to change, whereas others have suggested that self-esteem is multi-dimensional and hierarchical (Fleming & Courtney, 1984; Shavelson, Hubner & Stanton, 1976). This latter viewpoint suggests that self-esteem fluctuates across different life domains. For example, a person may have high self-esteem in one domain (e.g., academic achievement) but low self-esteem in another domain (e.g., physical appearance). Vallerand, Pelletier and Gagné (1991) point out that someone can feel competent in one domain but this feeling of competence does not necessarily generalize to other domains, nor is this domain-specific confidence necessarily reflected in the person's overall, global self-esteem. Vallerand et al. demonstrated that self-esteem in one domain may change, while global self-esteem remains relatively unaffected. Yet global self-esteem is not necessarily of paramount concern when considering affect related to self-esteem. Roberts and Munroe (1994), for example, discovered that a more appropriate framework for understanding an individual's susceptibility to depression required a multi-dimensional model of self-esteem.

Wells and Marwell (1976) identified evaluation and affect as the critical elements of self-esteem. Evaluation involves the cognitive appraisal of various attributes of the self, whereas the affective component is the feeling attached to the particular attribute being evaluated. Thus, it is possible for a person to have a negative evaluation of themselves in a particular domain of functioning, but the affect associated with this evaluation may not necessarily be negative as well. The affect associated with the evaluation will vary as a function of the importance of the attribute in question. The American pragmatic philosopher and psychologist, William James (1890), described how the importance of an attribute moderates the emotion associated with the evaluation:

> I, who for the time have staked my all on being a psychologist, am mortified if others know much more psychology than I. But I am contented to wallow in the grossest ignorance of Greek. My deficiencies there give me no sense of personal humiliation at all. Had I 'pretensions' to be a linguist, it would have been just the reverse. (p. 296)

Higgins (1987) developed a theory linking what he called self-discrepancies to affect. He defined the self-concept as the collection of traits and characteristics a person believes he/she has. Higgins claimed that an individual's level of self-esteem depends upon the extent to which the self-concept is positive or negative. In this theory, the relationship between self-esteem and affect is said to result from the discrepancy between the person's actual self-concept and their ideal self, or the standards against which they measure themselves. For example, Higgins (1987) proposes that depression is related to the discrepancy between an individual's actual self-concept and his/her perceived ideal, whereas anxiety results from a discrepancy between the individual's actual self-concept and the standards for behaviour he/she has set. Subsequent research has demonstrated that the magnitude of these self-discrepancies determines the extent to which an individual feels the associated negative affect (Higgins, Klein & Strauman, 1985, 1986; Strauman & Higgins, 1988).

These findings suggest that people differ with regard to the attributes they consider when evaluating themselves. People who consider certain attributes to be of similar importance may nevertheless have different associated levels of self-esteem depending on their evaluation of themselves with regard to these attributes. Therefore, self-esteem can be expected to vary within and between individuals depending on specific situations, roles, and events (Burke, 1980; Campbell & Tesser, 1985). For example, Salovey and Rodin (1991) found that negative emotions are more likely to result from lowered self-evaluations in an important, self-defining domain than in a domain the person considers to be less important. Similarly, Savin-Williams and Demo (1983) found that the joint effects of situation, activity, and other participants elicited various levels of self-evaluation within their sample of adolescents. More specifically, Fleming and Watts (1980) found support for the view that self-esteem is a multidimensional construct and they further suggested that variations in the salience of different domains influence the self-concept.

SOURCES OF SELF-ESTEEM

As we have seen, a major determinant of self-esteem is the evaluative component, or the extent to which the person considers themselves to have measured up to their standards. In order to understand how people arrive at such evaluations, we must examine the potential sources of the inferred standards against which they judge themselves. Clarifying the process of evaluating the self, and investigating the information that people use when forming and assessing their self-concept, should enable us to identify the important determinants of positive and negative self-evaluations.

Cooley (1902) maintained that people evaluate themselves based on their perception of social feedback. According to this view, social interactions determine how an individual decides what factors or attributes are important in organizing thoughts about him/herself, and feedback from others communicates to an individual whether he/she possesses each attribute to an acceptable degree. Whether or not the perception of this feedback is accurate, an individual will, to some degree, come to internalize the standards of others. This internalization leads to an ongoing awareness by the person of whether or not they have met the standards, even when the people who set the standards are no longer present (Mead, 1934). That is, once the template of self-standards has been created, the presence of those people who helped form this template is no longer required for the individual to continue evaluating him/herself against these established standards. For example, parents are among the most important people providing the feedback that helps shape a growing child's standards, and these standards typically remain influential long after the child has become an independent adult.

However, feedback is also received from various other sources on a variety of dimensions. For example, standards for acceptable physical appearance come primarily from the media, and feedback on academic performance comes from both teachers and the levels achieved by others. Thus, self-evaluations may differ according to the particular facet of the self-concept that is being considered, and different sources of information may be used to arrive at differing self-judgements for the various aspects of functioning. An individual may employ the standards set by his/her teacher when evaluating academic performance, but may access peer feedback when determining an evaluation of physical appearance. It also follows that the salience of particular aspects of the self-concept may fluctuate according to the environmental context and the access to relevant others from whom the standards are inferred. We can expect a young person to be primarily, if not exclusively, concerned with their physical appearance on a night of a school dance when feedback from peers is likely to be highly accessible. Yet this same person might, at another time, be completely focussed on academic self-esteem, particularly if report cards are due to be distributed.

In contrast to Cooley's (1902) "looking-glass self", or the social interactionist perspective of self-evaluation development, James (1890) suggested that individuals evaluate themselves against a standard of their own choosing. According to this view, if a person fails to meet this standard, the evaluation of the self is negative and the associated feelings are negative. Correspondingly, if people meet or surpass their own standards, they will evaluate themselves positively and the result will be high self-esteem. As previously mentioned, James recognized that different people have different aspirations, and hence, they have varying standards. Consequently, some people may consider as a success what others would consider to be a failure. Thus, James defined a person's self-esteem as the ratio of successes to aspirations.

James' perspective of the sources of self-esteem is clearly quite different from that of Cooley. James viewed self-esteem as the result of autonomous processes, whereas Cooley emphasized the importance of social feedback. Harter (1993) incorporated both perspectives in her explanation of the development of self-esteem. She described findings indicating that different important domains of functioning are differentially related to an individual's sources of social feedback. For example, Harter showed that people's self-confidence about their physical attractiveness is largely dependent on feedback from others, whereas their confidence in academic functioning derives more from a comparison of their actual functioning with their standards for acceptable achievement. Harter, therefore, captured James' emphasis on the importance of relevant life domains and linked this concept to Cooley's notion of the "looking-glass self".

SELF-ESTEEM AND SEXUAL OFFENDERS

Some researchers have proposed a link between self-esteem and aggressive behaviour. For example, Tanay (1969) found that the majority of his sample of homicide offenders exhibited self-rejecting attitudes. When Russell and Hulson (1991) assessed abusive partners, they found that both husbands and wives who were abusive tended to have low self-esteem. More specifically, Baumeister, Smart and Boden (1996) suggest that low self-esteem may play a role in sexual violence because low self-esteem leads these men to channel their violent tendencies into attacks on targets they perceive to be weak and helpless (i.e., women and children).

Comparing the characteristics of people low in self-esteem (Baumeister, 1993a) with the known features of sexual offenders (Marshall, Anderson & Champagne, 1996) suggested that there may be compelling commonalities. Table 4.2 describes some of the features of people who have low self-esteem that either match identified features of sexual offenders, or indicate problems relevant to treatment.

Table 4.2   Some relevant features of people low in self-esteem

See themselves as unattractive
Expect people not to like them
Seek poor quality partners
Have poor relationships with others
Lack empathy
Engage in cognitive distortions
Divert blame from themselves
Experience frequent emotional distress and negative affect
Underestimate their abilities
Expect to do poorly and to fail
Set lower goals for themselves
Unlikely to practice scheduled tasks
Readily give up adherence to prevention programs

Derived from: Baumeister (1993a); Marshall (1996a); Marshall, Anderson & Champagne (1996).

Not surprisingly, then, several theorists (Finkelhor, 1984; Groth, 1979) have claimed that low self-esteem and sexual offending are related and there is evidence in support of this claim. Marshall, Anderson and Champagne (1996) have described a reasonably extensive literature establishing that low self-esteem is a common feature of sexual offenders. Table 4.3 summarizes the findings from our research on the self-esteem of child molesters in social situations. In this series of studies, we (Marshall, Barbaree & Fernandez, 1995) only assessed one group of rapists, but they too showed low levels of self-esteem (mean = 118.27). In addition, there is evidence suggesting a relationship between low self-esteem and other factors that are known to distinguish sexual offenders. For example, Marshall, Hudson, Jones and Fernandez (1995) found that sexual offenders exhibit deficits in empathy, and Hutton (1991) found that individuals low in self-esteem have difficulties empathizing with others. In their examination of this relationship, Marshall, Champagne, Brown and Miller (1997) found that low self-esteem was significantly correlated with empathy deficits in a sample of child molesters.

The relationship between low self-esteem and difficulties displaying empathy may be linked to more general problems in social competence. Baumeister (1993b) described the difficulties that people with low self-esteem experience in their social relations. Similarly, sexual offenders have been found to display problems in their relationships with others (Marshall, Barbaree & Fernandez, 1995; Stermac, Segal & Gillis, 1990). For example, sexual offenders indicate that they experience far more loneliness and a greater lack of intimacy than do violent offenders and males from the community (Seidman, Marshall, Hudson & Robertson, 1994). Marshall (1989a) suggested that this lack of intimacy may lead offenders to seek out feelings of closeness through sex, even to the extent of forcing sexual interactions with victims. Cortoni and Marshall (1995, 1996) demonstrated that sexual offenders use sex (including their deviant activities) as a way of coping with

Table 4.3   Social self-esteem of child molesters

	Child molesters	Nonsex offenders	Nonoffenders
Marshall & Mazzucco (1995)	119.25	—	138.13
Marshall, Barbaree & Fernandez (1995)	109.54	—	126.02
Marshall & Fernandez (in press, b)	102.67	—	—
Marshall, Champagne, Brown & Miller (1997)	110.34	—	127.61
Marshall, Cripps, Anderson & Cortoni (in press)	124.83	152.83	139.79

distressing states induced by, among other things, loneliness resulting from a lack of intimacy. Unfortunately, this strategy of seeking intimacy through sex leaves the offender's need for intimacy unfulfilled but does provide sexual gratification and temporary relief from distress. As a result, the offender may continue his abusive behaviour in an attempt to allay unpleasant feelings as well as to gratify both his sexual desires and his need for intimacy. Evidence provided by Ward, Hudson and McCormack (1997) indicates that sexual offenders exhibit numerous intimacy skill deficits, such as an inability to express physical affection, lack of self-disclosure, and poor conflict resolution skills. These difficulties produce problems in the romantic relationships of sexual offenders and tend to undermine their self-confidence.

Because it triggers such unpleasant emotional responses, those with low self-esteem understandably attempt to avoid further derogation to their self-evaluations. As we will see, one way individuals manage this is by distorting input, but they also achieve this goal through their selective associations with other people. Individuals low in self-esteem tend to establish social and romantic relationships with others who are also low in self-esteem (Byrne, 1971). By so doing, they avoid comparisons with people who display positive attributes and hence avoid feelings of inadequacy. For example, a male who is low in self-esteem may avoid a partner who is very attractive, as physical attractiveness correlates highly with self-esteem, particularly in females (Harter, 1993; Silberstein, Striegel-Moore, Timko & Rodin, 1988). Thus, men with low self-esteem may purposely seek relationships with women they find relatively unattractive in order to avoid rejection (Murstein, 1972). Unfortunately, seeking out a partner who is least likely to reject them may not result in the establishment of the sort of relationship that may enhance intimacy and reduce loneliness. Indeed, many sexual offenders cite unfulfilling relationships as a factor in their decision to commit an offence (Marshall, 1989a; Ward, Hudson & McCormack, 1997).

Marshall and his colleagues (Marshall, 1989c; Marshall, Hudson & Hodkinson, 1993; Marshall & Mazzucco, 1995; Ward, Hudson, Marshall & Siegert, 1995) have suggested that the loneliness and intimacy deficits of sexual offenders derive from inadequate attachment styles. In support of these claims, Ward, Hudson and Marshall (1996) found that most sexual offenders display insecure adult attachment patterns, with child molesters being anxiously dependent and highly sensitive to rejection. Because insecure attachment patterns develop early in life and are associated with parent–child interactions (Goldberg, 1991), it would be expected that sexual offenders would report more problematic interactions with their parents during their childhood. Literature reviews (Marshall, 1989a; Marshall & Barbaree, 1990) have shown that sexual offenders had poor quality attachments with their parents and Smallbone and Dadds (1998) have shown that, while poor relations between a child and his mother leads to more general antisocial behaviour, inadequate attachments with the father predicts later sexually coercive behaviour. More to the point of the present issue, Marshall and Mazzucco (1995) demonstrated that the degree of disruption in the relationships between sexual offenders and their parents was inversely correlated with their adult self-esteem; that is, greater parent–child disruptions produced lower self-esteem. Finally, Marshall, Champagne, Brown and Miller (1997) found that among sexual offenders self-esteem was positively correlated with intimacy and negatively correlated with loneliness.

In addition, the cognitive distortions typically displayed by sexual offenders (Ward, Hudson, Johnston & Marshall, 1997) may be related to their sense of self-esteem. These cognitive distortions represent the offenders' use of "self-serving biases", which are commonly displayed by all people (Bradley, 1978; D.T. Miller & Ross, 1975; Zuckerman, 1979). These cognitive processes allow people to interpret events, their own behaviour, and the behaviour of others in a way that preserves their view of themselves. Information that contradicts a person's view of himself/herself will be perceived as threatening, particularly if the individual has low self-esteem. In fact, Wills (1981) declared that individuals with low self-esteem will be more likely to use self-serving biases even in their interpretations of negative events because they have a greater need for security in their sense of self-worth. Self-serving biases protect low self-esteem individuals by allowing them to maintain their already tenuous grip on a tolerable, although negative, self-evaluation. Included in these self-serving distortions among sexual offenders are their attempts to deny and minimize the nature and severity of their crimes (Barbaree, 1991; Marshall, 1994a). Obviously, these attempts are meant to protect sexual offenders from further negative appraisals by others and, in this sense, they serve to protect the already fragile sense of self-worth these men have.

Thus, deficits in self-esteem among sexual offenders appear to be related to a variety of other deficits these men display. Table 4.4 describes the magnitude of the observed interrelationships between self-esteem and other relevant features of sexual offenders.

Table 4.4 Relationships between self-esteem and other deficits in child molesters

	Social self-esteem
Intimacy	0.66
Loneliness	−0.60
Empathy for own victim	0.57
Emotion-focussed coping	−0.59
Deviant sexual arousal	−0.36

Adapted from Marshall, Champagne, Brown & Miller (1997); Marshall (1997b); and Marshall, Cripps, Anderson & Cortoni (in press).

As can be seen, self-esteem is related to many of the targets that are currently addressed in treatment programs with sexual offenders. Therefore, enhancing the self-esteem of these men may facilitate changes in these other critical features. Research with other psychological problems has indicated that enhancing self-esteem increases the likelihood of obtaining successful outcomes. For instance, W.R. Miller (1983) found that bolstering the self-esteem of problem drinkers was a necessary prerequisite for achieving behavioural change. In studies of relapse rates among people attempting to maintain dieting, both Ciliska (1990) and Heatherton and Polivy (1991) report that enhancing the self-esteem of dieters markedly reduced relapse rates.

There are, however, other reasons for thinking that it may be valuable to increase the self-esteem of sexual offenders if we aim to effect positive changes in treatment with these men. Researchers agree that there is an affective component linked to self-esteem such that low self-esteem leads to the experience of negative emotions. Beck (1967) asserted that negative thoughts about the self lead to depression and Tarlow and Haaga (1996) have demonstrated a relationship between low self-esteem and depressive symptoms. Similarly, Harter (1993) has described her consistent finding that low self-esteem, depression, and feelings of hopelessness are significantly related. Since negative emotional states have been found to immediately precede offences among sexual offenders (Pithers, Beal, Armstrong & Petty, 1989), and McKibben, Proulx and Lusignan (1994) have shown that similar negative emotions prompt deviant fantasizing among these men, low self-esteem may indirectly facilitate the commission of these crimes by way of generating negative emotions.

RELEVANCE OF SELF-ESTEEM TO TREATMENT

Similar to the way in which people with low self-esteem attempt to avoid rejection in their sexual relationships, they also attempt to avoid rejection in other interpersonal interactions. Sexual offenders, particularly those with low self-esteem, entering group therapy, are typically convinced they will receive negative feedback from and be rejected by other group members because of the nature of their particular crimes. Not knowing the details of other people's offences, many sexual offenders are convinced that their crimes are the most severe, such that other group members will view them as the most "sick" or "evil". Understandably, they want to avoid such feelings and this may increase whatever reluctance sexual offenders have about honestly reporting their crimes and accepting full responsibility for what they have done.

Although such processes may be more relevant for offenders with low self-esteem, it may be difficult in the context of treatment groups to distinguish those with high self-esteem from those with low self-esteem, particularly if they have recently experienced the negative impact of ad-judication. Self-esteem fluctuates over time and across situations and events (Burke, 1980; Campbell & Tesser, 1985; Wells & Marwell, 1976). Men who have been incarcerated for committing a sexual offence are certainly in a situation that can be expected to have a negative effect on their self-evaluations, at least in the short term. They are condemned by others, including other nonsexual offenders, and at the same time they are often facing the loss of support from loved ones, loss of their job, and perhaps even loss of their home. These sudden changes can be expected to further erode the offenders' sense of self-worth, even those who were formerly high in self-esteem. Therefore, issues relevant to the therapeutic process with people who have low self-esteem ought to be relevant to the treatment of all sexual offenders.

Spencer, Josephs and Steele (1993) noted that people with low self-esteem have fewer ways to reaffirm their integrity in the face of threats to their self-image. They must, therefore, adopt some tactics that reduce the likelihood of negative feedback. One way that sexual offenders could do this would be to simply avoid participating in group discussions. This tactic would impede behaviour change and would leave the therapist with little basis on which to judge the benefits of treatment. Sexual offenders may, in addition, adopt other tactics during therapy. For example, offenders who have sexually assaulted their own children may talk about the victims in negative terms, constantly referring to their poor behaviour at home, their lying, stealing, sexual promiscuity or school truancy. These offenders may, at the same time, focus on presenting themselves in a positive way by neglecting to discuss previous criminal behaviour, deviant sexual fantasies, or other relevant yet unfavourable information.

Spencer et al. (1993) also indicated that people with low self-esteem cannot readily access their own positive attributes to relieve the negative feelings caused by a threat to their self-image; therefore, those with low self-esteem must use other strategies in response to threat. One alternative strategy described by Spencer et al. is to engage in stereotypic and preju-diced behaviours involving negative views of others. In this way a person low in self-esteem diminishes the effect of comparisons with others. It follows from this reasoning that those low in self-esteem may be more likely to exhibit prejudice when they are in a context that evokes self-evaluative thoughts or interpretations.

In the context of a sexual offender treatment group, displays of prejudice can take the form of statements attributing negative characteristics to the group from which they chose their victims. Negative statements about women serve, in the view of rapists, to justify their sexually aggressive behaviour by suggesting that women either deserve to be raped or actively provoke rape. Similar negative remarks about police officers or the system in general serve to deflect consideration of the harm an offender's crime has caused by effectively portraying himself as a victim. Such displays of negative attitudes toward entire groups of people can be frustrating to hear, but attempting to understand the function of these attitudes can help direct a therapist's responses.

One of the implications of accepting responsibility for having committed a sexual offence is that the behaviour must be integrated with the offender's existing self-concept. People often have difficulty integrating behaviours that do not fit within their self-schema, and dissonance theory (Festinger, 1957) states that an individual holding two psychologically inconsistent ideas will experience a state of tension. The way in which people reduce this tension is to reduce the discrepancy between the cognitions. For sexual offenders, this means that they have to think of their abusive behaviour differently, to be perceived as congruent with their self-concept, or they have to think of themselves differently, to perceive their identity as congruent with their offensive behaviour. We have discussed the role of denial and minimization in the effort by sexual offenders to reframe their offences in a way that is consistent with their self-perceptions. But there are many offenders who will reduce their dissonance levels by altering their self-concept to conform to the behaviour. Since individuals with low self-esteem do not readily access positive self-attributes to affirm their sense of self-worth, they will be more likely to conclude that their offending behaviour is representative of their real self. Many offenders who take responsibility for their offences refer to themselves as "sick" or "evil". In these cases, it is clear that the offender has been unable to separate his view of his behaviour from his view of himself, and he will conclude that he is, therefore, a bad person. The offender will, as a consequence, experience shame, which has been shown to reduce a person's belief that behaviour change is possible (Bumby et al., in press). In this respect, the therapist must attempt to shift the offender's focus away from construing himself as bad and toward seeing himself as someone who has positive attributes but who has committed bad behaviour. When an offender views himself in this way, he may feel guilty about having done something wrong, and guilt has been shown to motivate behaviour change (Bumby et al., in press).

Campbell and Lavallee (1993) note that people low in self-esteem are more likely to have poorly defined self-concepts, further supporting the notion that offenders with low self-esteem will be more likely to readily form negative self-concepts when required to discuss their offence. With such negative aspects of their self-schemas most salient to them, these offenders can be expected to have difficulty discussing the other, more positive, aspects of their life. Additionally, incarcerated offenders have been removed from their usual environment, so their roles as fathers, husbands, employees, etc., will not be as conspicuous. Yet it is important for offenders to be able to access their positive attributes, so therapists must introduce strategies that will overcome these dysfunctional responses and facilitate the enhancement of the offender's sense of self-worth.

As we noted earlier, individuals with low self-esteem feel more threatened by negative feedback than do individuals with high self-esteem. The implications of this threat of negative feedback in the context of treatment groups for sexual offenders suggests that they may be more resistant to accepting challenges to their perspectives. When an offender feels threatened by challenges, he will be unlikely to focus on an adaptive response. Consequently, therapists must attempt to challenge sexual offenders in a firm but supportive manner. This, of course, denies the value of a confrontational approach which, not surprisingly, has been shown to impede change in sexual offenders on treatment-relevant functioning (Beech & Fordham, 1997).

Esses (1989) proposed that negative moods affect the accessibility of information encoded in memory. This effect of mood on retrieval of memories is pertinent to work with sexual offenders. When attempting to determine the factors that contributed to the decision by sexual offenders to abuse a woman or a child, we must rely on their recall of their past. If an individual is in a negative mood when attempting to recall childhood events, his family of origin, or his environment at the time he committed his offence, he may tend to access primarily negative memories. This excessively negative slant may lead an offender to perceive himself as a victim and he may draw more collusive responses rather than constructive feedback from other group members. Again, carefully avoiding a therapeutic approach that instills a negative mood state in offenders should reduce this disadvantageous response style.

Providing feedback in a manner that enhances, rather than degrades, a client's self-esteem is crucial for motivating clients to do the necessary work during the course of their therapy. Degrading a client's self-esteem can be the result of the client interpreting feedback as an indication that he has failed. People with low self-esteem already expect to do poorly (Shrauger, 1975) and they believe criticism more than they believe praise (Tice, 1993). Individuals with low self-esteem have also been found to be less motivated and to exhibit poorer performances on tasks following what they perceive to be failure feedback (Baumeister & Tice, 1985). Thus, if feedback is provided in a manner that encourages an offender to perceive himself as a failure, he will be less likely to turn in homework in the future, or may take much longer to complete a program due to lack of motivation. Because those with low self-esteem are disinclined to make commitments to change (Rodin, Elias, Silberstein & Wagner, 1988), the lack of motivation will only be exacerbated by an ineffective therapeutic relationship that results in the client feeling worse about himself than he did before participating in the treatment group.

The relationship between enhanced self-esteem and motivation to practice tasks can be understood in terms of self-efficacy. Bandura (1977) suggested that an individual's self-efficacy, or the belief in his/her ability to carry out the relevant behaviour, can be enhanced in the following ways: directly engaging in the behaviour, observing a model successfully engaging in the behaviour, being verbally persuaded to carry out the behaviour, and by feeling calm enough to evaluate his/her capabilities with optimism. Obviously, then, to enhance feelings of self-efficacy, a therapist must have established a trusting therapeutic relationship with the client, such that the client will believe the therapist's persuasions and will attempt behaviours that may otherwise seem intimidating. The therapist must work with the client to overcome a fear of failing at a task, and then set tasks that are not too difficult so that the client will have a successful experience. Beech and Fordham (1997) found supportive group therapists were more likely to conduct cohesive groups that focus on practical tasks and decision making. While the supportive therapeutic environment may not be sufficient for producing changes in client behaviour, it does seem necessary.

Just as the problem behaviour, sexual offending, occurs in the context of predisposing individual factors and precipitating environmental circumstances, behaviour change is also affected by similar factors. A therapist who works with sexual offenders within any environment must be attuned to the individual differences that clients bring with them into therapy. Moreover, a therapist must be aware of the differences in the clients' external environments. Clients receive feedback other than that delivered by the therapist and group members, and it may be difficult for some clients to integrate extremely negative feedback (e.g., from the media, other nonsexual offenders, family members) with the feedback they receive in the group sessions. Therapists should encourage clients to discuss their own specific situations as they go through the process of enacting behavioural and attitudinal changes. After all, the gains made in therapy must generalize to other settings if the therapy is to be successful, so clients must feel they can effectively deal with situations outside the group therapy setting.

THE ENHANCEMENT OF SELF-ESTEEM

More complete descriptions of our approach to enhancing the self-esteem of sexual offenders can be found in Marshall (in press c) and Marshall, Champagne, Sturgeon and Bryce (1997). Here we will provide a brief synopsis of the elements in our program that we have designed to specifically enhance low self-esteem.

In the context of what has already been said in this chapter, it will perhaps not surprise the reader that we specifically adopt those therapist characteristics that have been demonstrated to facilitate behaviour change. With respect to self-esteem, we particularly emphasize a respectful, empathic and rewarding approach to our clients, and we explicitly distinguish them from their offensive behaviour. We have also worked hard to encourage all other institutional staff to behave in similarly respectful ways toward our clients, and we encourage all group participants to model our style of interaction with each other. The administration at our institution has been particularly helpful in directing all staff to behave respectfully toward sexual offenders and to encourage those who enter treatment. This has been very helpful and has provided our clients with the opportunity to blossom within this supportive environment.

Since our institutional setting is a thoroughly rehabilitation-oriented prison, all inmates are required to upgrade their education or work toward such upgrading. Inmates typically display the normative range of intelligence, but have markedly low educational attainment. The underlying assumption (both the institution's and ours) of this educational program is that bringing educational attainment up to the level of the inmate's intellectual capacity will enhance his confidence and provide him with skills that should improve his post-release opportunities. We also have our clients increase the range and frequency of their social activities, and we encourage them to engage in more pleasurable activities when possible. In our previous research, we (Khanna & Marshall, 1978) have demonstrated that simply increasing social and pleasurable behaviours results in an enhancement of the confidence of low self-esteem individuals.

We also assist each client in generating a list of 8–10 features of themselves that are both positive and attractive. These features do not have to be remarkable, since most of us are liked for a collection of rather ordinary characteristics. These positive features are listed on a pocket-sized card that the client carries with him at all times. He is instructed to read each of the features at least three times on three different occasions each day and to persist in this even though it may appear to be mechanical. It is often necessary to deal with rather negative views that clients have toward this procedure. Not only do clients frequently complain that it is mechanistic, and they think, as a consequence, that it will not produce benefits, they also express some reluctance at complimenting themselves. We point out that this is not an uncommon feeling in our society where we are frequently admonished not to be boastful and that this has the effect of inhibiting us from privately complimenting ourselves. Group discussion of this issue typically leads to an acceptance of this procedure, particularly when we are able to provide evidence of its efficacy (Marshall & Christie, 1982; Marshall, Christie, Lanthier & Cruchley, 1982).

Finally, we encourage our clients to attend to their personal appearance and self-presentation. There is clear evidence that people's self-esteem is markedly affected by their belief about their appearance (Harter, 1993), and a person's self-presentation obviously influences the feedback they are likely to get from others. As an incentive to follow this advice, we point out that their appearance and self-presentational style will likely influence parole boards and institutional transfer boards, both of which our clients wish to favourably impress.

Our evaluation of these procedures (Marshall, Champagne, Sturgeon & Bryce, 1997) revealed highly significant improvements in our clients' self-esteem, and revealed that these changes were strongly correlated with changes in other treatment targets. Although correlations cannot be taken to imply causality, in the case of our observed correlation between increases in self-esteem and reductions in deviant arousal it does appear to reflect a causal influence. In that study, we deliberately withheld any attention (procedural or discussion) to deviant fantasies during treatment, and yet our program markedly reduced deviant responding at phallometric assessment. While it might not have been the enhancement of self-esteem alone that produced these changes, it certainly appears to have contributed.

In any case, it is clear that addressing our clients in a respectful and empathic manner while offering specific procedures to enhance their self-esteem, is effective and appears to at least facilitate improvements in other target areas.

Chapter 5

COGNITIVE DISTORTIONS

A lie would have no sense unless truth were felt as dangerous.
Alfred Adler, 1870–1937

The idea that sexual offenders distort information in a way that facilitates their offending behaviour entered treatment approaches with these men, rather unsystematically, in the late 1970s. It was not until Abel, Becker and Cunningham-Rathner (1984) published their views on cognitive distortions that therapists and researchers concerned with sexual offenders began to approach these issues in a more careful way. What has resulted since then, unfortunately, is not overwhelmingly impressive. There has not been more than a limited amount of research on the nature and extent of the cognitive distortions of sexual offenders, nor has anyone yet evaluated more than limited aspects of the attempts to correct these distortions. Recent theoretical developments (Johnston & Ward, 1996; Langton & Marshall, in press; Ward, Hudson, Johnston & Marshall, 1997; Ward, Hudson & Marshall, 1995) may provide the bases for more systematic research, and they have certainly helped to clarify what cognitive distortions are. In fact, the first question we must ask here is just that: What do researchers and clinicians mean when they speak of cognitive distortions? We will address that issue in conjunction with a limited review of the relevant literature; we will then turn to an examination of the way in which therapists have addressed these issues; and, finally, we will describe the limited evaluations that are available.

THE NATURE OF COGNITIVE DISTORTIONS

It may be important to distinguish lying (i.e., distorted presentation) from misperceptions (i.e., distorted ways of seeing the world). Should we consider a sexual offender's presentation as indicative of cognitive distortions if we believe him to be lying? Put more specifically, are cognitive distortions illustrative of deliberate and conscious distortions of information or should we limit the use of this descriptor to only those beliefs, attitudes, and perceptions that are accepted as true by the offender? In the latter interpretation, most, if not all, aspects of denial would not be seen as distortions. The views of a sexual offender regarding his victim's behaviour prior to, during, and after an assault, and his offence-supportive beliefs about women and children, may or may not involve conscious and deliberate distortions. However, all people search for, and readily accept, information that supports their beliefs, behaviours, and goals, and they ignore disconfirmatory evidence (Harris, 1991). We remind our readers here that the distorting processes thought to be characteristic of sexual offenders do not differentiate them from the rest of us; it is the content of their distortions, and the goals manifested by their behaviours, that differentiates them. This view of cognitive distortions is similar to Ward's (in press) idea that the distortions of sexual offenders reflects their more general implicit theories about their victims. According to Ward, these implicit theories guide the way sexual offenders organize and interpret the behaviours of their victims. However, the question remains: Are sexual offenders aware of their distorting processes, or are these distortions guided by schemata of which they are at best only vaguely aware?

According to Ward (in press), the cognitive distortions of sexual offenders are manifestations of what he calls "implicit theories" they hold about people. These underlying theories are, Ward suggests, relatively coherent, and can be thought of as schemata guiding the processes of perception and interpretation of information. It is well established that people organize and interpret unfamiliar material so that it matches their beliefs (Williams, Watts, Macleod & Mathews, 1997); that is, they distort information to fit their beliefs. It should, therefore, be no surprise to find that sexual offenders do the same. These underlying beliefs have been described as schemata (Ingram & Kendall, 1986) or propositions (Nisbett & Ross, 1980) and, as a result of guiding the interpretation of input, they serve to direct behaviour (Nasby & Kihlstrom, 1986). Ward says that the implicit theories of sexual offenders can be concerned with assumptions about people in general, theories about women and children, or specific beliefs about particular victims. These self-serving theories are like those of other people (Snyder, 1984), and this fits with Abel's (Abel et al., 1984) idea that distortions allow the sexual offender to continue abusing others without guilt.

Langton and Marshall (in press) have also examined cognitive distortions within the framework of an information-processing analysis of cognitions. They also note the importance of schemata in guiding the processing of information from the environment and consequently the selection of behavioural responses. In their analysis of the cognitions of rapists, Langton and Marshall matched particular cognitive components (structures, propositions, operations, and products) with the five rapist types identified by Knight and Prentky's (1990) taxonomic system.

While these views expressed by Ward and Langton and Marshall have not yet been subjected to empirical examination, they have clear, testable predictions and offer a way to reduce the heterogeneity so evident in the cognitive distortions of sexual offenders. This heterogeneity presents a problem for both research and clinical work so any theories that reduce this variability may be helpful.

Even if the offender consciously distorts his perceptions and beliefs initially (as Abel et al., 1984, seem to suggest) as a way to allow himself to offend without guilt, he may, once offending becomes an entrenched behaviour, come to believe these self-serving distortions. Beliefs, attitudes, and perceptions are shaped by experience. No doubt we all more readily accept those views that are self-serving (Stangor & Ford, 1992), and once accepted, these cognitive responses become entrenched precisely because they meet our needs. As we noted, the difference between sexual offenders and the rest of us is not in their habit of cognitively distorting, but rather, in the goals these distortions serve. Hopefully the goals of nonoffenders, including their sexual goals, are prosocial.

Denial and minimization

Several authors have outlined what they consider denial and minimization to mean. Happel and Auffrey (1995) described denial has having 12 possible features, although other authors (e.g., Barbaree, 1991) construe many of these features as minimizations. For example, denial of responsibility (one of Happell and Auffrey's features) represents an attempt to shift responsibility for the offence to some other person (e.g., the victim, the victim's parents) or to some personal state (e.g., intoxication) or personal experience (e.g., childhood sexual abuse). Thus, denial of responsibility is essentially an attempt by the offender to minimize his culpability. Similarly, attempts to minimize the nature and extent of the abuse (at least two of Happel & Auffrey's features) are described by others simply as minimizations rather than as denial.

In Happel and Auffrey's denial list, and in Barbaree's minimizations, victim harm is identified. This is also true of both Abel's measure of cognitive distortions (Abel et al., 1989), and Bumby's (1996). These measures include questions about victim harm which require the offenders to accurately perceive the harm. In so far as they do not see the victim as harmed, the offenders are said to be distorting their perceptions. Identification of harm is an essential first step in an empathic response (Marshall, Hudson, Jones & Fernandez, 1995) and has, therefore, been seen by many as part of the problem of lack of empathy among sexual offenders (Hanson, 1997; Pithers, 1994). As we will see in the chapter on empathy, our research (Fernandez, Marshall, Lightbody & O'Sullivan, in press) has convinced us that the apparent lack of empathy in these offenders is simply a failure to acknowledge or recognize victim harm and should, therefore, be construed and treated as a cognitive distortion.

In any case, it is considered essential by the majority, if not all, sexual offender therapists to overcome issues of denial and minimization, whether they are seen as cognitive distortions or not, if effective progress is to be made with these men. From this perspective, these issues should be the first step in treatment as it is difficult to see how other problems could be addressed unless the offender admits full responsibility. However, since Hanson and Bussière (1998) have shown that denial is not a predictor of the likelihood of recidivism, it may be that this assumption is unfounded. No matter how logically compelling a position may be, it is to data that we should be responsive.

Denial and minimization have been found to occur in the majority of sexual offenders. Maletzky (1991) reported that 87% of these offenders denied all or part of their crimes; Sefarbi (1990) found 50% denied committing an offence and their families supported them; Barbaree (1991) observed that 54% of rapists and 66% of child molesters categorically denied having offended, and 98% of all his sexual offenders either denied or minimized their offences. Obviously, these are very common problems. Table 5.1 lists our way of conceptualizing the features of denial and minimization among sexual offenders.

The last two features listed in Table 5.1 require some discussion. It seems to us that clinicians and researchers are not as clear as they might be on either of these issues. Some clinicians appear to accept that all sexual offences are preceded by both elaborate planning and extensive sexual fantasies involving all or some of the details of the offender's actual crime. Accordingly, in treatment, these clinicians attempt to have their clients admit to detailed plans and fantasies that led to their offences or they assist them in identifying covert planning. Indeed, in some cases, the offender is all but bullied into accepting that he planned his offences in some detail. No doubt the intention of these clinicians is therapeutic, but, are they correct in assuming that all sexual offences are preceded by meticulous planning and elaborate fantasizing by the offender? In our view, the evidence on this issue is neither extensive nor convincing. This is partly because little evidence on

Table 5.1 Features of denial and minimization

Complete denial

    False accusation

- police out to get me
- victim hates me
- victim's mother using it to deny access or to get back at me

    Wrong person

- it must have been someone else

    Memory loss

- I'm not like that so I doubt that it happened
- could have happened but I can't remember

Partial denial

    Wasn't really sexual abuse

- victim consented
- victim enjoyed it
- she was a prostitute or promiscuous
- victim said he/she was older
- I was only massaging the victim
- I was putting medicated cream on his/her genitals
- it was only play
- it was love
- it was educational

    Denial of a problem

- I did it but I am not a sex offender
- I will never do it again
- I don't have any interest in kids or forced sex
- I don't have deviant fantasies

Minimizing the offence

- frequency less than victim claims
- no coercion/force/threats
- intrusiveness less than victim claims
- no other victims

Minimizing responsibility

- victim was seductive/provocative
- victim's parents were neglectful
- I was intoxicated
- I was severely stressed/emotionally disturbed
- my partner wasn't satisfactory sexually
- I have a high sex drive
- victim said no but really meant yes

Denying/minimizing harm

- friends or family tell me victim was not harmed
- victim's current problems not caused by me
- I was loving and affectionate so couldn't have caused harm
- I was not forceful so couldn't have caused harm

Denying/minimizing planning

- I acted on the spur of the moment
- things just unfolded
- victim initiated it

Denying/minimizing fantasizing

- I do not have deviant sexual fantasies
- I did not think about abusing the victim prior to actually offending

planning or fantasizing has been produced, and because what evidence is available has relied on the offender's self-report. The self-reports of sexual offenders are often suspect and it is difficult for researchers with strongly held convictions not to inadvertently influence the reports of these offenders.

Of course, it is difficult to accept that no planning at all took place, so it is perhaps reasonable to explore the possibility. It may be that the offender does not wish to admit to planning, or was not fully aware that allowing things to unfold was in fact an active decision on his part, or that other forms of passive planning occurred. However, the claim (we might say "accepted doctrine") that all sexual offending is preceded by fantasy not only flies in the face of the evidence, it appears to reflect some confusion over masturbatory-related fantasizing and sexual thoughts prompted by the sight of a potential victim. From general human experience, it appears likely that a man who has engaged in some form of sexual encounter with another person, at least thought about the act or the other person in a sexual way prior to the actual encounter. No doubt the same is true for sexual offending. These thoughts, however, may have been fleeting and not at all organized, so when challenged, an offender may honestly, although inaccurately, claim not to have thought about having sex with the victim. Interviewers need to be particularly clear about what it is they are asking offenders in these cases, and researchers certainly need to clarify both to their subjects and to their readers just what it is they mean when they address sexual thoughts or fantasies.

The evidence regarding the number of sexual offenders who admit to having sexual fantasies prior to offending has not helped us resolve this question, although it is clear that far from all admit to fantasizing (Abel, Becker, Cunningham-Rathner, Mittelman & Rouleau, 1988; Marshall, Barbaree & Eccles, 1991; Pithers, Beal, Armstrong & Petty, 1989). Of course, as we noted, these data may simply reflect untruthfulness on the part of some of these offenders, but, until that is shown to be the case, we have to rely on the available evidence. This evidence definitely does not justify pressing all sexual offenders into admitting to having engaged in deviant sexual fantasizing prior to (or even after) the offence. The conviction by many clinicians that deviant fantasizing is characteristic of all sexual offenders, and must be revealed and resolved in treatment, is yet another manifestation of the well-entrenched belief that sexual offending is primarily, if not exclusively, motivated by sexual desires. We are sceptical of this viewpoint.

Misperceptions and inappropriate beliefs

As noted above, sexual offenders characteristically (and almost invariably) misperceive their victim's behaviour. At least prior to their first assault, child

molesters perceive their victim's actions as sexually provocative and as ma-
nifesting sexual interest. Of course, they have a vested interest in perceiving
things this way, but it is apparent that most of them do so without consciously reframing their victim's actions. Rapists often claim that their victim
led them on and simply changed her mind either at the last minute or after
the fact. Whether this is what they perceived at the time or is a *post hoc*
reformulation is not clear, but they do seem to misperceive women's cues.
For example, Lipton, McDonel and McFall (1987) demonstrated that rapists
persistently misread social cues from women in simulated first-date vignettes, but did not misread cues from men in a similar non-date social
interaction. In particular, the rapists read as positive and encouraging, cues
from women that were clearly meant by the women to be discouraging and
negative. Even during the assaults, sexual offenders perceive their victims as
enjoying, or at least acquiescing, in the activities. Child molesters characteristically interpret an absence of evident responses by their victims as
indicating a sexually compliant, if not enthusiastic, response to the sexual
activities. Rapists also often see these sorts of responses as indicative of
sexual interest. Victims quite commonly attempt to shut down their responses during a sexual assault for fear that any response they make might
trigger an escalation in violence by their assailant. Such an absence of responding is typically perceived by the offender as a sign that the victim is
not distressed and is often interpreted as evidence that she/he is enjoying
the sexual elements of the assault. Interestingly, Hudson et al. (1993) found
that rapists and child molesters were poor at identifying emotions in others.
These deficits were most evident in their misidentification of anger, disgust,
and fear, all of which they tended to construe as more positive. These, of
course, are just the sort of emotions that victims are likely to portray during
an assault. It may be, then, that the misperceptions noted above are just that,
misperceptions, rather than *post hoc* rationalizations. It is, however, difficult
to determine just which is the case, and it may not be necessary for practical
purposes to concern ourselves over the issue. For theoretical and etiological
purposes, on the other hand, these distinctions between purposeful reformulation and unconscious misperceptions are important.

Another interesting and valuable way to think about distorted perceptions and beliefs among sexual offenders is to consider the role that sexual
fantasies play (Wright & Schneider, 1997). Wright and Schneider point out
that the evidence indicates that sexual fantasies contain several elements
(Leitenberg & Henning, 1995), many of which are aimed at bolstering the
offender's self-esteem in the face of his clearly deviant behaviour. They
describe their notion about the role of sexual fantasies as "motivated self-
deception" (Wright & Schneider, 1997). When Wright and Schneider
examined their theory, they found that, indeed, the fantasies of sexual
offenders contained elements portraying their victims as compliant with,

and enthusiastic about, the sexual elements of the offence, and as strongly sexually motivated and provocative. Wright and Schneider claim that these features of fantasies cultivate distorted beliefs so well that the offenders come to see reality as matching their fantasies and thereby entrench their distorted beliefs about the actual world.

After the assault is over, the offender may be in a position to judge the effects on the victim. If he is the father of the victim, he will almost certainly have knowledge of the victim's post-offence behaviour. Even if he is removed from the home (or the victim is removed), the incest offender is usually told by others how the victim is managing. All too often these other sources (e.g., the offender's spouse, family or friends) present an account of the victim that is meant to please the offender and is supportive of his view that no harm was done. Nonfamilial child molesters and rapists often get similar feedback from friends and family that characterizes the victim as unaffected by the assault(s), or they see the victim in court and construe her/his behaviour as indicative of an absence of problems. Victim statements to the contrary are taken to mean the victim is lying or was pressured into making these statements by the police or the prosecutor.

Much of the work examining the relationship between attitudes and sexual coercion has been conducted on males who have not been legally identified as offenders. McFall (1990) suggests that the tendency to sexual aggression is continuously distributed among men, and so it is appropriate to use non-offenders to examine this relationship. While this assumption has some merit, there are problems with studies of this kind, not the least of which concerns the requirement that these nonoffender subjects report their likelihood of being sexually coercive or their actual history of being sexually assaultive.

In Malamuth's research (Check & Malamuth, 1983; Malamuth, 1981; Stille, Malamuth & Schallow, 1987), for example, nonoffender males are asked to indicate their likelihood of forcing a woman to have sex (or raping her) if they were sure they could get away with it, and their responses are related to various expressed attitudes. Since the respondents are not provided with any details under what sort of circumstances this forceful encounter might occur, and they are not told what constitutes forcefulness, it seems certain that the meaning of their responses will present difficulties in interpretation. One respondent might consider how he would respond in the normal circumstances of his everyday life, while another might imagine how he would behave if stranded on a desert island for several years with a lone female. While both might indicate the same degree of likelihood, the meaning of their responses for their tendency to rape would be quite different. Since the researchers have no idea of the contextual bases for their subjects' responses, they are not in a position to make meaningful interpretations of the data. Similarly, in this sort of research, typically no definition is provided of what is encompassed by the terms sexual coercion, forcefulness, or rape. Again, different respondents can be expected to impose their own definition. This makes interpretation all the more problematic, since presumably men who are inclined to rape are likely to have a more restrictive definition of forced sex than do more gentle males. As a result of these considerations, we will ignore research on nonadjudicated sexually aggressors. This is not to imply that such men should be more generally disregarded in our attempts to understand sexual coercion, but rather that the current ways in which these males are identified, and their potential responses examined, is unsatisfactory.

The measures of attitudes, beliefs, and perceptions about women, children, their sexuality, and the use of force in interpersonal relations are quite transparent in the sense that it is readily apparent what the socially appropriate responses are. It is therefore no wonder that the evidence bearing on the attitudes and beliefs of rapists and child molesters is inconsistent (Segal & Stermac, 1990; Stermac, Segal & Gillis, 1990). Some studies have found that rapists do not differ from other males in their attitudes toward women or in their acceptance of rape myths (Field, 1978; Segal & Stermac, 1984). In fact, in at least one study rapists have been observed to have more positive attitudes than other men (Sattem, Savells & Murray, 1984). Stermac et al. quite reasonably suggest that employing a measure of the tendency to respond in a socially desirable manner might allow researchers to control for, or separate out, this tendency. However, such measures are of dubious quality and it is not clear that they are measuring the sort of tendencies we are concerned about (Holden & Fekken, 1989). In our clinical work we have found that the responses of rapists and child molesters in treatment are far more revealing of inappropriate attitudes than is evident in their responses to various measures of any one of the many cognitive distortions. Our clinical assessment procedures rarely reveal the sort of negative attitudes we see clearly during treatment, despite our attempt to control for socially desirable response sets.

Whatever the results of research are, the belief remains entrenched in the literature and in clinical practice that sexual offenders have a variety of distorted or inappropriate attitudes and beliefs. Rapists are thought to harbour negative views of women, to endorse violence against women, and to accept rape myths. Child molesters are believed to view children as desiring sex with adults, as sexually responsive, and as obliged to do what adults want regardless of whether or not it upsets them. Several studies have, in fact, discerned such views in rapists and child molesters (Bumby, 1996; Hall, Howard & Boezio, 1986; Hanson, Gizzarelli & Scott, 1994; Hayashino, Wurtele & Klebe, 1995; Marolla & Scully, 1986; Stermac & Segal, 1989), although in one of these studies (Hall et al., 1986), while the rapists differed from community subjects, they responded in the same way as did nonsex offenders. Marshall and Hambley (1996) also found that rapists scored higher than the normative range on both the Rape Myth Acceptance Scale (Burt, 1980) and Check's Hostility Toward Women Scale (Check, 1984).

In an attempt to overcome the limitations imposed by the use of questionnaires, Hartley (1998) selected offenders who were making successful progress in treatment, thereby increasing the probability that they would be forthcoming; she also conducted extensive interviews with each subject. Hartley found clear evidence of distortions among incest offenders, including the idea that because they did not have intercourse, it was not really sex and therefore did not harm the child, that the relationship was really more like two adults interacting, and that it was their patriarchal right to have sex with their child. Hanson et al. (1994) also discerned a sense of entitlement among incest offenders. Neidigh and Krop (1992) used open-ended questions to encourage child molesters to elaborate their beliefs, attitudes and ideas about their offences. The commonest beliefs these offenders reported concerned extenuating circumstances (e.g., drunk at the time), no harm to the victim, and enjoyment of the sexual contact by the victim.

According to Finkelhor (1984), child molesters feel emotionally congruent with children. Howells (1979), for example, using the repertory grid technique, found that child molesters viewed children as less threatening and more submissive than adults, although these findings were not replicated by Horley (1988) using an identical methodology. This sense of emotional congruence with children by child molesters was further explored by Wilson and Langevin (1998). They developed a measure of this concept which was completed by various groups of males: men who had molested boys, men who had molested girls, father/daughter incest offenders, rapists, and non-sex offenders. Only the men who had sex with boys expressed a preference for interacting with children on the child's level, while the incest offenders elevated their victims to adult status, as Hartley had found earlier.

Cognitive deconstruction

Baumeister (1991) developed a theory about escape from the self whereby people avoid the negative implications of self-awareness when they attempt to alleviate an aversive state by engaging in some forbidden behaviour. He suggests that there are hierarchical levels of meaning that we attach to our actions and that these levels range from highly abstract to concrete levels of interpretation. When we are engaged in an activity that is acceptable to ourselves and others, we generally operate at the abstract or similarly high level of meaning; that is, we are fully aware of what we are doing and its implications for our sense of self. When, however, we choose to act in a way that is unacceptable to ourselves or others (e.g., using drugs or engaging in offensive sexual behaviours), we operate at a lower more concrete level of awareness, focussing only on our immediate needs while disregarding the needs of others and even the long-term consequences to ourselves. Baumeister describes this as a state of cognitive deconstruction, and says it allows us to enact unacceptable behaviour without feeling guilt or shame which would otherwise prevent us from acting in this way. Ward, Hudson and Marshall (1995) have applied Baumeister's idea to an analysis of the behaviour of sexual offenders. While this idea makes some sense in terms of at least some offenders, it has not yet been empirically evaluated.

CHANGING DISTORTED COGNITIONS

While this review of the evidence concerning the existence of cognitive distortions in sexual offenders may be seen by some as not overwhelmingly convincing, we are persuaded that cognitive distortions of one kind or another need to be addressed in treatment. Whatever is lacking in data from controlled studies is, we believe, more than convincingly provided in clinical work with sexual offenders. Therapists have to be constantly providing feedback to these clients about the inappropriateness of their attitudes and perceptions. Such corrective processes necessarily go on throughout the offender's participation in treatment as newly emerging attitudes are expressed and as clients backslide into familiar ways of perceiving their offences. However, it is in the initial stages of therapy that these distorted views are most evident and most consistently challenged.

Murphy (1990) has suggested that the appropriate way to modify these distorted perceptions and beliefs is to adopt a cognitive restructuring approach (Meichenbaum, 1977). This involves providing clients with: (1) a rationale for the role these cognitions play in maintaining their deviant behaviour; (2) corrective information and education; (3) assistance in identifying their specific distortions; and (4) challenges to these distortions.

After our clients have been provided with an outline of, and rationale for, the nature of the treatment program, they begin the treatment process by describing in detail their offence(s). Initially, clients are asked to describe either their first offence, if they can clearly recall it, or a more recent offence they can remember well. There are several goals involved in this process. It allows us to begin the process of building an offender-specific, typical offence chain. This process continues throughout treatment until the chain is finally detailed in the ultimate step in the program; that is, the relapse prevention component. However, having the client provide details of his offence also reveals a whole range of misperceptions and distorted attitudes and beliefs about his victim, his offence, and about other more general issues (e.g., negative attitudes toward women in general, a sense of entitlement about children).

The expression of cognitive distortions within this context allows them to be examined and challenged in the way that Murphy (1990) suggested. Whenever a distortion becomes evident the therapist asks the other group members what they think of the target offender's statement. This not only begins the process of having all group members actively participate in the treatment of each other, from which they learn more about their own offences and from which they build their self-confidence, it also trains them to think critically about their own beliefs, attitudes, and perceptions. The therapist models an appropriately firm but supportive style of challenging and provides corrective feedback to the challenges of other group members. Therapists working with sexual offenders within the Correctional Services of Canada are routinely supplied with detailed victim statements, police reports, and court records concerning each offender's case. This information is, of course, very helpful in providing the therapist with a firm basis for challenging the offender's description of his assaults, although challenging distorted thinking about nonfactual matters (e.g., what the victim was thinking or feeling) does not require independent information.

Since each group member must present his version of his offence, this process not only allows him to be challenged and rethink the issues, it also provides the opportunity for considerable vicarious learning. In particular, when an offender challenges another participant, he typically does so by offering illustrations from his own offending experience or his own thinking. Most offenders find it difficult to challenge others without drawing on their own experience, and this makes them rethink their way of viewing their offences and the way in which they perceive others. Cognitive restructuring, then, is an active process rather than having the therapist behave as an instructor. As we said earlier, our view is that the treatment of sexual offenders is best done as a therapeutic process rather than conducted within a psycho-educational style.

These individual disclosures are typically repeated over several sessions and extensive discussions ensue regarding the offender's interpretation of the victim's behaviour, his own behaviour, and his expressed or implied attitudes and beliefs. Again, the offender's interpretations and beliefs are challenged and restructured by the group. As noted, these challenges and restructuring go on throughout the program as evidence of distortions continues to emerge. While this is true for almost all sessions, it particularly occurs in the empathy component and in the intimacy/attachments segment.

Unfortunately, we could not find any reports of the results of modifying general cognitive distortions or attitude changes, but there is evidence that denial and minimizations can be overcome. Before considering that evidence, we need to note an issue of some importance concerning denial and minimization. Many therapists see denial as a serious obstacle to effective treatment (Conte, 1985; Langevin & Lang, 1985) and, as a consequence, many treatment providers exclude deniers from their sexual offender programs (Schwartz, 1995). This, however, is neither legally appropriate (Cohen, 1995) nor therapeutically sensible. The problem of denial, as we will see, can be addressed in treatment, and every effort should be made to involve the offenders in treatment since they constitute a future threat of injury to innocent people.

Barnard, Fuller, Robbins and Shaw (1989) used phallometric results to challenge sexual offenders who denied or minimized aspects of their offence. However, they did not report details of how many of these offenders changed their positions. Barbaree (1991), Marshall (1994b), Schlank and Shaw (1996), and Brake and Shannon (1997), on the other hand, not only provided descriptions of their procedures for challenging denial and minimizations, they also generated data demonstrating the effectiveness of this procedure.

In addition to the procedures described above, Barbaree and Marshall made an effort to limit the number of deniers in each treatment group so that the admitters could challenge them without threatening their own position. As well, since both these researchers work within Correctional Services of Canada, they not only have independent evidence of the offences, they also have considerable leverage over the offenders. For example, deniers and minimizers who remain intractable are advised they will be unlikely to be granted the early parole that is typically available to offenders in the Canadian federal system. In Marshall's case, deniers are also advised that, should they remain resistant, they will be removed from the program and consequently, since this is a programs institution, they will be transferred to a nonprogram prison, which for sexual offenders is an extremely unpleasant consequence. This sort of leverage facilitates cooperation at a level not likely to be present in community programs or in prison systems that do not have these behavioural contingencies available. Partly, no doubt as a result of these consequences, but also hopefully as a result of their procedures, both Barbaree and Marshall demonstrated that their approach to deniers and minimizers was very effective. For instance, in Marshall's (1994b) evaluation, 25 deniers were reduced to 2 upon completion of the program, and one of these later returned to treatment as an admitter. Similarly, minimizations were reduced in both frequency and strength; pre-treatment, 32% of the group were minimizing to significant degree (3.7 on a 6-point scale), while after treatment only 11% were still in the minimizer category and the degree of minimization had also been reduced (0.5 on the 6-point scale).

Shaw and Schlank (1992) presented early data on their program for deniers. They have these offenders complete their victim empathy and relapse prevention components in a "nonthreatening manner" as preparation for entering the more general program. More recently, Schlank and Shaw (1996) have provided a detailed account of the value of this procedure. They received referrals of deniers who had been unresponsive to regular sexual offender treatment. Schlank and Shaw advised these deniers that the program was simply meant to prepare them for treatment. Subjects signed a contract agreeing to attend each of 16 sessions. Initial discussions centred on the reasons why offenders deny, and the therapists attempted to provide face-saving ways in which the offenders could change their positions. Ten victim empathy sessions followed these initial sessions which were, in turn, followed by an introduction to the basic concepts of relapse prevention. In the relapse prevention section, the initial focus was on habits the offenders wished to change, such as cigarette or marijuana smoking, or being verbally abusive to their partner. They then applied these principles to a hypothetical sexual offender whose case was similar to their own. These procedures reduced the number of deniers by 50%.

Also employing a pretreatment program, Brake and Shannon (1997) were able to show that their procedures produced a significant reduction in denial in 54% of their participants. These offenders participated in a six-component program. The first component involved honouring the offender's past denial (i.e., acknowledging that denial has served a purpose) but pointing out that it has outlived its benefits. In this way, they attempt to provide the offender with a face-saving way to change his position. The second component attempts to encourage optimism about the potential to change, while in the third component they explain the purposes denial serves and reframe it in a way that encourages the offender to change. The fourth component extends this reframing and the fifth introduces empathy for the victim. Finally, the therapist asks permission to challenge the offender's view, and then engages challenging by successive approximations. Brake and Shannon also use polygraphy as a last resort and only toward the end of their denier's program.

As a final point in considering the value of procedures for overcoming denial, we note that there is no evidence that changing a denier's status to that of an admitter has any effect on subsequent recidivism. Despite the commonsense conclusion that, given the extent of denial and minimization and its implications for subsequent effective participation in treatment (i.e., the problems of these offenders cannot easily be addressed unless they admit some degree of culpability), Hanson and Bussière (1998) found that denial did not predict subsequent sexual recidivism. On the basis of this observation, Thornton (1997) suggested that it may not be necessary to move sexual offenders past their denial, but rather, treatment of criminogenic needs may be all that is necessary. We are in the process of examining this suggestion. Maletzky (1991, 1993) reports that the majority of sexual offenders who complete his program did not subsequently reoffend, whether or not they admitted their guilt, so we can be hopeful that our experimental program might work.

Chapter 6

EMPATHY

When people understand each other in their innermost hearts, their words are sweet and strong, like the fragrance of orchids.

I Ching, 12th century BC

THE CONCEPT OF EMPATHY

Empathy has been a topic of interest in discussion and research for at least the last century (Pithers, 1994). Despite this long history, however, there has been little agreement as to its essential elements. Researchers have done little to consolidate the theories and definitions of empathy despite the fact that it is generally agreed that empathy plays an important role in regulating behaviour (Moore, 1990) and has been judged to be so critical to human behaviour by some that it has been described as the core of what it means to be fully human (Zahn-Waxler & Radke-Yarrow, 1990).

Among the many approaches to empathy, it has been described as a shared emotional experience (Deutsch & Madle, 1975), the understanding of affect in another (Moore, 1990), and a response to another person's affect or circumstance (Deutsch & Madle, 1975). There is some disagreement as to whether an empathic person must simply understand another person's feelings, or if a vicarious emotional response is also necessary. There is also much debate over whether empathy is biologically based or learned. While some researchers consider empathy to have developed in the most recently evolved areas of the brain, others consider empathy to be a purely learned emotional response. These latter theorists also believe there may be a number of different types of empathic responses that we are emotionally capable of displaying (Clarke, 1980; Hoffman, 1977; Zahn-Waxler & Radke-Yarrow, 1990).

Empathy has, unfortunately, been studied under a variety of topics, such as person perception, role-taking, recognition of affect in others, and social cognition. As a result, the procedures used to measure empathy in these studies are often so different that it is difficult to determine if the same concept is being examined. To further confuse the issue, the debate regarding empathy has also involved disagreement over whether it is a purely cognitive response, an emotional response, or some combination of these.

The cognitive component of empathy was originally described by Dymond (1948) as involving the ability to correctly identify the feelings and thoughts of another person, and to accurately take the perspective of the other person. In contrast, Stotland (1969) described empathy in terms of the emotional component which included sharing the feelings of an observed person. It appears, however, that contemporary theorists consider both cognitive and emotional responses to be important components in the empathic response (Davis, 1983; Eisenberg & Miller, 1987; Hanson, in press; Marshall, Hudson, Jones & Fernandez, 1995; Moore, 1990).

According to Davis (1983), there are four components that comprise the empathic response: perspective-taking and fantasy (the cognitive components of empathy), and empathic concern and personal distress (the emotional components of empathy). Similarly, Williams (1990) proposed a multidimensional approach to empathy that included both cognitive and emotional components as well as communicative and relational elements. Marshall, Hudson et al. (1995) have suggested that empathy is an unfolding four-stage process that involves the following elements: emotional recognition, perspective taking, the experience of a compassionate emotional response, and taking action to comfort or reduce suffering. They proposed that an apparent lack of empathy might result from deficits at any or all of these stages. In fact it is possible, and in the case of sadistic sexual offenders, very likely, that some people may accurately recognize the distress of others, and may even be able to take the perspective of another person, but may, nevertheless, not feel compassion and not take ameliorative action. Indeed, sadists should, by definition, be pleased to recognize and prolong the distress of others. In any case, Marshall et al.'s model, and the other similar multicomponent models of empathy, should encourage more detailed analyses of empathic responding, not just in sexual offenders, but in all people.

EMPATHY AND AGGRESSION

Empathy has long been considered a mediator of prosocial behaviour (Feshbach, 1987; Moore, 1990) as well as a fundamental motivator in eliciting altruism and in inhibiting aggression (Clarke, 1980; Miller & Eisenberg, 1988). The capacity to understand another's viewpoint or to be empathic with the feelings of someone else is considered essential for prosocial and altruistic acts. Alternatively, a deficiency in comprehending the feelings of others is related to negative social behaviour (Miller & Eisenberg, 1988). Miller and Eisenberg (1988) proposed that if an aggressor could vicariously experience the negative reaction of his/her victim, then this should result in a lower inclination to continue the aggression at present or in the future. Zahn-Waxler and Radke-Yarrow (1990) also believe that an aggressor who feels another's distress will be less likely to continue to hurt others and more likely to help. Feshbach's (1987) study on parental empathy indicated that parents who physically abuse their children are less sensitive to their child's feelings and needs, and tend to have low scores on empathy scales. As well, parents who are low in empathy tend to have children who have low empathy scores and problems in self-regulatory behaviour. Children who are securely attached are better able to empathize with others and are able to inhibit negative social acts, while performing more prosocial behaviours (Zahn-Waxler et al., 1990). These authors suggest that parental empathy fosters positive social response patterns and facilitates the development of adaptive behaviour in children.

In recent years, both researchers and clinicians have begun to focus on the issue of empathy, or the lack thereof, in sexual offenders. It has been suggested that sexual offenders are able to carry out their assaults, despite clear indications of distress by their victims, because they lack empathy for them (Fernandez, Marshall, Lightbody & O'Sullivan, 1999; Langevin, Wright & Handy, 1988; Malamuth, 1988; Marshall, O'Sullivan & Fernandez, 1996). Some theorists have proposed that descriptions of scenes in which a woman is hurt or humiliated inhibits sexual arousal in nonrapists but not in rapists (Barbaree, Marshall & Lanthier, 1979; Quinsey, 1984). This is supported by findings indicating that if a woman is depicted as enjoying rape, as is shown in many pornographic films, then many men (including nonrapists) demonstrate sexual arousal to the scene (Malamuth & Check, 1980, 1983; Malamuth, Heim & Feshbach, 1980; Quinsey & Chaplin, 1984).

Related support for this view comes from Mosher and Sirkin's (1984) study of nonsexual aggression in which it was found that high scores on their Hypermasculinity Inventory (HI) predicted both low scores on measures of empathy and responses reflecting indifference to the suffering of others. It has also been found that hypermasculinity scores are positively correlated with self-reported likelihood of raping (Smearson & Byrne, 1987), and Mosher and Anderson (1986) found a significant correlation between hypermasculinity scores and a reported history of actually engaging in sexual assault. A subscale of the Hypermasculinity Inventory, named the Calloused Sex Attitudes subscale, reflects a lack of empathy toward victims of sexual assault. Clearly then, a person low in empathy is deficient in a major factor that inhibits aggression toward others. It is this lack of inhibitory processes that is considered critical in allowing sexual offenders to abuse their victims.

MEASURES OF EMPATHY

Measures of empathy should be, but are not always, operational definitions derived from the theoretical understanding of empathy articulated by the designers of the tests. Some measures clearly are derived from theoretical notions made explicit by the test designer. For example, Hogan (1969) argues that empathy involves strictly cognitive processes (e.g., perspective-taking ability) and his measure is said to reflect this. Mehrabian and Epstein (1972) emphasize the emotional features of empathy and their measure assesses these features. Davis (1983), on the other hand, construes empathy as a complex of cognitive and emotional processes, and he has constructed a measure that attempts to evaluate these various features. One problem, then, with the measures of empathy that has been used with sexual offenders, which may make comparisons across studies problematic, is that the different measures assess different aspects of the processes thought to underlie empathic responding. Of course, not only do these conceptualizations differ, they may all be wrong.

The assessment of empathy has undergone many changes in the recent past. Hanson (in press) described four methods for the assessment of empathy in sexual offenders: (1) inferences made from a detailed offence and social history (collected through official records, questionnaires, and interview rating scales); (2) direct observation; (3) measures of cognitive distortions and justifications; and (4) self-report questionnaires that purport to directly examine empathy. The majority of research with sexual offenders has used the fourth method. The three most commonly used self-report questionnaires of general empathy have been Hogan's Empathy Scale (Hogan, 1969), the Emotional Empathy Scale (Mehrabian & Epstein, 1972), and the Interpersonal Reactivity Index (Davis, 1983) (for a more detailed review of these measures, see Hanson, in press). Unfortunately, each of these measures has its own constellation of problems. Chlopan, McCain, Carbonell and Hagen (1985) reported that both the Hogan Empathy Scale and the Emotional Empathy Scale have adequate reliability and validity but appear to measure different aspects of empathy. They suggest that while the Hogan Scale is based on a cognitive view of empathy (the recognition and understanding of another person's emotions), the Emotional Empathy Scale emphasizes a vicarious emotional response to another's affect. Interestingly, contrary to Chlopan et al.'s (1985) findings, Cross and Sharpley (1982) found that two-thirds of the items in the Hogan Empathy Scale failed to significantly correlate with the total score. Consistent with this observation, a factor analysis of the Hogan Scale by Johnson, Cheek and Struther (1983) found four factors: even-temperedness, sensitivity, self-confidence, and non-conformity, of which only sensitivity appears to be related to empathy. In addition, Hanson (in press) noted that because the Hogan Scale included a broad mixture of items that distinguish socially skilled people from unskilled people, some of the items have no face validity in terms of their relation to empathy (e.g. "I prefer a shower to a bathtub").

As described earlier in the paper, the Davis Interpersonal Reactivity Index (Davis, 1983) assesses the four aspects of empathy that Davis believes comprise the empathic response. Davis has generated data supporting the reliability of the measure and the stability of the four factors across repeated administrations. The scores on this measure have also been shown to be consistently, but moderately, correlated with other measures of empathy. Marshall, Hudson et al. (1995) suggested that, of the three measures most typically used to measure generalized empathy, the Davis (1983) measure seemed to be the most psychometrically sound. They note, however, that, to date, all of the psychometric evidence on the measure has been generated by the author of the test and the needs to be replicated.

Perhaps the most important feature of these measures of empathy is the fact that they assume that empathy is a trait manifest across persons, situations, and time. There are many problems with the notion of traits (Mischel, 1968) and, in any case, it seems unlikely that people are consistently empathic or not toward everyone in all situations. Very few people displayed empathy for the Nazis on trial at Nuremburg for crimes committed during World War 2, and yet some of the accused appeared quite distressed. In fact, novelists and movie makers rely on the fact that their readers and audience will display empathy for some characters but not for others. Indeed, the problem some potential therapists, who may otherwise be quite empathic, have about working with sexual abusers is that, far from feeling any empathy for these offenders, they feel anger and contempt. Perhaps sexual offenders also feel empathy for some people under some circumstances, but not for others. Thus, measures of generalized or ubiquitous empathy seem unlikely to reveal deficits specific to sexual offenders. It would seem more appropriate to examine the empathy of sexual offenders toward specific individuals or groups of individuals rather than toward either everyone in general or toward nonspecific individuals. We will return to this issue in a moment, but first, let us consider what has been found using these general measures with sexual offenders.

GENERALIZED EMPATHY IN SEXUAL OFFENDERS

The literature on child abuse has often presupposed deficits in child molesters' ability to empathize with children. Williams and Finkelhor (1990) reviewed the characteristics of incestuous fathers and reported that they are deficient in both bonding and empathy. This is supported by Parker and Parker (1986) who found that a greater number of incestuous fathers (56% as compared to 14% for nonincestuous fathers) reported being absent from the household during most of the first three years of their victim's lives. Parker and Parker reported that incestuous fathers, even when they were at home, were more likely than other fathers to avoid child care activities such as diapering and feeding during these formative years. Absent fathers, and those who avoid intimate child care, are unlikely to form the bonds with their children that might prevent abuse. This, however, suggests a more specific empathy deficit; that is, empathy is lacking toward their own child but may be present toward others. Life history interviews with child molesters have indicated that they see their victims as objects and focus on their own pleasure or satisfaction (Gilgun & Conner, 1989). Despite this interest in the area of sexual offender empathy, few empirical data have been generated that support the assumption of a generalized deficit.

Using the Hogan Empathy Scale, Rice, Chaplin, Harris and Coutts (1990) reported data indicating that a group of rapists incarcerated in a maximum security hospital was less empathic than a group of nonoffender males. This was supported in a subsequent study by Rice, Chaplin, Harris and Coutts (1994), who found that rapists scored lower on the Hogan Scale and endorsed more rape myths than did community controls. Unfortunately, Seto (1992) failed to replicate these findings with rapists imprisoned in Canadian penitentiaries. Seto initially found differences between rapists and nonoffenders on Hogan's Scale, but the results disappeared when level of education was used as a covariate. These discrepancies are not surprising when we consider the populations used in the Rice et al. studies. Rapists from a maximum security psychiatric facility typically display very poor social skills and a substantial number meet the criteria for psychopathy. They might, accordingly, be expected to display little empathy for other people. On the other hand, far fewer rapists from a general prison population meet the criteria for psychopathy (Serin, 1995), and this might be expected to result in fewer empathic deficits.

Mehrabian and Epstein's (1972) Emotional Empathy Scale has been even less successful in discerning empathy deficits among sexual offenders. In a study of 96 mixed sexual offenders (exhibitionists, incest offenders, pedophiles and rapists), Langevin et al. (1988) found that scores on the Emotional Empathy Scale did not discriminate these offenders from a normative group of college students. Sexual offender subgroups were not differentiated by total empathy scores or by any of the items, and empathy scores were not related to violence revealed in the offence histories. Similarly, Hoppe and Singer (1976) found that the Emotional Empathy Scale did not discriminate between sexual offenders and other types of offenders, and Rice et al. (1994) reported that the scale failed to distinguish rapists from community controls.

Although the Davis (1983) Interpersonal Reactivity Index (IRI) was designed to overcome some of the difficulties associated with these other scales, it has not been widely used with sexual offenders. In a study assessing pre- and post-treatment empathy in sexual offenders, Pithers (1994) found that rapists demonstrated poorer empathy at both pre-treatment and post-treatment than did pedophiles, but the total scores on the IRI for both groups increased following victim empathy training. An important point to note here, however, is that the average score of both groups of sexual offenders at pre-treatment was within the same range as that reported for normative subjects. In contrast, Hayashino, Wurtele and Klebe (1995) found no differences between incestuous offenders, extrafamilial child molesters, incarcerated nonsexual offenders and laypersons on any scales of the IRI. Hudson et al. (1993) found that outpatient child molesters had lower scores than community controls on the IRI total score and the fantasy subscales, but the responses of incarcerated child molesters were similar to those of the normative sample. The data indicating empathic deficits in community-based child molesters, but not in imprisoned offenders, suggest that the incarcerated child molesters may have been dissimulating.

In fact, the problem with self-report measures of any kind is that respondents may simply answer in a way that describes their tendencies as prosocial. This would be expected to be particularly true with sexual offenders who typically present themselves in an exculpatory fashion. The Hudson et al. study also reported that IRI scores (except for the personal distress subscale) correlated with the offenders' ability to identify emotions from pictures of adults and drawings of children. Hanson (in press) suggested that, while the Perspective-Taking and Empathic Concern subscales of Davis' measure seem promising for the assessment of empathy in sexual offenders, they may be too general. As previously mentioned, rather than assessing generalized deficits, it may be preferable to look at empathy toward specific persons (Marshall, Hudson et al., 1995).

The three general empathy measures described previously follow the standard "trait" approach to empathy reflected in most of the literature. As a rule, empathy has been conceptualized as a fixed disposition that is demonstrated unvaryingly across time and place. Consequently, a respondent is construed as either an empathic person or an unempathic person. Most theorists who propose that sexual offenders are deficient in empathy seem to suggest that they suffer from a generalized deficit. As we saw from Pithers' (1994) study evaluating treatment effects, even therapists appear to share this view. The question, however, is "Do sexual offenders in fact display generalized deficits in empathy?" Our examination of the rather limited evidence on the use of general measures does not encourage confidence that we will find a lack of empathy toward all people among sexual offenders.

Recently, there has been a trend toward identifying situations in which sexual offenders are more or less likely to show empathy. Marshall, Hudson et al. (1995) strongly encouraged researchers to focus on studies of victim-specific empathy. They suggested that we should not expect general empathy deficits in sexual offenders. While some sexual offenders, such as those who score high on measures of psychopathy, might reasonably be expected to demonstrate little empathy toward anyone, most sexual offenders, so Marshall et al. suggested, should be empathic in a variety of nonsexual offence-related situations.

A number of measures have been developed that allow us to evaluate this approach to conceptualizing empathy. Hanson and Scott (1995) have designed the Empathy for Women and Empathy for Children tests in which written vignettes are used to assess perspective-taking deficits in sexual offenders. The tests contain 15 vignettes that describe interactions between men and women or between adults and children. In order to avoid self-report biases, the series of vignettes include both deviant and nondeviant themes. Thus, offenders are not able to appear nondeviant by rating all vignettes as inappropriate. Fernandez, Marshall, Lightbody and O'Sullivan (1999) described a measure of empathy for child molesters that required subjects to identify various harmful effects experienced by children as a result of either sexual molestation or some other trauma. They suggested this measure would allow for the separate appraisal of empathy within different contexts. Following the development of this test, Fernandez et al. (1999) have generalized a similar measure of empathy specifically for rapists. Other measures have also been developed that permit us to assess sexual offenders' empathy toward victims of sexual abuse. These measures include having rapists rate the reactions of women in videotaped vignettes of dating situations (Lipton, McDonel & McFall, 1987; Murphy, Coleman & Haynes, 1986) and having child molesters respond to written descriptions of adult and child sexual interactions (Beckett, Beech, Fisher & Fordham, 1994; Stermac & Segal, 1989).

VICTIM-SPECIFIC EMPATHY IN SEXUAL OFFENDERS

Despite the scarcity of empirical data demonstrating that the empathic deficits of sexual offenders are victim specific, some evidence has been generated that lends support to this idea. In an evaluation of emotional recognition skills (the first stage in Marshall, Hudson et al.'s, 1995, model of empathy) Hudson et al. (1993) found that sexual offenders and violent offenders had difficulty identifying surprise, fear, anger, and disgust in others. Because these emotions reflect the types of reactions one would expect from a victim of sexual assault, the offenders' inability to accurately identify them should prevent them from displaying empathy toward victims. Interestingly, the nonsexual, violent offenders in Hudson et al.'s study demonstrated the greatest accuracy of emotional identification, while the sexual offenders were the least accurate. Hanson (1996) offered an explanation for this finding by suggesting that offenders who are overtly violent are likely to find an uncaring, adversarial relationship reward and, therefore, accurately identify, and enjoy, distress in their victims. In a second study in the Hudson et al. report, it was found that child molesters performed more poorly than a group of community males at identifying the emotions of both adults and children.

Scully (1988) examined the perceptions 47 rapists had of their own and their victims' responses to their assault. Fifty-eight percent of the rapists acknowledged at least some understanding of the victims' feelings. However, although most of the rapists in the study could recognize at least a few of the victims' feelings, and they were apparently able to respond emotionally to this recognition, they, nevertheless, had no empathy for the victims. In a study by Deitz, Blackwell, Daley and Bentley (1982), empathy toward both victims of rape and toward the rapists was examined in a group of nonoffender males. It was found that subjects who demonstrated high empathy toward rape victims reported less desire to actually commit rape than men who demonstrated lower empathy toward the victim. In a later study, Deitz and his colleagues reported that empathy toward both the victim and the offender predicted nonoffender male subjects' perceptions of the victim, the offender, and the offence (Deitz, Littman & Bentley, 1984). Low empathy males saw the victim as more responsible, the offender as less culpable, and the offence as less serious, than did the high empathy men. Wiener, Wiener and Grisso (1989) found that the views expressed by nonoffender males on the measure used in the Deitz et al. studies influenced the subjects' processing of information given by witnesses in a rape trial. Again, low empathy males were less likely than high empathy males to believe witnesses who supported the victim's version of events.

Written vignettes of adult and child sexual interactions were used in a study by Stermac and Segal (1989). These authors reported that, in vignettes describing the child as showing few overt signs of resistance, child molesters tended to underestimate the child's distress; rapists and nonoffenders, on the other hand, equally accurately estimated the child's distress. Beckett et al. (1994) similarly found that child molesters, when asked to respond to written vignettes of adult and child sexual interactions, underestimated the harmfulness of the sexual offences. As with the Stermac and Segal (1989) study, the sexual offenders in Beckett et al.'s study were more likely to minimize the harmfulness of sexual assaults that did not involve obvious force.

Hanson (in press) suggested that, while promising, the Stermac and Segal (1989) and Beckett et al. (1994) methods of assessment were open to self-report bias. In an attempt to control for this, Hanson and Scott (1995) designed the Empathy for Women and Child Empathy Tests. The tests include written vignettes of heterosexual adult interactions and adult–child interactions respectively. Some of the interactions described in the tests are sexually abusive, some are nonabusive, and some are ambiguous. Hanson and Scott pointed out that if respondents overestimated the distress of the woman or child, then this would suggest they were attempting to "fake good". Where there were underestimates of distress, Hanson and Scott claimed, this would indicate empathic deficits.

On the Empathy for Women test, the authors reported clear group differences between the sexual aggressors and comparison groups: the rapists tended to underestimate the women's distress in the vignettes. Responses to the Child Empathy Test demonstrated that child molesters who were in treatment more accurately identified distress than did those who were untreated. In addition, the incest offenders tended to overestimate the distress of children, suggesting they were attempting to "fake good". Unfortunately, however, the internal consistency of the Child Empathy Test was low and no overall group differences between sexual offenders and a comparison group were found. Currently this test is being revised in an attempt to improve some of its psychometric properties.

Fernandez et al. (1999) designed a Child Molester Empathy Measure to examine empathy in three contexts: (1) toward a child who had been disfigured in an accident; (2) toward a child who had been sexually abused by an unspecified assailant; and (3) toward the offenders' own victim(s). An initial study demonstrated that the measure was internally consistent (i.e., all items appeared to be measuring the same thing) and had good test–retest reliability. It was found that child molesters showed lower empathy scores, relative to a group of nonoffenders, toward the child who had been sexually abused by another offender, but not toward the child who had been a victim of the car accident. Most importantly, the child molesters exhibited their greatest empathy deficits toward their own victim(s). In a series of studies, we (Marshall, Champagne, Brown & Miller, 1997; Marshall, Champagne, Sturgeon & Bryce, 1997; Marshall, Hamilton & Fernandez, 1998; Marshall, O'Sullivan & Fernandez, 1996) have essentially replicated these findings, confirming that the empathy deficits in child molesters primarily involve their attitude and feelings toward their own victim. The results of our studies are summarized in Table 6.1.

Fernandez and Marshall (1998) modified this measure to allow the appraisal of empathy in rapists. This revised version evaluates the empathy toward a woman across the same set of circumstances as the earlier measure. Once again, an initial study revealed high internal consistency and satisfactory test–retest reliability. In an examination of the value of their Rapist Empathy Measure, Fernandez and Marshall found, oddly enough, that the rapists demonstrated more empathy than a group of nonsexual

Table 6.1 Empathy scores on Fernandez et al.'s measure

	Accident victim	General sexual abuse victim	Own victim
Child Molesters			
Marshall, O'Sullivan & Fernandez (1996)	284.94	262.31	176.27
Marshall, Champagne, Brown & Miller (1997)	279.70	278.30	178.10
Marshall, Champagne, Sturgeon & Bryce (1997)	280.66	283.25	192.94
Fernandez et al. (1999)			
Study 1	274.38	273.16	159.46
Study 2	277.62	284.76	173.59
Rapists			
Fernandez & Marshall (1998)	349.96	356.37	276.48
Nonoffenders			
Marshall, Champagne Brown & Miller (1997)	289.30	345.40	—
Fernandez et al. (1999)	286.48	334.90	—
Fernandez & Marshall (1998)	285.44	345.11	—

offenders toward women in general (i.e., toward the accident victim). Rapists also displayed the same degree of empathy as the nonsexual offenders toward the woman who was sexually assaulted by someone else. However, like the findings with child molesters, the most marked empathy deficits were found in these rapists toward their own victim(s). Table 6.1 describes the data we have generated on both rapists and child molesters using our measures.

One important point of note in these studies concerns the variance found among the sexual offenders. For instance, the child molesters displayed the same variability in empathy toward the accident victim as did the nonoffenders, but their empathy scores toward their own victim revealed twice this degree of variability. Thus, some of the child molesters displayed appropriate empathy toward their victims, while others were quite unempathic. The rapists, on the other hand, displayed the same level of variability across all three women, and the variance in their scores did not differ from the nonoffenders. Apparently, in terms of empathy for their victims, child molesters are a good deal more heterogeneous than are rapists.

The results of these studies strongly suggest that empathy deficits in sexual offenders are best examined in relation to particular people (i.e., victims of sexual abuse) or in particular circumstances (i.e., when victimization is occurring). Fernandez's measures are aimed at the former (i.e., empathy for victims), while Hanson's tests attempt to examine the latter (i.e., empathy for victims during abuse). Perhaps some of the variance in Fernandez's studies of child molesters results from the fact that these offenders are able to inhibit empathy (or ignore signs of distress) during their offence, but some, when they reflect on what they have done, may subsequently feel empathy for their victim. If this is true, then it may be best to use two measures (e.g., Hanson's and Fernandez's) in order to fully capture the empathic problems of child molesters.

The findings of the above studies clearly suggest that the majority of sexual offenders have trouble empathizing with their victims. However, we suggest that these apparent deficits in empathy are not necessarily evidence of a lack of empathy at all, but rather, they may reveal yet another facet of the cognitive distortions that are so characteristically evident in sexual offenders. If sexual offenders have empathic skills that are equal to those of nonoffenders (i.e., they are just as empathic toward a disfigured accident victim and on general measures of empathy they look normal), and yet they display little empathy toward their own victim, then it is tempting to construe the latter apparent deficit as either a deliberate withholding of empathy, or more likely, as a deliberate and successful attempt to deny having done any harm to their victims. This denial may result from either shutting out or distorting their perceptions of the victim's distress during the assault and subsequently ignoring or distorting post-assault signs of distress. Indeed, there is evidence that sexual offenders deny harming their victims (Abel et al., 1989), and this is usually considered to represent distorted perceptions.

Sexual offenders, like most people, tend to perceive things in a self-serving way. In their case, sexual offenders want to continue offending without feeling any personal distress, and the best way to achieve this is to see their victims as unharmed by the abuse. Persistently construing their victims in this way which is often, unfortunately, supported by the offender's family and friends, allows sexual offenders to convince themselves that their offences are exceptions to the general rule that sexual abuse causes damage to victims. In our model of empathy, emotional recognition is the necessary first step. Thus, the denial of harm prevents the unfolding of the empathic process and results in an apparent deficit in empathy that, in most cases, is victim-specific.

Other researchers have also pointed out that empathy deficits in sexual offenders are inextricably linked to cognitive distortions. Hilton (1993), for example, has suggested that lack of empathy could readily "be woven into the bed of cognitive distortions" by the offenders, promoting further minimizations and justifications of their offensive behaviour. Likewise, Hanson (in press) points out that measures of cognitive distortions are an alternative route to identifying empathy deficits. It has also been shown that treatment aimed at increasing empathy toward sexual assault victims decreases cognitive distortions in sexual offenders (Bumby, 1994; Pithers, 1994; Schewe & O'Donohue, 1993). A look at many of the current victim-specific empathy questionnaires (Beckett et al., 1994; Fernandez et al., 1999; Hanson & Scott, 1995) reveals that these measures include many items that could readily be interpreted as revealing cognitive distortions (i.e., items that address minimization of harm to the victim). For example, sexual offenders claim that their victims are not harmed by the experience, or actually enjoy the interaction (Abel, Becker & Cunningham-Rathner, 1984; Snowdon, 1984).

Consequently, we suggest that, to date, empathy research on sexual offenders has actually been addressing a very specific set of cognitive distortions; that is, those related to the harm caused to the victim. This would help explain the lack of evidence indicating a generalized empathy deficit among sexual offenders. If empathy deficits reflect the offenders' attempts to specifically justify their offences to themselves and to others, in order to avoid feelings of guilt and loss of self-esteem, we should not expect these cognitive distortions reflecting a perceived lack of harm to victims to generalize to other situations. There would be no need for the offender to rationalize away empathic responses to situations that do not threaten his own sense of self-worth, such as toward people (or women or children) in general. Certainly, future research examining empathy in sexual offenders will need to take a closer look at this issue.

In pursuit of this possibility, we (Marshall, Hamilton & Fernandez, 1998) compared the responses of child molesters, nonsex offenders, and nonoffender males on our measure of victim empathy and Abel et al.'s (1989) measure of cognitive distortions. Once again we found that child molesters were primarily deficient in empathy toward their own victim; they also manifested far greater signs of cognitive distortions than did either of the other two groups. Most importantly, the child molesters' victim-specific empathy deficits were strongly correlated with their scores on the measure of cognitive distortions. This, of course, is consistent with our hypothesis that apparent empathy deficits in these offenders are no more than distortions about the harmful consequences of their abuse.

Whether empathy deficits are seen as cognitive distortions or not, it is generally accepted that these problems are significant factors in sexual offending. Much more needs to be done before we can be said to understand the nature and extent of these issues. In particular, researchers need to examine more fully the specificity of empathy deficits in sexual offenders. In addition, the role that emotional and harm recognition play in sadistic offenders has yet to be explored, but is obviously quite important. We look forward to future studies elucidating these complex issues. The results of such studies will, of course, better inform treatment, although the majority of programs currently attempt to train these offenders to be more empathic. It is to those issues that we now turn.

EMPATHY ENHANCEMENT

Empathy enhancement is practiced in 94% of all sexual offender treatment programs in North America (Knopp, Freeman-Longo & Stevenson, 1992), despite the poverty of evidence that sexual offenders actually lack empathy, or that these treatments are effective. The inclusion of empathy-enhancing components in treatment is based on the belief that the attitudes of sexual offenders toward their victims will change if they understand how the victim feels, and the subsequent development of empathy will inhibit future sexual abuse (Williams & Khanna, 1990). It is also believed that empathy will increase the offender's motivation to engage his relapse prevention plans (Hildebran & Pithers, 1989). However, none of these rationales has yet been empirically validated.

Treatment components aimed at enhancing sexual offenders' empathy are quite varied, and it is not always clear what the precise goals are of these treatment processes. Many reports of these treatment components discuss empathy as though it were a trait manifest toward all people that is either present or absent. However, when the elements of treatment are described, it appears that most programs are aimed at enhancing empathy for either all victims of sexual abuse, or simply the offenders' own victims. In fact, all too frequently the descriptions of treatment do not make clear precisely which of these two goals are the aims of empathy training. We (Marshall, O'Sullivan & Fernandez, 1996) have also been guilty of this and, in our case, and we presume also in others, it was due to both a lack of clarity in our earlier thinking about the nature of empathy deficits in sexual offenders, and to a fuzziness in our ideas about what it was we should aim for. While our notions about empathy deficits are now somewhat more clear, we are still unsure about what it is we need to address. We are now convinced that apparent empathy deficits in most sexual offenders are due to either a failure to recognize harm (i.e., a particular form of cognitive distortions) or to pleasure in the sadistic offenders as a result of the recognition of harm (again, a distorted way of viewing the world). Consequently, our current treatment component addressing empathy deficits focuses on the recognition of harm for the majority of our offenders. We believe that sadistic offenders constitute such a different group that they need specialized and separate treatment from most sexual offenders. Not that we have any profound remarks to make about appropriate treatment for these sadists, except that antiandrogen interventions seem essential. Clearly, far more research is required before we can attempt to understand sadists, much less design adequate treatment for them. For the rest of this discussion we will focus on nonsadistic offenders who, fortunately, comprise the majority of sexual offenders seen in most settings.

When programs aim at enhancing empathy most seem unclear about what it is they are attempting to do. From the research reviewed in the previous section, we might hope that empathy for victims would be the main target. Some empathy treatment components encourage offenders to role-play the part of the victim in order that they might come to appreciate the ways that victims perceive the abuse (Mendelson, Quinn, Dutton & Seewonarian, 1988). Other programs have the offender write an account of the offence from the victim's perspective and read it aloud to the treatment group (Hildebran & Pithers, 1989). Some programs discuss the feelings, thoughts and reactions of a group member who has disclosed his own sexual victimization (Murphy, 1990). Knopp (1984) described a role-play variant of covert sensitization in which the offence is reconstructed with the offender taking the role of the victim. The idea behind this procedure is to link the act of victimizing with the victim's presumed imagery of the offence.

Hildebran and Pithers (1989) describe their attempts to enhance sexual offenders' empathy for sexual abuse victims. They suggest that, because empathy has both cognitive and emotional components, once it is entrenched in the offender it will function at both these levels to block offending. By instilling empathy in sexual offenders, so Hildebran and Pithers claim, the sequence leading to an offence will be prevented from fully unfolding. Even when the offender fails to acknowledge that he has begun a chain of behaviour leading to an offence, empathy will provide the emotional connection with the victim that will abort this sequence. This is much like our early contention (Barbaree, Marshall & Lanthier, 1979) that empathy would inhibit arousal to deviant and hurtful sexual acts. In fact, Hildebran and Pithers thought that empathy training was so important, they implemented it as the first step in treatment and only allowed those offenders who successfully developed empathy to move on to the next stage in the program.

The topic of empathy is introduced in Hildebran and Pithers' program by having offenders read a collection of descriptions by victims of the effects of sexual abuse. The offenders write a report on this and read it to the group at the next session where they are challenged by others. Next, the group watches videotapes depicting the damage to victims of sexual abuse, which are subsequently discussed by the group. Offenders then write an account of their abuse from the victim's perspective and read it to the group. All of these sessions are videotaped to provide feedback to the offender. Those offenders who have themselves been sexually abused are then required to discuss with the group both their abuse and its effects.

For those offenders who display resistance to recognizing victim harm, Hildebran and Pithers design role-plays. First the offender plays himself acting out the concrete details of his offence. He then switches to the role of the victim and, throughout these role-plays, he is repeatedly asked about his feelings and wishes. Again, these sessions are videotaped in order to provide feedback to the offender. One of the potential problems with these sort of role-plays is the possibility that such realistic enactments may provoke sexual arousal in the observing group members. It is not clear what sort of precautions Hildebran and Pithers take to deal with this possibility. Finally, the group meets with adult survivors who describe their problems and the suffering they have experienced as a consequence of being sexually abused.

Pithers (1994) described an evaluation of this component of treatment. He had offenders complete both Davis' IRI and Burt's Rape Myth Acceptance Scale. On both these measures sexual offenders displayed significant improvements after treatment. However, since Davis' IRI is a nonspecific measure of empathy that is unrelated to sexual offending, it is not clear that Pithers' program increased the capacity of his offenders to recognize the harm they had done to their victims and to respond to it appropriately.

We (Marshall & Fernandez, in press, a) described in detail our earlier version of empathy training, so we will give only a brief account of it here. First, it is important to note that many other features of our program contribute to the enhancement of empathy. For example, the initial task offenders have in our program is to disclose in detail their offence. This requires them to not only give an account of what they did, but also to describe what they were thinking and feeling throughout the assault. Challenges occur throughout this disclosure, many of which concern an offender's failure to recognize the harm he was doing and his lack of empathy. In addition, as was noted in the chapter that outlined the overall features of our program, we do not take a components approach to treatment. Consequently, although there are sessions that focus primarily on empathy, the relevant issues are addressed throughout the program whenever it seems appropriate. For example, even after completing the empathy section, some offenders have made less than the full changes we expect, while others subsequently take backward steps. The former cases are recorded and we raise issues repeatedly with them in later sections of the program. For those who slip back, this generally becomes evident when other topics are discussed and we immediately address the issues. In addition, in some of the later components we revisit empathy. For example, an important feature of effective intimacy skills in the capacity to be empathic. In this case, empathy is related to dealing with a partner rather than a victim, so it is revisited with a somewhat different slant.

The specific features of our empathy component involve addressing each aspect of our staged model. Initially we attempt to increase the offenders' ability to recognize emotional states. Some of our offenders have problems with this because they are not able to identify their own emotions. Consequently, our first step requires each offender to describe to the group an emotionally distressing event from his past. Often enough this concerns his own physical or sexual abuse as a child which, of course, is particularly valuable for the group to hear and discuss because it alerts them in a very personal way to the damaging effects of abuse. Whatever the nature of the past distressing experience, the presenting offender must, at the end of his description, identify the emotions he felt when presenting.

Discussion of these presentations requires, in addition to a general discussion, that each other group member offers an appraisal of the description, and also identifies both the target person's emotions and his own emotional response to the description. Each response is appraised by the therapist who assists the group in identifying the degree to which each respondent has displayed empathy toward the target person. Since every offender must describe an emotional experience, and appraise every other person's description, there are repeated opportunities for both direct and vicarious learning. These opportunities are typically more than enough to make offenders sufficiently aware of both their own and other people's emotional responses. However, when an offender is having trouble developing emotional recognition, he is given as homework the task of writing a description of another distressing experience which is then read to the group and followed by discussion.

The next step requires the group to identify the possible harmful effects of sexual abuse on the victims. Each offender in turn is required to mention at least three or more potential effects which the therapist writes on a flip-chart. When an offender indicates that he cannot think of any additional effects, or when he simply indicates agreement with what others have said, he is told to think about it until all the rest are finished, then add his original comments. If he is still unable to generate any additional harmful effects, he is given as a homework task the job of identifying at least three additional problems victims might experience.

Once the list on the flip-chart is completed by all group members, each offender is required to identify from this list the effects that might have occurred to, or might in the future occur to, his victim. Again, all other group members appraise each offender's description of the effects he expects have been or will be experienced by his victim. The descriptions are often challenged and revised as a result of feedback from the group.

We then have each offender describe his actual offence (or one of his offences, if he has several) from the victim's perspective. If this description is unsatisfactory, we will have the offender role-play his victim's responses during specific aspects of the offence. The role play is subsequently discussed by the group, and the offender is helped in appreciating the victim's likely responses. Repeated role-plays may be necessary for a resistant offender to fully accept the harm he has done. In these role-plays we do not have the offender elaborate every intrusive sexual behaviour since we do not want any group member to become distracted by sexual arousal to the scene. This is not always easy to manage and great care must be taken when using role-plays of the offence. We therefore try to avoid employing offence role-plays where possible.

Each offender is then required to write two hypothetical letters: the first from the victim to him, and the second as a response to the victim's letter. The first letter should identify the anger, confusion, loss of trust, and guilt experienced by the victim and any other distress or problems that might be expected. This letter is read aloud by the therapist to the group and then discussed for its adequacy. Rarely is the letter acceptable at the first attempt as there are typically various exculpatory intrusions. These are challenged, and the offender is required to rewrite it and go through the same process again and again until he gets it in satisfactory form. The offender's letter of response should indicate that he takes full responsibility for the abuse, accepts and legitimizes the victim's distress, notes that, unlike himself, most other people are trustworthy, and he should express regret for his actions. Again, this response letter often includes inappropriate comments, such as a request for forgiveness. These inappropriate remarks are challenged by the group and the offender is required to rewrite the letter until it is deemed satisfactory.

Finally, actual victim accounts are provided for each offender to read as homework with in-depth discussions occurring in the following sessions. Each offender describes both the victim's emotions and his own emotional responses to having read the account. These descriptions are discussed and challenged, if necessary, by the group.

This component was evaluated with child molesters by taking pre- and post-treatment assessments using our empathy measure (Marshall, Champagne, Sturgeon & Bryce, 1997; Marshall, O'Sullivan & Fernandez, 1996). The results of these appraisals revealed significant increases in empathy for both children abused by someone else and for the offender's own victim. Table 6.2 describes the results of these evaluations. In fact, the post-treatment mean scores of the offenders' empathy for these two groups of victims matched the original normative group's responses to the child abused by an unknown assailant. Perhaps even more impressive is the fact that the variance displayed by the child molesters at post-treatment for both these children approximated that of the normative group. Obviously, this treatment component achieved the goals we were aiming for.

However, this component is quite time consuming and does not lend itself well to the open-ended group format which we prefer. Fortunately, as we saw in the research section of this chapter, our findings of primarily victim-

Table 6.2 Treatment changes in empathy among child molesters

	General sexual abuse victim		Own victim	
	Pre-treatment	Post-treatment	Pre-treatment	Post-treatment
Marshall, O'Sullivan & Fernandez (1996)	262.31	328.69	176.27	344.83
Marshall, Champagne, Sturgeon & Bryce (1997)	283.25	320.03	192.94	324.81

specific empathy deficits led us to reconstrue these deficits in a way that encouraged a restructuring of our empathy component. As a result of our data, we came to view these apparent empathy deficits as cognitive distortions rather than as empathy deficits. Specifically, we believe that offenders misconstrue the responses of their victims during the offence as indicating either passive, nondistressed acceptance, or as positive compliance. Any subsequent problems the victims experience are similarly misconstrued as unrelated to the offence. Since recognition of distress is the essential first step in the unfolding empathic response, we decided to examine the possibility that simply having the offenders recognize and accept the harm they had done might be sufficient.

Accordingly, we markedly abbreviated our empathy component so it involved only two elements, both of which we have already described. First, we have the group generate a list of problems that result from sexual abuse and these are discussed and related to each offender's victim as outlined above. Next, they write and present for discussion the hypothetical letters; one from the victim and the other a response from the offender to the victim. We are presently in the process of evaluating this more concise component, but the results to date are encouraging. This abbreviated component more readily fits into our open-ended group approach and also flows more easily from the previous cognitive distortions component. It also allows us to process more offenders because they can move through the program more efficiently.

Finally, on the issue of training empathy in sexual offenders the concern is often expressed that all we may be doing is teaching them the right things to say. In this view we have modified the cognitive, but not the emotional, aspect of empathy. In fact, some have questioned the possibility of training anyone to be empathic. For example, Hilton (1993) argued that teaching "cognitive" empathy may not generalize to "emotional" empathy. She cited examples of offenders who are able to demonstrate an understanding of empathy in descriptions of their own victimization, but who nevertheless continue to offend. Hilton points out that psychopaths "epitomize cognitive empathy without the emotional link" and she suggests that some sexual offenders may be taught to identify and mimic others' feelings rather than truly embody what we would consider empathy. It is no doubt possible that Hilton and other critics of empathy training with sexual offenders are correct, and certainly their challenges must be taken seriously.

Hilton (1993), however, seems to be talking about empathy as if it were a trait, and, as we have seen, this may not be the problem for most sexual offenders. Nevertheless it remains true that all we have after treatment is the offender's account of his recognition of harm and feelings of concern. We have not yet found a way to appraise the emotional depth of any remarks made by offenders (nor, for that matter, by anyone else) and it would be no surprise at all to learn that they had not been fully truthful, given their invidious position. For the present, we see no choice but to rely on the therapists' judgements about the veracity of offenders' reports and the depth of their empathic expressions. In any case, surely the acquisition of understanding (i.e., the cognitive component of empathy) is a necessary precursor to feeling distress over the harmful effects of behaviours so, at the very least, we appear to have moved our offenders in the right direction.

Clearly, both in terms of the assessment and treatment of empathy deficits in sexual offenders, and the ways in which we construe such deficits, we have much more work to do. However, we believe the interest in these issues over the recent past encourages the view that we are on the right path and that a reasonably consensual view of this problem will emerge within the next few years. When our view of empathy in sexual offenders is clarified, appropriate measures should follow, as should effective and efficient treatment methods. For the moment, we encourage researchers and clinicians to take a multimethod approach to the assessment of empathy.

Chapter 7

SOCIAL FUNCTIONING

RACHEL MULLOY AND WILLIAM L. MARSHALL

Department of Psychology, Queen's University, Kingston, Ontario, Canada K7L 3N6

Alas, is even Love too weak
To unlock the heart, and let it speak?
Are even lovers powerless to reveal
To one another what indeed they feel?

Matthew Arnold, 1822–1888

Issues to do with the social functioning of sexual offenders have been persistently raised over the years. For example, Mohr, Turner and Jerry (1964), in their extensive study of child molesters, noted that these men did not interact effectively with adults, but spent a good deal of their social activities with children. Fisher (1969; Fisher & Howell, 1970) found child molesters to be "sexually and emotionally inadequate in relating to adult females." In their report, Pacht and Cowen (1974) indicated that sexual offenders were deficient in establishing satisfactory relationships with adults and they saw this deficit as leading these men to attempt to form relationships with children.

In the early 1970s, as cognitive behavioural treatments began to emerge, Marshall (1971) illustrated the value of addressing social deficits with non-familial child molesters. He pointed out that if we wished these men to change the direction of their sexual interests from children to adults, simply modifying their sexual preferences would not necessarily ensure they had the requisite skills to meet their needs with adult partners. Marshall proposed training sexual offenders in heterosocial skills, most specifically, relationship skills. Shortly thereafter, Barlow (1974) wrote a paper outlining the need to increase the social skills of men he called sexual deviates (which unfortunately included homosexuals). Barlow followed this with the development of a heterosocial behaviour checklist to assess the social skill deficits of these men (Barlow, Abel, Blanchard, Bristow & Young, 1977). Marshall, Christie and Lanthier (1979), in a descriptive study of a sample of incarcerated rapists and child molesters, reported some social deficits in sexual offenders, and other authors also suggested that this was an important problem related to the crimes of offenders (Clark & Lewis, 1977; Laws & Serber, 1975). It was suggested that not only did the lack of adequate social skills prevent sexual offenders from meeting their needs in acceptable partnerships, but also that such deficiencies made them fearful of adult contact. Consistent with this latter view, Howells (1979), using the repertory grid technique, found that child molesters saw adults as domineering, overbearing and threatening, whereas children were seen by these men as compliant, submissive and nonthreating.

Observations such as these led cognitive behaviour therapists in the 1970s and 1980s to include a social skills training component in their treatment programs (Abel, Blanchard & Becker, 1978; Barnard, Fuller, Robbins & Shaw, 1989; Crawford, 1981; Marshall, Earls, Segal & Darke, 1983; Perkins, 1977; Rowan, 1988), and specific interventions were described to enhance social competence (Burgess, Jewitt, Sandham & Hudson, 1980; Crawford & Allen, 1977; Serber & Keith, 1974; Whitman & Quinsey, 1981). There is some, but limited, evidence that these specific interventions achieved their goal. Crawford and Allen (1977), for instance, showed that, in terms of their responses to various questionnaires and simulated role-plays, sexual offenders displayed improved skills after treatment which were maintained at 2-year follow-up (Crawford, 1981). However, as Crawford (1981) noted, as yet there is no evidence that these programs have any effect on subsequent recidivism. Furthermore, most of these earlier social skills components focussed primarily on training conversational skills, assertiveness, and reducing social anxiety (e.g., Edwards, 1972; Maletzky, 1991; Stevenson & Wolpe, 1960; Travin & Protter, 1993), which are certainly important, but do not exhaust the extensive aspects of effective social functioning. Relationship skills, for example, involve far more than simply being able to confidently carry on a superficial conversation. Relationships typically develop over time and usually involve greater intimacy as they develop. Furthermore, even in conversation with nonintimates it is necessary to be able to accurately read the subtle cues emitted by the conversational partner (McFall, 1982). McFall (1990) also pointed to other aspects of the complex of skills needed for effective social functioning. Other than McFall's own work, however, very little has been done to examine these facets of social skills. For instance, Lipton, McDonel and McFall (1987) found that rapists consistently misread negative social cues from women as encouraging signs of the women's interest in them. However, not only do sexual offenders misread cues from other people, they are also poor at judging and predicting their own behaviour (Segal & Marshall, 1986).

Despite the continued enthusiasm shown by cognitive behaviour therapists for increasing the social skills of sexual offenders, there is not a clear body of evidence confirming that they suffer from such deficits. For instance, while Segal and Marshall (1985) found some limited overall deficiencies in social functioning among incarcerated sexual offenders, no unique deficits were identified, and rapists, in particular, were found to function reasonably well. Similarly, Overholser and Beck (1986) were unable to find significant differences in the assertiveness of child molesters and rapists compared to nonsex offenders and nonoffenders, although the trend was for the child molesters to appear most deficient. Only Stermac and Quinsey (1985) were able to find assertiveness deficits in rapists, but their sample came from an institution housing the criminally insane, whom we might expect to be generally more deficient than sexual offenders housed in prisons or attending community clinics.

When we consider possible social skills deficits in sexual offenders, it is important to note that many of these men will be returning to a milieu wherein standards for social competence may be different from those evident in the social strata from which most therapists come. For example, Marshall, Barbaree and Fernandez (1995) demonstrated that sexual offenders have quite different standards for acceptable social behaviour than do nonoffenders, and that even among nonoffenders, standards differ from what is usually described as socially appropriate behaviour. Using video-taped scenes, Marshall et al. required subjects to make judgements about the appropriateness of the responses of males to an unreasonable demand by another man. They found that child molesters judged clearly unassertive behaviour to be the most appropriate, rapists judged clearly aggressive behaviour to be the most appropriate, and demographically matched non-offender males did not differentiate unassertive, assertive, and aggressive responses; only university males identified polite but firm assertive behaviour to be the most appropriate response. This clear evidence of quite different standards in the demographically matched nonoffenders compared to the university males, suggests that we must be careful not to train clients to our standards, but rather, assist them in developing skills that will make them effective within their own milieu. We must be careful, therefore, not to impose our standards on our clients, or we may make them into social misfits within their life circumstances.

As Gordon, Marshall, Loeber and Barbaree (1977) noted some time ago, we need a clearer identification of just what it is we expect when we claim that sexual offenders have social deficits so that we can more definitively examine the hypothesis that they are deficient in these skills. McFall's (1982, 1990) conceptualization provides an ideal framework for analyzing the social skills of sexual offenders, but we also need to extend our examination beyond simple conversational interactions. As a step in that direction, we have begun to systematically examine problems in adult relationships among sexual offenders.

INTIMACY PROBLEMS

A number of authors have, over the years, drawn attention to the possibility that sexual offenders may have difficulties in establishing and developing intimacy with adults (Bancroft, 1978; Fagan & Wexler, 1988; Tingle, Barnard, Robbin, Newman & Hutchinson, 1986). These suggestions, combined with our clinical observations of apparent problems in relationships among our offenders, prompted us to reconsider what we were doing in treatment. For example, when we initially evaluated our treatment program for exhibitionists, we found rather disappointing results (Marshall, Eccles & Barbaree, 1991). This early program for exhibitionists focussed primarily on sexual motivation and consequently failed to address more than limited aspects of social functioning. We modified this program so that it focussed primarily on relationship skills, and we found this modified approach to be more effective than the earlier version (Marshall, Eccles & Barbaree, 1991). These results encouraged us to more seriously consider the possibility that relationship issues may be relevant to understanding and treating all sexual offenders.

In an attempt to integrate these ideas, Marshall (1989a) outlined a theory suggesting that deficits in their capacity to achieve satisfaction in intimate relations with consenting adults caused sexual offenders to seek sexual satisfaction with either children or nonconsenting adults. Marshall (1989a; 1993; 1994a; Marshall, Hudson & Hodkinson, 1993) suggested that insecure attachments to their parents provided sexual offenders with an inadequate template for other relationships. These insecure parent–child relationships, Marshall suggested, produced a fear of intimacy, as a result of rejection or neglect by their parents, and also failed to provide them with the skills and confidence necessary to meet their needs in appropriate peer-aged relations. This, in turn, so Marshall suggested, made these offenders feel emotionally lonely, which is a state that generates self-interest and aggression (Check, Perlman & Malamuth, 1985; Zilboorg, 1938). It is easy to see how this may lead a man to decide to engage in sexual abuse.

A central idea of Marshall's theory is that sexual offenders identify intimacy with sex, so they think that sexual behaviour of any kind will meet their unresolved needs. Of course, sexual offenders are not the only men who identify intimacy with sex, but other men may seek to resolve this, for example, by having numerous affairs. According to Marshall's theory, sexual offenders, as a result of their difficulties in peer-aged relationships, unfortunately turn to offending as a distorted way of dealing with this largely unrecognized need to seek intimacy. However, since intimacy needs are best met in equitable relations (Birchler & Webb, 1977; Reiss & Lee, 1988), sexual offending will necessarily produce no more than transitory satisfaction, if any at all. Those sexual offenders who better understand the broader nature of their needs (i.e. those who recognize their lack of intimacy) will attempt to establish a more involved relationship with their victim, which almost necessarily means they will molest children. Consistent with this idea, Finkelhor (1986) and Ward, Hudson and France (1993), found that a significant number of child molesters described their desire to offend as motivated by a need for affection and intimacy.

Obviously there are many implications to Marshall's theory, the most obvious of which are that sexual offenders should display intimacy deficits and experience chronic loneliness. Subsequent research has confirmed these expectations, and Table 7.1 summarizes the findings from some of these studies. Seidman, Marshall, Hudson and Robertson (1994) evaluated intimacy and loneliness in both incarcerated and community-based sexual offenders. They found that rapists, nonfamilial child molesters, incest offenders and exhibitionists all exhibited loneliness and a lack of intimacy in their lives. Garlick, Marshall and Thornton (1996) also found that rapists and child molesters were lonely and had low levels of intimacy, and these offenders tended to blame women for their problems in relationships. Marshall and Hambley (1996) and Marshall, Champagne, Brown and Miller (1997) essentially replicated these findings. Not only did Bumby and Hansen (1997) also repeat these findings, they showed that rapists and child molesters were afraid of intimacy. In addition, Bumby and Hansen expanded their evaluation of intimacy problems to include not only the subjects' romantic or sexual partners, but also their family and friends. Most interestingly, they found that both rapists and child molesters had little intimacy with anyone. Thus their problems in relationships are manifest in all aspects of their social functioning; little wonder, then, that sexual offenders score very high on measures of loneliness.

In addition to the support these findings offer for our theory, the following results demonstrated that sexual offenders have had the sort of childhood relationships with their parents that we expected. Antisocial behaviours in general, for example, have been shown to be most accurately predicted by poor quality parent–child relationships (Kolvin, Miller, Fletting & Kolvin, 1988; Loeber & Stouthamer-Loeber, 1986). More specifically, Smallbone and Dadds (1998; in press) found that while poor quality relations with mothers predicted general antisocial behaviour, poor paternal attachments predicted sexual coercion in adulthood. Awad, Saunders and

Table 7.1   Results of research on intimacy and loneliness

Study	Intimacy	Loneliness
Seidman et al. (1994)		
Study 1		
Rapists	88.0[1]	51.4[4]
Child molesters	95.6	51.2
Incest offenders	129.3	48.6
Exhibitionists	108.0	48.9
Nonoffenders	140.4	37.7
Study 2		
Rapists	18.7[2]	44.6
Child molesters	20.4	46.4
Violent nonsex offenders	19.1	37.4
Nonviolent nonsex offenders	25.0	37.1
Garlick et al. (1996)		
Rapists	278.7[3]	42.8
Child molesters	238.6	49.8
Nonsex offenders	300.8	36.6
Marshall & Hambley (1996)		
Rapists	19.02[2]	39.83
Nonoffenders	21.85	41.54
Marshall, Champagne, Brown & Miller (1997)		
Child molesters	85.31[1]	46.84

[1]Miller's Social Intimacy Scale (Miller & Lefcourt, 1982)
[2]Waring's Intimacy Scale (Waring & Reddon, 1983)
[3]The Psychosocial Intimacy Questionnaire (Tesch, 1985)
[4]The Revised UCLA Loneliness Scale (Russell, Peplau & Cutrona, 1980)

Levene (1984) reported serious disruptions in parent–child bonds among adolescent sexual offenders, with one-third of the parents being described as rejecting and one-third as abusive to their sons, while half of the fathers were described as emotionally detached. Similar poor quality attachments were found by Saunders, Awad and White (1986) between parents and their sons who later became sexual offenders. Paternal separation and physical abuse by parents was observed among adolescent sexual offenders by O'Reilly et al. (1998), and Prentky et al. (1989) found inconsistent parental care to typify the childhoods of adult sexual offenders. Various other studies have likewise found disruptive parent–child relations, physical, sexual and emotional abuse, and neglect by parents to be common features of the childhoods of adult sexual offenders (Burgess, Hartman & McCormack 1987; Dwyer & Amberson, 1989; Finkelhor, 1984; Firestone, Bradford, Greenberg, Larose & Curry, 1998; Langevin et al., 1984).

Interestingly, both Lisak (1984) and Mullen, Martin, Anderson, Romans and Harbison (1994) found that non-offender subjects who had been sexually abused as children had serious problems as adults in intimate relations. Since childhood sexual abuse is a common feature of sexual offenders (Hanson & Slater, 1988), these findings of a strong connection between such abuse and adult difficulties with intimacy, strongly suggest that sexual offenders will have intimacy problems and the evidence, as we have seen, certainly supports this speculation.

ADULT ATTACHMENTS

An alternative and perhaps more productive way to look at this issue is to consider the style sexual offenders typically employ in their adult romantic relationships. Ward, Hudson, Marshall and Siegert (1995) adopted this approach in order to expand on Marshall's earlier work on intimacy. The general approach to examining adult attachment styles has been derived from the literature on parent–child attachments (Bartholomew & Perlman, 1994). Accordingly, we will introduce our discussion of adult attachments by placing it in the context of childhood attachments.

Attachment theory conceptualizes "the propensity of human beings to make strong affectional bonds to particular others" and explains "the . . . emotional distress to which unwilling separation and loss give rise" (Bowlby, 1969, p. 127). Attachment behaviour describes the actions of people in relation to their attachment figure: someone to whom the person turns for affection and comfort, when feeling stressed, anxious or frightened. For children, this person is usually a parent (Bowlby, 1969); for adults, the primary attachment figure is most frequently a romantic partner or close friend (Hazan & Zeifman, 1994). Our concern here is primarily with adult attachments to a romantic or sexual partner.

According to Hazan and Zeifman (1994), behaviour toward such figures is characterized by *proximity seeking* (needing to be close and/or make contact), seeing them as a *safe haven* (turning to the figure for comfort, support or reassurance) and as providing a *secure base* (using the figure as a base from which to engage in non-attachment behaviours). In addition, attachment figures are said to be capable of generating *separation protest*, which involves displays by the child of resistance to, and being stressed by, separations from their parent. All of these are survival behaviours, no doubt developed through our evolutionary history (Ginsberg, 1997), that maximize an infant's chances of being protected and cared for by others (West & Sheldon-Keller, 1994). Attachment behaviours are said to characterize humans throughout their life span. From Bowlby's theory, patterns established during the formation of attachment in parent–child relationships tend to structure later adult attachment patterns (Bartholomew, 1993). In Bowlby's (1969) description, these early attachment experiences provide a template for all later relationships.

The attachment system is organized and regulated by social input. Infants quickly learn from their caregivers what to expect and how to behave in relationships. From this early experience, children develop mental representations, or internal working models. These are "complementary . . . models of attachment figures and of the self through which the history of specific attachment relationships is integrated into the personality structure" (Bretherton, 1985, p. 3). Bowlby (1969) describes these models as consisting of expectations about whether or not others are likely to respond supportively in times of need (i.e. their model of others) and whether or not they themselves are the kind of people that others are likely to respond to helpfully (i.e., their model of the self). Theoretically, then, there is a strong link between the development of internal working models of attachment, early relationship experiences, and adult relationship styles.

Children's behaviours are not just generated by the nature of their relationship with their parents, but also by the way in which their parents impose their ideas about acceptable behavior. For example, the open expression of negative feelings by parents and their tolerance of such expressions in others shows a lack of fear of these emotions, and a confidence that they can be controlled (Bowlby, 1977). This openness not only provides a model for the growing child, it also creates an atmosphere favourable to the development in the child of self-control. On the other hand, pressure on children to conform to unrealistic, covert, and distorted parental expectations, Bowlby believed, results in the adoption by the child of the parent's false models of both the self and the nature of relationships. In conjunction with these pressures there is also a clear parental disregard for the child's needs. These experiences, along with the resulting false models and the attendant feelings of insecurity and incoherence, markedly increase the likelihood that the child will develop problems in the appropriate expression of emotion. When a child's responses are ignored, the lesson for the child is that his/her feelings, needs, and wants are invalid or irrelevant. Where parents are intolerant of negative feelings and emotions, children do not learn how to experience such emotions in a moderate and organized fashion (Bowlby, 1969).

Once developed, internal working models (of the self, others, and relationships) tend to be resistant to change (Kirkpatrick & Hazan, 1994; Scharfe & Bartholomew, 1994) which is partially because they appear to operate automatically. This does not imply, however, that internal working models are incapable of change. It is simply more difficult to change the representations in response to disconfirming information than it is to interpret information so as to fit existing mental representations. Evidence indicating similarities between parental and adult romantic attachment patterns, and perceptions of similarity between an individual's opposite-sex parent and his or her romantic partner, support this view (Collins & Read, 1990). Thus, changes in internal working models may only occur slowly and infrequently (Kirkpatrick & Hazan, 1994; Scharfe & Bartholomew, 1994; Swann, Hixon & De La Ronde, 1991). When an individual's attachment does change, it tends to be in response to relationship experiences that are directly relevant to the internal working model (Kirkpatrick & Hazan, 1994; Scharfe & Bartholomew, 1994).

It has been suggested that individuals tend to choose partners and experiences consistent with their beliefs about themselves and others (Collins & Read, 1990). There is a greater-than-chance probability that when one partner in a relationship is securely attached, the other partner will also be securely attached (Owens, et al., 1995). It is not yet clear, however, whether people choose each other on the basis of similarity of attachment patterns, or whether the attachment patterns of partners grow more similar over time. Some concordance has also been found between individuals' views of themselves and their romantic partners' perceptions of them (Swann et al., 1991). Taken together, these findings offer further support for the stability of internal working models by providing evidence for the mechanisms by which such stability may be achieved.

Researchers who have examined the way in which adults form relationships have distinguished different individual styles of relating. Borrowing from the parent–child attachment literature, these researchers have identified styles that consistently discriminate those who have secure adult relationships from those whose style does not produce secure intimacy. Bartholomew (1993), in particular, has been at the forefront of this research.

Bartholomew's four-category model

Bartholomew and Horowitz (1991) suggest there are four adult attachment patterns which are essentially extensions of the attachment patterns found between children and their parents (Ainsworth, Blehar, Waters & Walls, 1978). These models of self and others have been shown to be consistent across various domains of functioning (Griffin & Bartholomew, 1994).

Adult attachment styles

Bartholomew and Horowitz's (1991) model of attachments is presented in Table 7.2.

Individuals with a *secure attachment style* have a positive concept of both themselves and others. They are confident about their ability to make friends and interact well with others. Secure people genuinely like and

Table 7.2 Bartholomew and Horowitz's attachment model

Attachment Style	View of Self	View of Others	Relationship behaviors	Level of intimacy
Secure	Positive	Positive	Seeks closeness Reciprocity Tolerant	High
Preoccupied	Negative	Positive	Emotionally labile Dominating Intense	Inconsistent but limited
Fearful	Negative	Negative	Fearful of disclosure Lacks trust Emotionally unexpressive Passive	Superficial
Dismissive	Positive	Negative	Uncaring Uncomfortable with feelings Avoids closeness Non-disclosing	Almost none

Adapted from Bartholomew (1990).

appreciate other people and are able to trust them. They can realistically assess the quality of friendships and romantic relationships, and deal with problems in a constructive fashion. Secure people do not dominate and are not dominated by others; they are able to balance their involvement in relationships with their individual needs.

There are three types of insecure adult attachment styles.

Preoccupied individuals have a negative self-concept, and do not feel confident about their ability to deal with problems without the help of others. They have a positive concept of others and are likely to be in intense romantic relationships on a continuous basis, although they may change their specific romantic partner quite often. They are very emotionally expressive, sometimes to the point of histrionics. This preoccupied pattern is associated with intense involvement in relationships and a dominating interpersonal style.

People with a *fearful* style have a negative concept of themselves. They have low self-confidence and tend to blame themselves for problems in their lives. They also have a negative concept of others. They find it frightening to go to others for help and to trust the people around them, although they would like to. Fearful people are very aware of their feelings, but find it difficult to express them, especially around other people. When they do have relationships they tend to be passive.

Individuals with a *dismissing* style have a positive self-concept and a strong sense of self-confidence. They are likely to say they do not care what others think of them, and associated with this, they have a negative concept of others and do not seek out other people for help or support. These dismissing people are not comfortable with feelings or their expression and tend to avoid others in times of stress. Not surprisingly, they are rarely strongly emotionally involved in their relationships, and are not likely to put up with things they do not like.

Adult romantic attachments

Most adults cite their romantic partner as their primary attachment figure (Hazan & Zeifman, 1994). The concept of adult romantic love is closely related to that of attachment. Behaviours such as needing to be close to people and to care for them (Kelley, 1983) parallel the attachment concepts of proximity seeking and safe haven (Hazan & Zeifman, 1994). Research has found that different attachment patterns tend to be associated with different romantic relationship qualities. Because most of this research has been conducted using an earlier three category model (Hazan & Shaver, 1987), the findings will be discussed using that model. The primary difference between this earlier model and that of Bartholomew is that the *anxious/ambivalent* category approximately corresponds to Bartholomew's preoccupied pattern of attachment, while the *anxious/avoidant* category encompasses both the dismissing and fearful patterns.

Secure attachment tends to be associated with a general high quality of intimate relationships. The relationships of secure people are characterized by happiness, trust, friendship, enjoyment of closeness, little jealousy, and few emotional extremes (Kobak & Hazan, 1991; Shaver & Hazan, 1987). Secure lovers support their partners, and are able to accept them, including their flaws. Their relationships tend to be long-lasting (Hazan & Shaver, 1987; Senchak & Leonard, 1992) and they have higher levels of commitment and interdependence (Simpson, Rhodes & Nelligan, 1992) than do insecurely attached lovers. Finally, secure partners display higher levels of relationship satisfaction than do insecure partners (Senchak & Leonard, 1992).

Insecure individuals tend to experience more unhappiness in their relationships than do secure individuals (Bartholomew, 1993) and this is associated with lower levels of trust, less commitment, dissatisfaction, and an absence of interdependence (Simpson et al., 1992). Compared to secure people, those with an anxious–avoidant pattern are less likely to accept their partners' faults, and are more likely to be jealous and to respond with emotional extremes (Shaver & Hazan, 1987). They are also less likely to commit to their relationships (Feeney & Noller, 1990). Anxious/ambivalent people are characterized by obsessive, preoccupied and jealous forms of love (Feeney & Noller, 1990; Levy & Davis, 1988; Simpson et al., 1992). They have a very strong desire to be in a relationship and frequently fall in love at first sight (Hazan & Shaver, 1987). In sum, it has been found that the relationships of people with differing attachment patterns differ qualitatively in a number of ways.

Attachment characteristics have been found to be associated with many aspects of interpersonal functioning. For instance, securely attached people are generally happy and healthy, and function well in most other aspects of their lives (Bartholomew, 1993). Insecure patterns, on the other hand, have been associated with various forms of psychopathology, including personality disorders, anxiety, and depression (Davila, Burge & Hammen, 1997).

Attachments and sexual offending

Ward, Hudson, Marshall and Siegert (1995) outlined a theoretical model linking dysfunctional attachment styles to specific characteristic patterns of sexual offending. Indeed, rather than linking sexual offender types (e.g., rapists and child molesters) to particular insecure attachment styles, Ward, Hudson and McCormack (1997) later suggested that attachment styles offer a better way to classify sexual offenders than do offence types.

What Ward, Hudson et al. (1995) suggested was that the preoccupied attachment style should be linked to sexual offenders who seek to establish a nonthreatening, intimate relationship with their victims; the fearful style should identify sexual offenders who engage in impersonal, and frequently single contact sex with their victims; while the dismissive style should be associated with a coercive and physically assaultive pattern of sexual offending. Thus, according to this view, preoccupied sexual offenders should seek immature victims by grooming them over time and by developing a quasi-romantic relationship with these children. Fearful offenders should be more likely to engage in either short-term, impersonal contacts with children, or rape women using only sufficient forcefulness or threats to achieve their goal. Finally, dismissive offenders, who it will be remembered have a negative view of others, would be expected to be aggressively sexually assaultive against either women or children.

While this theory has many advantages, not the least of which is that it makes clearly testable predictions, there are some problems in its match with Bartholomew's (1990) model of adult attachment styles from which it is said to derive. Specifically, in terms of sexual offending behaviours, the fearful–avoidant pattern was described as follows:

> We can also expect them to be unconcerned about their victims' feelings so they will feel little empathy toward their victims and experience little in the way of guilty feelings about their offending. Similarly, they will be self-

focussed during their offenses and will not feel constrained to use force if necessary to achieve their goals. (Ward, Hudson et al., 1995, p. 12)

This description is at odds with Bartholomew and Horowitz's (1991) conceptualization of the fearful pattern as involving individuals who lack assertiveness and are socially inhibited. Bartholomew and Horowitz note that subjects rated high on fearfulness are relatively warm and are characterized by introversion, unassertiveness, and exploitability. These features do not fit with the cold, self-focussed, and forceful individual depicted by Ward, Hudson et al. (1995). Ward et al.'s description does fit, by contrast, with the dismissive pattern. Research has indicated that individuals with this latter style are hostile, excessively cold, and lack nurturance and expressiveness (Bartholomew & Horowitz, 1991). In addition, the description by Ward, Hudson et al. (1995) of the dismissive pattern, although generally consistent with research findings, does seem to be discrepant in one specific feature. Ward et al. state that these individuals blame others for their lack of intimacy and this may be identified with Garlick et al.'s (1996) findings that sexual offenders blame women for their loneliness. Ward et al.'s position suggests that dismissive individuals desire close relationships, whereas this pattern is actually associated with downplaying the importance of other individuals who are perceived as rejecting (Bartholomew & Horowitz, 1991). Bartholomew (1993) makes it clear that the central characteristic of the dismissive pattern is a defensive denial of the need or desire for intimate contact. The conceptualizations by Ward, Hudson et al. (1995) of the interpersonal and offending characteristics associated with the different attachment patterns are thus partially flawed, and need to be revised.

The general proposition, however, that insecure attachment patterns will be associated with sexual offending has received clear support in several studies (Bumby & Hansen, 1997; Cortoni, 1998; Hudson & Ward, 1997; Jamieson & Marshall, in press; Smallbone & Dadds, in press; Ward, Hudson & Marshall, 1996; Ward, Hudson, & McCormack, 1997). In addition, child molesters tend to be over-represented in the fearful pattern, and to some extent, in the preoccupied pattern. By comparison, rapists have been found to be more likely to be dismissive. The difference in offence types between these two groups indicates, as suggested by Ward, Hudson et al. (1995), that fearful offenders may also be different from dismissive offenders in the ways in which they victimize. Higher levels of offence violence have been found to be associated with those sexual offenders having the dismissive pattern, whereas those with the fearful avoidant style were less violent than securely attached sexual offenders (Jamieson & Marshall, in press; Ward et al., 1996). This is interesting, because being violent is not an identifying characteristic of the dismissive pattern. One possible explanation is that the uncaring, self-centred aspects associated with the dismissive pattern could lead to the use of aggression. Such characteristics are also associated with psychopaths (Hare, 1991), who tend to be violent in their offences. It is, therefore, possible that the association between sexual violence and the dismissive pattern is due to variables associated with both; that is, callousness and lack of empathy.

Despite the problems we have identified with Ward et. al's theory, there appears to be no doubt that attachment styles are an important area of dysfunction in sexual offenders. However, more work is needed to examine whether or not these insecure attachment styles are linked to specific sexual offending patterns as Ward, Hudson et al. (1995) originally suggested. Nevertheless, if we wish our sexual offending clients to meet their needs in more prosocial ways, we will have to assist them in altering their current way of engaging in romantic adult relationships.

TREATMENT OF INTIMACY DEFICITS

We have developed, evaluated and described a treatment component aimed at enhancing intimacy and reducing loneliness (Marshall, Bryce, Hudson, Ward & Moth, 1996). The original article describes these procedures in detail, so we will give only an outline here.

There are, of course, aspects to the other components of our program that are relevant to the establishment of intimacy or to the adoption of an effective attachment style. For instance, the clients have had practice in disclosure to others of quite intimate aspects of their lives in both the cognitive distortions component and in the emotional expression section of the empathy component. They have also learned more about empathy in general and have developed attitudes that are more likely to lead to harmony with others. Self-confidence has also been enhanced, and this is a crucial feature of people who are able to develop good quality intimate relations (Brehm, 1992).

As a first step in this component, we examine the origins of the capacity for intimacy. We discuss with the group their relations with their parents and their early romantic relationships. We point out to them that much of their distrust of others in relationships has arisen from these experiences, although their own need to be secretive as a result of sexual offending, and their dysfunctional style of relating, has almost certainly caused their adult partners to withdraw from them. We emphasize the benefits of being more open, and more equitable and supportive in relationships. Couples involved in equitable relationships have sex more frequently and derive greater sexual and more general satisfaction than do less equitable couples (Reiss & Lee, 1988; Traupmann et al., 1983). We point out that since equitability cannot be achieved in sexually abusive interactions, they can never meet the full range of their needs through offending. Because mutually enjoyable leisure activities seem to both increase equitability and cement good quality relationships (Birchler & Webb, 1977), we assist the participants in identifying a range of activities they might enjoy and share with a partner. Finally, in this opening segment, we outline Bartholomew's (1993) attachment styles and each client is assisted in both defining his current style and its dysfunctional consequences. Happiness in relationships, we emphasize, is not just a matter of chance. Selecting an appropriate partner and working at the relationship are essential to forming satisfactory intimacy.

Since most of our clients identify intimacy with sex, we address the issue of sexual relations early in this component of treatment. Presumed differences between the sexuality of men and women are discussed and the results of research are presented in an informal way. Essentially many of the differences observed in research (e.g., men are more physically focussed and less concerned about the relationship aspects than are women, and men tend to be more concerned about the frequency of sex) begin to disappear when men pass the age of 40. Effective communication about sex is essential to satisfaction (Metts & Cupach, 1989) and satisfaction is impeded by various dysfunctional beliefs about sex (e.g., only vaginal intercourse with the man on top is appropriate). Acquired fears about sex are discussed and procedures are outlined for overcoming these anxieties (e.g., desensitization and sensate focus strategies). An essential feature of the correctional institutions where we work is the opportunity to have reasonably regular conjugal visits where our clients can practice what they are learning. Since all inmates can have three 2-hour open visits and they can communicate by telephone several times each week, our offenders also have repeated opportunities to practice effective communication skills.

Jealousy is a common problem in relationships (Salovey & Rodin, 1988) and is, if anything, exaggerated in sexual offenders. Suspicious jealousy (i.e., unfounded jealousy) commonly results from lack of self-confidence, so our more general procedures for enhancing self-esteem are relevant here and we ensure that our clients make the connection. Also, suspicious jealousy is most likely to arise when the client is himself unfaithful. Apparently unfaithful people assume that their partners will have the same tendencies.

In terms of general relationship skills, it may be necessary for some clients to complete a more extensive social skills training program prior to entering the present component; however, most clients appear to have sufficient basic conversational skills to function effectively within their own milieu. We emphasize to our clients the importance of seeking a compatible partner, and we discuss with each client what characteristics might make a potential partner suitable. They are also advised to progress slowly in developing a relationship and they are assisted in distinguishing initial infatuation from the later development of a more enduring companionship love. Throughout this component we stress the value of reflecting on, and learning from, past relationships. What they can change is their own behaviour and expectations, but only if they profit from their experience. Once again we stress, as we do throughout this component, the need for effective communication, and we provide repeated opportunities to role-play communication skills.

Of course many of our offenders are currently in a relationship. Sometimes this is a continuing relationship that has not been severed by the disclosure of their offence, and sometimes it is a relationship that has been initiated after they were charged and convicted, or even after they were imprisoned. In these cases it is a matter of working on their current relationship rather than developing a new one. However, they all profit from every aspect of the processes outlined here, and what they learn might cause them to reflect on the value of their present relationship. Their opportunities to interact with their partners by telephone, in open visits, and during conjugal visits, provide them with the chance to practice the skills they are learning and these opportunities certainly facilitate learning. However, many of the skills they are acquiring can be practiced with acquaintances in the institution, and we strongly encourage them to expand their range of friendships and to see intimacy as lying along a continuum.

Since we (Barbaree, Marshall & Connor, 1988) have shown that sexual offenders are not good problem solvers, we also outline appropriate problem solving behaviours. However, as we noted earlier, almost all sexual offenders are also required to participate in a cognitive skills program, and an important component of this is problem solving. We simply provide the opportunity for them to apply these skills to their relationships.

Evaluation of the intimacy component

In our evaluation of the effectiveness of this component in achieving the goals we set out to obtain, we were restricted somewhat by the limits of available measures, particularly the measures of intimacy. These measures tend to depend upon an evaluation by the respondents that is based on how effectively they have achieved intimacy over time. Despite their reasonably extensive visiting opportunities, they have had, from pre-treatment to post-treatment, a limited time in which to implement the skills they have hopefully acquired, so it may be hard for them to see any enduring change. This is not quite so true of the measure of loneliness we use, since it more readily evaluates current feelings. Nevertheless, being in prison may exaggerate a sense of loneliness.

Even with these limitations, however, we demonstrated that the intimacy/relationship component achieved its goals. We (Marshall, Bryce, et al., 1996) showed that the sense of intimacy of our participants was enhanced and their loneliness reduced. It is important to note, however, that despite the fact that improvements in intimacy were statistically significant, they were only marginally so, and could certainly not be considered dramatic improvements from a clinical standpoint. Their post-treatment intimacy scores, while significantly higher than their pre-treatment scores, remained well below the normative mean. This was not true for their loneliness scores which were slightly better than the normative mean at post-treatment. Perhaps the sense of loneliness is more responsive to change than is intimacy, which may require more prolonged opportunities to enact the skills of intimate relationships. A post-release follow-up evaluation may be the only way to properly evaluate enduring change in intimacy, but we have not yet been able to complete that assessment.

Chapter 8

SEXUAL PREFERENCES

Sex multiplies the possibilities of desire.

Luis Buñuel, 1900–1983

The quintessential feature of the early behavioural approach to treating sexual offenders was the modification of deviant sexual preferences. These preferences, it was assumed, resulted from an early accidental pairing of deviant sexual stimuli and sexual arousal (McGuire, Carlisle & Young, 1965). Conditioning processes initiated by this pairing, and implemented by masturbating to fantasies derived from these original circumstances, entrenched, so it was claimed, a disposition to engage in deviant sexual acts whenever an opportunity arose or was created. Almost invariably associated with this view, and possibly essential to it, was the idea that sexual offending is driven by sexual motivations. That is, offenders engage in sexual abuse in order to satisfy their sexual desires. From these two views, it was concluded that sexual offenders have distinctive sexual preferences that match their actual offending behaviours. Child molesters were said to prefer sex with children, rapists were thought to prefer forced nonconsensual sex, and exhibitionists exposed themselves because they derived greater sexual pleasure from this act than they did from normative sexual behaviours.

Although these views were rarely articulated clearly (see, however, McGuire et al., 1965, and Abel & Blanchard, 1974), they appear to underpin the early enthusiastic use of phallometry in the assessment of sexual offenders (Abel, Barlow, Blanchard & Guild, 1977; Freund, 1967; Kolarsky, Madlafousek & Novotna, 1978). In the application of treatment, this perspective encouraged the use of little more than behavioural procedures aimed at changing sexual preferences (Abel, Levis & Clancy, 1970; Laws, Meyer &

Holmen, 1978; Maletzky, 1974; Marquis, 1970; Quinsey, Bergersen & Steinman, 1976). As we have seen, behavioural approaches have expanded to include, in both assessment and treatment, a variety of other factors including cognitive processes, social functioning, empathy, and relapse prevention. However, sexual preferences remain a central feature of most programs and are thought by some researchers and clinicians to be crucial to the proper assessment and treatment of sexual offenders (Quinsey & Earls, 1990).

Despite the continuing emphasis placed on sexual preferences, it is now apparent that most researchers do not expect all sexual offenders to display deviant preferences at phallometric assessment (Freund, 1991). The problems for determining the discriminant validity of phallometric assessments that arises as a result of this currently accepted notion, concern what proportion of sexual offenders are expected to display deviant arousal and what features of the offenders define those who will have deviant preferences. Of course, if we could know in advance which offenders would be deviant, there would be no need to do phallometric assessments. This circularity notwithstanding, there remains the problem of what it is we expect phallometry to reveal. At present there does not appear to be a clear answer to this question other than that there ought to be group differences in arousal patterns between sexual offenders and other males.

PHALLOMETRIC ASSESSMENTS

There are a number of general issues concerning phallometric assessments that influence results and that differ across different studies, thereby limiting the value of comparisons. Marshall and Fernandez (in press) have provided a detailed examination of the literature, and they pointed to several problems in attempting to assimilate findings. For example, in order for the results of any test to be comparable over different settings or studies, the procedures must be the same, or at least nearly the same. Unfortunately, it is difficult to find two phallometric studies from different settings that used comparable testing procedures. Stimuli differ in content, duration of presentation, and format (slides, audiotapes or videos), and the instructions given to subjects, and in the way in which responses are scored also differ. Features of the subjects differ, such as their chronicity, viciousness, and sexual intrusiveness, and they vary in the number of victims they have abused. Furthermore, little or no effort is made to control for transitory features of the subjects, including their mood, prior use of intoxicants, and time from last ejaculatory release. Some degree of standardization, then, needs to be achieved if we are to attempt to integrate findings from different settings.

In addition to these problems, there are various threats to the meaning of the results of phallometric assessments, the most important of which is the vulnerability of the test to attempts by subjects to distort their responses. Faking has been considered a problem for many years, and it is not necessarily obvious when a subject is trying to present himself as having more prosocial sexual interests. Cognitive strategies aimed at distorting actual interests are the hardest of all to overcome, and although procedures to obviate this have been developed (Malcolm, Davidson & Marshall, 1985; Quinsey & Chaplin, 1988), it is not clear that they always achieve their goal (Proulx, Coté & Achille, 1993).

The essential first step in establishing the value of a test is to demonstrate its reliability (Kline, 1993). For phallometric testing, there are two aspects to reliability that are of primary concern: (1) internal reliability, and (2) test–retest reliability. Internal reliability (or consistency) refers to how well each item produces the same response as all other items in that category. If we have a set of child stimuli, for example, they should all produce much the same response in each subject. This, however, is probably unattainable since, if the sexual preference hypothesis makes any sense, we should expect different subjects to respond differentially to the different features of each child stimulus (e.g., pose, colour of hair, facial features, body maturity). What few studies there are of internal consistency have serious methodological problems (e.g., all of them either collapse across different stimulus categories or across different subject groups) so it is impossible to say anything at all about how phallometry measures up on this criterion.

The studies of test–retest reliability are not much better. A thorough search of the literature detected only three studies, none of which had a test–retest interval of more than 1 week. Wormith (1986) reported a test–retest coefficient of $r = 0.53$ for his child molester test, while Davidson and Malcolm (1985) found a coefficient of $r = 0.65$ for their rape index. While these coefficients reflect marginally acceptable levels of reliability, Barbaree, Baxter and Marshall (1989) found quite unacceptable reliability using rape stimuli. In fact, Barbaree et al. were able to achieve satisfactory levels of test–retest reliability only after eliminating all subjects who showed less than 75% of full erection to the stimuli; this resulted in the rejection of, coincidentally, 75% of all rapists. These results are certainly not encouraging, particularly since the test–retest period was only 1 week.

Since standardization and reliability are considered essential, a psychometrician might abandon at this point further consideration of phallometry. However, there is an extensive body of literature bearing on the discriminant validity of these tests, and it would be remiss of us not to at least consider this literature.

Criterion validity

Criterion validity refers to how well test responses differentiate groups that are known, or expected, to differ on the feature being assessed. In such studies of phallometry, researchers typically compare particular types of sexual offenders (e.g., rapists, child molesters, exhibitionists) with either other types, or nonsex offenders, or nonoffenders. The sexual offenders are expected to demonstrate either greater arousal than other subjects to stimuli that depict their offence targets, or less arousal to appropriate stimuli, or some combination of both, depending upon the particular version of the sexual preference hypothesis the researcher holds (see Barbaree & Marshall, 1991, for a discussion of the various versions of this hypothesis and their implications). Overall, phallometric assessments have not fared as well as might be hoped (Marshall & Fernandez, in press). Before we consider that evidence, however, let us consider the ecological validity of phallometric assessments.

Blader and Marshall (1989) pointed out that evaluations of the preferences of rapists simply measure their sexual responses to stimuli depicting forced nonconsenting sex, whereas, in the actual enactment of rape the offender not only becomes sexually aroused but also engages in overt forceful behaviour. Thus, Blader and Marshall note, ecologically appropriate evaluations would involve examining the possibility that rapists can become sexually aroused while at the same time enacting an aggressive response toward a female. While this proposed paradigm may not seem to be easily secured, Blader (1987) was able to arrange experimental circumstances that permitted the simultaneous measurement of sexual arousal and aggressive behaviour directed at a woman. Under the usual phallometric procedures, Blader found no differences in sexual preferences between rapists and normals. Using his experimental procedure, Blader found that only rapists were able to produce the two responses (i.e., sexual arousal and aggression) in concert; the sexual arousal of nonrapists was inhibited by their enactment of aggression. Furthermore, the rapists only displayed these concurrent behaviours when they were previously angered by a female (Blader, 1987). Blader's procedure requires far more time than does the usual phallometric evaluation, and it involves deception (i.e., convincing the subject that he really is punishing a woman) and the evocation of aggression. In these respects, while Blader and Marshall's (1989) challenge to the ecological meaning of phallometric evaluations of rapists was demonstrated to be sound, a viable alternative assessment procedure that could be used in clinical settings was not provided.

Perhaps the most important point of Blader and Marshall's analysis is that rape involves more than just sexual arousal in response to external cues. Rather, the topography of rape seems to involve sexual arousal occurring within a context in which the offender is also emotionally aroused in nonsexual ways. Groth (1979; Groth & Burgess, 1977a), for example, considers rape to be a pseudosexual act that serves as a vehicle for expressing anger toward women and perhaps serves to resolve a host of other negative emotional states. Consistent with this view, Amir (1971) and Groth and Burgess (1977b) have provided clinical evidence that even when rapists clearly premeditate sexual assault they rarely experience sexual arousal until *after* the victim is secured. In their examination of the factors that immediately precede rape, Pithers, Beal, Armstrong and Petty (1989) found that anger toward women was present among 77% of rapists, and Yates, Barbaree and Marshall (1984) have shown that angering normal men increases their arousal to rape scenes. Also, 60% of the rapists in another study (Marshall & Darke, 1982) reported that humiliating and degrading the victim was their primary goal. In addition, Proulx and his colleagues (McKibben, Proulx & Lusignan, 1994; Proulx, McKibben & Lusignan, 1996) have demonstrated that negative mood states increase the frequency with which rapists engage in deviant fantasizing. Finally, Barbaree, Marshall, Yates and Lightfoot (1983) demonstrated that alcohol intoxication produced significantly more arousal to rape scenes in normal males than did a placebo condition. Presumably these transitory states overcome any inhibitions men may feel about rape and this allows them to externalize their distress by responding to cues of raping a woman. No doubt a host of other affective and cognitive states occur immediately prior to a rape and find expression in the behaviours of the rapists during the assault. As we noted earlier, such affective, somatic and cognitive states are not controlled for in phallometric assessments despite the demonstrated influence of these states. However, the main point here is that these various studies strongly suggest that sexual motivation is not the only, or even the primary, force that drives sexual offending.

Similar analyses could be applied to the phallometric evaluations of child molesters, but we will mention only one aspect of the possible failure to generate ecologically valid assessments of these offenders. Child molesters are typically presented with visual images of children that may or may not be erotic in nature. Other than the fact that no researcher has ever attempted to determine whether the children in these images, or the way in which they are posed in the stimuli, are attractive to the child molesters under examination, there is the problem of the relevance of such stimuli for incest offenders. A number of studies (Frenzel & Lang, 1989; Freund, Watson & Dickey, 1991; Marshall, Barbaree & Christophe, 1986; Quinsey, Chaplin & Carrigan, 1979) have shown that incest offenders respond to these visual images in much the same way as do normal males, while nonfamilial child molesters display significantly greater deviant sexual arousal. It is necessary, therefore, to offer an explanation for these seemingly contradictory observations.

Studies of animal and human learning demonstrate that generalization of responding is a function of the organism's experience with the class of stimuli (Honig & Urcuioli, 1981; McIntosh, 1974). For instance, if a pigeon is repeatedly reinforced for pecking at only a particular shade of red, it will not thereafter show generalization to other colours or even to other shades of red. If, on the other hand, the pigeon is simply reinforced for pecking at coloured keys regardless of the specific colour, it will subsequently peck at any coloured key even if it has not seen that particular colour before. Since incest offenders typically offend against only one or two victims, and do so repeatedly over a number of years, they should not respond to images of novel children, much as our first pigeon did not respond to other colours; that is, incest offenders should not be expected to show deviant arousal to unfamiliar children. Some nonfamilial child molesters, on the other hand, have had sexual experiences with numerous children, although rarely more than once with the same child (Abel & Rouleau, 1990); this sort of experience should lead to a generalized disposition to be aroused by all children. In phallometric assessments these child molesters should, much like our second pigeon, show generalized arousal to the unfamiliar children in the visual images. Other nonfamilial offenders, however, have far more limited experience and should, as a consequence, not display arousal to children at phallometric evaluation.

These predicted results are precisely what has been found. Nonfamilial child molesters with multiple victims appear deviant at assessment, while single-victim nonfamilial child molesters do not (Freund & Watson, 1991). As we have seen, incest offenders in most studies are similarly unresponsive to child stimuli. However, to complicate matters, Abel, Becker, Murphy and Flanagan (1981) and Murphy, Haynes, Stalgaitis and Flanagan (1986) both found that incest offenders responded more to audiotaped descriptions of sex with children than they did to similar depictions involving adults. Murphy and Barbaree (1994) quite rightly suggest that audiotaped descriptions allow the incest offenders to imagine their own victims, suggesting that clinical assessments should ensure that these offenders are instructed to imagine their own victims. Once again, we see that it is important to attempt to match as closely as possible the context of phallometric evaluations to the context of the offenders' pattern of abusing, and yet this has not been routinely done. Indeed, the stimuli used in most phallometric assessments are, at best, tenuously related to the subjects' offence targets.

In view of these reservations, it is perhaps not surprising that findings from phallometric studies have been somewhat inconsistent. For example, early small sample studies with rapists (Abel et al., 1977; Barbaree, Marshall & Lanthier, 1979; Quinsey, Chaplin & Varney, 1981) revealed deviant arousal, although in quite different ways across these studies. Quinsey et al.'s rapists were significantly more aroused by rape scenes than by consenting sex; Abel et al.'s subjects were equally aroused by rape and consenting sex; and the rapists in Barbaree et al.'s study were more aroused by consenting sex, although they showed greater arousal to rape than did normal subjects. Some subsequent studies have found rapists to be deviant compared to nonrapists (Earls & Proulx, 1987; Freund, Scher, Racansky, Campbell & Heasman, 1986; Rice, Chaplin, Harris & Coutts, 1994), while others have found no differences between rapists and other subjects (Baxter, Barbaree & Marshall, 1986; Hall, 1989; Langevin, Paitich & Russon, 1985; Murphy, Krisak, Stalgaitis & Anderson, 1984; Wormith, Bradford, Pawlak, Borzecki & Zohar, 1988). Lalumière and Quinsey (1993, 1994) argue that these differences result from the use of different stimuli, whereas Marshall and Fernandez (in press) claim they reflect differences in the samples of rapists examined. At present, this issue remains to be empirically resolved, but recently, Thornton (1998a) reported results suggesting that the only rapists who produce deviant responses at phallometric assessment are those who, on the basis of actuarial indices, are at high risk to reoffend. Since actuarial bases for estimating risk derive largely from the rapist's offence history, the high risk group will necessarily include sadists, or at least, quite vicious offenders. Blader and Marshall (1989) had previously suggested that the different findings from rapists across different settings might be attributable to the proportion of sadists in the different studies, and Thornton's data appear to offer some support for this view.

Finally, not only have studies produced different results with rapists, the responses of these offenders appear to be heterogeneous. In an analysis of a large sample of rapists and nonoffenders, Marshall (in press) found quite different patterns of responding to the various classes of stimuli. He reported five different nondeviant response profiles and five different deviant profiles. Most importantly, neither this profile analysis, nor the raw scores, differentiated the rapists from the nonoffender males.

With nonfamilial child molesters, phallometric assessments have produced their most consistent results which are, for the most part, in line with the sexual preference hypothesis; that is, nonfamilial child molesters appear to have a deviant sexual attraction to children. Numerous studies have reported stronger arousal to children or lower arousal to adults in child molesters than in other subjects (Abel, Becker, Murphy & Flanagan, 1981; Baxter, Marshall, Barbaree, Davidson & Malcolm, 1984; Frenzel & Lang, 1989; Freund, 1967; Freund & Blanchard, 1989; Marshall, Barbaree & Butt, 1988; Marshall, Barbaree & Christophe, 1986; Quinsey & Chaplin, 1988; Wormith, 1986). However, these data are not all as clear cut as they might appear. For example, Baxter et al. (1984) found that men who had molested postpubescent girls (aged 12–16 years) responded in much the same way as the rapists and not at all like the men who molested prepubescent girls. Also, Freund, Chan and Coulthard (1979) noted that those child molesters who deny having offended respond to phallometric evaluations in the same way as do normal males, and so also do single-victim child molesters (Freund, Watson & Dickey, 1991). In addition, in a detailed examination of each subject's individual response profile (i.e., the overall pattern of arousal to females aged 3 to 24 years), Barbaree and Marshall (1989) found five quite different patterns in their female-victim nonfamilial child molesters. Among these patterns were men who responded: (1) most to adult females; (2) equally to adults and teenagers; (3) equally to all ages of females; (4) equally to children and adults, but not to teenagers; (5) most to female children. These results were subsequently replicated by Becker, Kaplan and Tenke (1992), and we (Marshall, Barbaree, & Butt, 1988) found similar variability within men who had molested boys. Thus, there is clear heterogeneity in the responses of nonfamilial child molesters and it is, therefore, no wonder that different results are apparent across different studies.

Phallometric studies of exhibitionists have not consistently revealed deviant responding. Early studies of exhibitionists in Czechoslovakia by Kolarsky and his colleagues revealed deviant arousal in one study (Kolarsky & Madlafousek, 1983) but not in another (Kolarsky, Madlafousek & Novotna, 1978). Several North American studies (Freund & Blanchard, 1986; Langevin et al., 1979; Murphy, Abel & Becker, 1980) also failed to reveal deviant responding in exhibitionists. However, all of these studies used stimuli of questionable ecological relevance.

Employing ecologically appropriate images matched for context, Marshall, Payne, Barbaree and Eccles (1991) found that their 44 exhibitionists responded with significantly greater sexual arousal to adult consenting sex than they did to scenes of exhibiting. These exhibitionists produced a pattern of arousal similar to that of Marshall et al.'s nonoffenders. In summarizing the available data, Murphy (1997) concluded that there is little support for the idea that exhibitionists prefer exposing. He suggests that their responses at phallometric assessments indicate, if anything, "a deficit in inhibition to (exhibitionistic) stimuli" (Murphy, 1997, p. 33). Once again, sexual preferences for their deviant acts do not appear to characterize this group of sexual offenders.

Table 8.1 describes our findings concerning the heterogeneous responses of rapists, child molesters, and exhibitionists. An important feature of this table concerns a frequently neglected response from sexual offenders; that is, a significant number of them show little or no arousal at all to any of the stimuli. Thus, phallometric assessments do not consistently distinguish rapists, incest offenders, and exhibitionists from other males. However, they do differentiate nonfamilial child molesters with a reasonable degree of reliability, although even here considerable heterogeneity has been consistently observed (Barbaree & Marshall, 1989; Becker, Kaplan & Tenke, 1992; Freund,

Table 8.1 Phallometric responses of sexual offenders

	Non-responders	Nondeviant responders	Deviant responders
Rapist assessment			
Rapists	20	49	31
Nonoffenders	7	66	27
Child molester assessment			
Nonfamilial offenders	22	30	48
Incest offenders	34	38	28
Nonoffenders	15	70	15
Exhibitionist assessment			
Exhibitionists	—*	87	13
Nonoffenders	—*	95	5

*Not recorded
Note: All figures are percentages of each group.

Chan & Coulthard, 1979; Freund, Watson & Dickey, 1991; Marshall, Barbaree & Butt, 1988; Marshall et al., 1986).

MODIFICATION OF DEVIANT PREFERENCES

Despite the relatively unsatisfactory results with phallometric evaluations and the fact that sexual offenders rarely self-report deviant fantasies (O'Donohue, Letourneau & Dowling, 1997), therapists typically target presumed deviant preferences as part of a comprehensive program. In fact, early behavioural interventions targeted very little more than deviant arousal. Bond and Evans (1967), for instance, declared that if the sexual preferences of deviants were normalized, then no other interventions would be necessary. In this view, deviant sexual fantasies elicit deviant sexual arousal which, in turn, leads to deviant sexual behaviour. Thus, eliminating deviant fantasies should eliminate deviant behaviour.

Although this view has been modified over the years, nevertheless deviant sexual preferences remain a central target in the treatment of sexual offenders. Indeed, sexual offenders seem at times to be bullied by therapists into agreeing that they do have deviant sexual fantasies and that these fantasies precede their offensive behaviours. However, the available evidence does not support the apparent convictions of these enthusiastic therapists. For example, Pithers et al. (1989) found that only 17% of rapists reported having deviant sexual fantasies in the six-month period prior to their offence. Although 51% of the child molesters in Pithers et al.'s study reported deviant fantasies during this six-month period, that still leaves 49% who did not. These results are even more interesting given that

Pithers appears to be an advocate of the view that deviant sexual fantasies are a critical feature that leads sexual offenders to abuse others (see Pithers & Laws, 1993). In addition, Marshall, Barbaree and Eccles (1991) reported that, among their child molesters, 31.6% of those with female victims and 41.1% of those with male victims claimed not to have experienced deviant fantasies, at least until after they had first offended. While it is appropriate to be sceptical of the self-reports of sexual offenders, most of the child molesters in Marshall et al.'s study did admit to at least occasionally fantasizing deviant acts subsequent to the first offence, so it does not appear they were trying to hide the fact that they entertained deviant thoughts.

Aversion therapy

The procedures that have primarily been employed to modify deviant sexual fantasies include either some form of aversion therapy or one of the various forms of masturbatory reconditioning. While nausea-inducing substances were used as the unconditioned aversive stimulus in some early studies, the most common aversive events used in the treatment of deviant interests have been electric shocks or foul odours. In treating a man with sadistic sexual arousal, Laws, Meyer and Holmen (1978) delivered a foul odour each time the man signalled that he was fantasizing inappropriate scenes. This proved to be very effective. Marshall, Keltner and Griffiths (1974) developed a complex apparatus to deliver offensive odours in order to overcome the difficulty presented by the fact that foul odours linger. Their apparatus delivered mentholated air immediately after the termination of the foul odour, thereby allowing several trials per session. Marshall et al. effectively changed the evocative value of deviant sexual activities, as measured phallometrically, in several sexual offenders.

Electric aversion was the most popular procedure during the 1970s, but as Quinsey and Earls (1990) noted, by the late 1980s descriptions of this procedure had all but disappeared from the literature. An early report of electric aversion with child molesters by Bancroft and Marks (1968) found lasting benefits with only one patient. Quinsey, Bergerson and Steinman (1976) reported significant overall effects for electric aversion, but the magnitude of the effects was not striking. In perhaps the most powerful, and certainly the most well-controlled, demonstration of electric aversion, Quinsey, Chaplin and Carrigan (1980) showed that their signalled punishment procedure produced significant reductions in deviant responding at phallometric assessment. Despite these modest successes, electric aversion is rarely used any more, presumably because of the associated ethical concerns and because alternative less contentious procedures are now available.

Ammonia aversion

One of the problems that exhibitionists in particular present is that they are essentially bombarded by cues that elicit urges to expose in almost all circumstances of their life. Under these eliciting conditions, exhibitionists (and many other sexual offenders) are operating in what Ward, Hudson and Marshall (1995) call "cognitive deconstruction". In this state, people suspend abstract thought and contemplation of consequences, and focus only on the satisfaction of immediate desires. Obviously, this is a risky state for sexual offenders and one in which they are unlikely to abort an offence sequence. Exhibitionists tend to offend at very high rates and, while they may have routines that characteristically lead to offending, they also frequently expose under various other circumstances. Of course, other types of offenders may also be incited to offend by a broad range of eliciting stimuli, but exhibitionists are more typically incited at a greater frequency. Accordingly, it is useful to provide exhibitionists (and other similarly ubiquitously incited offenders) with strategies that they can self-administer to abort an offence sequence as it unfolds.

Marshall and Fernandez (1997) describe their use of ammonia aversion for this purpose. The client carries a small bottle of smelling salts which he is to open whenever an urge occurs, and take a quick, deep nasal inhalation. The effects of this are to interrupt and remove any current thoughts and feelings, giving the client the opportunity to reappraise what he is doing, consider the consequences, abort the sequence, and engage nonoffence-related thoughts and actions. Unfortunately, while this procedure makes good sense, and numerous offenders report that it helps them, there is no available evidence from controlled studies bearing on its value.

Covert sensitization

An alternative version of aversion therapy was first described by Cautela (1967). He proposed having the subject imagine the undesirable act followed by imagining negative consequences. Cautela called this covert sensitization, and Abel, Blanchard and Becker (1978) described its application to sexual offenders. While the evidence on the efficacy of covert sensitization with sexual offenders is not strong (Quinsey & Marshall, 1983), it is very popular and has been effectively combined with olfactory aversion in the treatment of exhibitionists and child molesters (Maletzky, 1980).

The consequences in covert sensitization with sexual offenders originally involved having the subject imagine becoming sick while fantasizing deviant acts or discovering repulsive sores on the body of the victim. These scenes represent unlikely consequences to sexual abuse and have been replaced by the sort of consequences many offenders catastrophize about after they have completed an offence. Marshall and his colleagues (Marshall & Eccles, 1995; Marshall & Fernandez, 1997) have outlined an application of covert sensitization that attempts to serve purposes additional to simply reducing attraction to deviant acts. They have the offender generate at least three behavioural and cognitive sequences that terminate in deviant behaviour and match the offender's typical modus operandi. For example, for one of our clients, the sequence began with him sitting at home feeling bored. The next step involved him thinking about going downtown to visit the local video-game arcade where he had in the past picked up boys. The next step had him riding downtown on his motorcycle which he used to lure boys into cooperating with his sexual desires. Once at the video-game arcade, his sequence involved looking for a potential victim (a compliant and needy boy), striking up a conversation, giving the boy money to play the games, and finally, offering to take the boy for a ride on his motorcycle. He then drove out to the country on the pretext that once there, the boy could drive the motorcycle safe from the eyes of the police. Of course, once they were out in the country, the boy was expected to trade sexual favours for the ride.

This whole sequence, broken down into five or six discrete steps, was then written in abbreviated form on a pocket-sized card which the offender carried with him at all times. On the back of the card were written catastrophic consequences that were meaningful to the offender. These consequences involved getting caught in the act by a policeman who treated the offender in a derogatory and physically rough manner, followed by being taken to jail where he was held overnight in a cell with several nonsex offenders who beat him up. Next morning, according to the script, his name appeared in the paper, his friends and family disowned him, and he was sentenced to a penitentiary for five years. The offender was instructed to read the offence sequence several times each day, followed by turning the card over and reading the consequences. Initially he was encouraged to read the offence sequence through to the terminal behaviour before reading the consequences, but over sessions he was told to abort the sequence progressively earlier and then read the consequences. In the final sessions he was to read only the first step in the sequence, where he contemplates the course of action leading to an offence, before reading the consequences.

This procedure is meant, as was the original version of covert sensitization, to associate consideration of the deviant act with unfortunate results in order to make it less attractive. In addition, the stepwise sequencing of the thoughts and behaviours that lead to the deviant act allows the association of the consequences to occur with earlier steps in the process, it being presumed that it will be easier to abort the sequence at the contemplation stage rather than at the terminal stage. Moreover, detailing the offence sequence in this way allows the offender to recognize the earliest steps in his offence pattern and this facilitates integration of this component of treatment with the later relapse prevention component.

Masturbatory reconditioning

Perhaps a more naturalistic approach to changing sexual preferences is to employ a reversal of the very procedures that are thought to instill deviant preferences. As we have seen, deviant preferences are thought to result from conditioning processes that involve fantasizing the deviant acts while masturbating. While there is no evidence that conditioning procedures either instill deviant preferences or are involved in their elimination (Marshall & Eccles, 1993; O'Donohue & Plaud, 1994), the idea that masturbating to deviant fantasies generates and maintains deviant behaviour is so well-entrenched that it has all but achieved the status of accepted dogma. Certainly, that was the view that held sway when early behavioural pioneers described what have become known as "masturbatory reconditioning" procedures.

Thorpe, Schmidt and Castell (1963) used what was later called the "thematic shift" approach with a homosexual client to increase sexual interest in heterosexual activities. This procedure was subsequently modified by Marquis (1970) who described its use with numerous sexual eccentrics. The client is told to adapt his usual masturbatory practice in the following way. He is to initiate arousal by, if necessary, fantasizing his deviant acts; he then immediately switches to fantasizing prosocial sexual activities. If he loses arousal during appropriate fantasizing, he is to switch back to deviant thoughts until he becomes rearoused, then switch back to normative fantasies, and so on until orgasm. Laws and Marshall (1991), in their review of the literature, noted that this technique had been employed in several reports but that most of these reports described either poorly controlled single-case studies or confounded thematic shift with other interventions such as aversion therapy. Laws and Marshall, therefore, concluded that there was no strong empirical support for the use of this technique. They then considered the value of several other approaches aimed at enhancing attraction to appropriate sexual behaviours and claimed that the strongest support, although not remarkable, was for Maletzky's (1980) "directed masturbation". In this procedure, the client is simply directed to masturbate exclusively to appropriate themes. Marshall (1974), and Kremsdorf, Holmen and Laws (1980), demonstrated in reasonably well-controlled single-case designs that this procedure effectively enhanced phallometrically evaluated arousal to appropriate sexual acts. Again, the evidence is limited but is supportive.

These procedures, however, as the reader has no doubt observed, might enhance normative sexual interests, but there is no good reason to expect this change to reciprocally inhibit deviant arousal despite the apparent expectations of those who originally designed the techniques. Borrowing from Knight Dunlap's (1932) original idea that the simple unreinforced repetition of a behaviour should lead to its extinction, Marshall (Marshall, 1979; Marshall & Barbaree, 1978; Marshall & Lippens, 1977) developed an approach for directly reducing the appeal of deviant fantasy. In the original version of this procedure that Marshall called "satiation", the client was to masturbate to orgasm, wipe himself clean, and then continue to masturbate for upwards of one hour while rehearsing aloud every variant he could think of on his deviant fantasies. The expectation derived from Dunlap's theorizing was that repeated unreinforced (i.e., the absence of sexual arousal) evocations of the deviant thoughts would lead to the extinction of their attractiveness. This seems particularly likely since post-orgasm men experience a period of time where they are refractory to sexual arousal (Masters & Johnson, 1966).

In two controlled single-case evaluations, Marshall (1979) demonstrated that satiation effectively eliminated deviant interests in two chronic predatory child molesters. Appropriate arousal, however, was only enhanced when directed masturbation was introduced, thus encouraging the combined use of these two procedures. Unfortunately, masturbatory satiation is so effectively aversive that refusals present a problem, although they are not as high as one might think. Accordingly, Laws, Osborn, Avery-Clark, O'Neil and Crawford (1987) modified the procedure by eliminating the requirement to masturbate post-orgasm. After their clients had ejaculated, Laws et al. simply had them repeatedly verbalize their deviant fantasies for up to 20 minutes. Laws et al. thought it was unwise to fantasize beyond 20 minutes as there might, thereafter, be some recovery of the capacity for arousal; this, of course, might serve to enhance, rather than reduce, the attractiveness of the deviant acts. Laws et al. demonstrated that their version, which they called "verbal satiation", was effective with several sexual offenders.

Subsequent research (Alford, Morin, Atkins & Schoen, 1987; Hunter & Goodwin, 1992; Hunter & Santos, 1990) has also provided convincing support for the use of satiation in one or other of its forms. Particularly interesting findings were reported by Johnston, Hudson and Marshall (1992). In their treatment of child molesters, Johnston et al. delayed all other aspects of treatment while they applied satiation combined with directed masturbation. Measuring sexual responses phallometrically before and after this combined intervention, Johnston et al. found dramatic reductions in arousal to deviant images (from 60.7% full erection to just 17.3% after treatment). Unfortunately, arousal to normative sexual images also dropped, although not to the same degree (from 53.4% to 32.6%). This latter observation, however, may not be as problematic as it first seems. If we calculate a deviant index by dividing arousal to deviant scenes by arousal to appropriate images, the pretreatment mean index is 1.13, which is clearly quite deviant; post-treatment the index is 0.53 which is well within the normative range. Usually relative arousal is seen as the critical feature, and 32.6% full erection to appropriate stimuli generated under laboratory conditions may be construed as sufficiently strong to encourage optimism.

A summary of the evidence bearing on the various procedures for modifying deviant sexual preferences, and their estimated current use, is provided in Table 8.2.

Table 8.2   Procedures for modifying deviant preferences

Procedure	Evidence	Current use
Aversion therapy		
Electric aversion	Encouraging support	Rare
Olfactory aversion	Limited support	Uncommon
Nausea aversion	Limited support	None
Ammonia aversion	Nil	Uncommon
Covert sensitization	Little support	Popular
Masturbatory reconditioning		
Directed masturbation or thematic shift	Limited support	Very popular
Satiation*	Reasonable support	Popular

*Current evidence and practical considerations appear to favour "verbal satiation" over the earlier "masturbatory satiation" version.

Implications for treatment

As we have seen throughout this section on the modification of deviant sexual preferences, the evidence in support of such procedures is not overwhelming, although it is reasonably strong for satiation. It is not that empirical investigations have failed to offer support for the various procedures aimed at changing sexual preferences, it is rather that there have been remarkably few controlled studies. Furthermore, most of the studies that do exist have confounded the results of the procedure under examination by utilizing other interventions concurrently. All of this is surprising given that deviant sexual preferences have for so long been seen as a critical feature of sexual offenders that must be altered for treatment to be effective. But is this true? Do we need to directly change sexual preferences to effectively treat sexual offenders?

One way to answer this question is to consider whether or not assessments of sexual preferences altered by treatment predict subsequent successes or failures. Rice, Quinsey and Harris (1991) found that among treated child molesters, post-treatment phallometric indices were essentially uncorrelated with recidivism ($r = -0.06$). Similarly, Proulx, Pellerin, McKibben, Aubut and Ouimet (1998) found no differences between the phallometrically determined deviant indices of rapists who did or did not reoffend after treatment. Another way to look at this issue is to consider the effects of treatment. For example, Rice et al. (1991) compared untreated child molesters with those treated in a program where the reduction of deviant arousal was the major component. In a long-term follow-up appraisal, Rice et al. found no difference between the recidivism rates of the treated and untreated offenders. Thus, focussing treatment on deviant preferences does not appear to produce lasting benefits.

Marshall (1997a) set out to more systematically appraise the value of modifying deviant arousal. He selected the 12 most deviant offenders from a sample of over 80 child molesters referred for treatment. At phallometric assessment, these 12 child molesters displayed an average pretreatment deviant index (deviant arousal divided by appropriate arousal) of 1.64 (range 0.9–3.6). Thus, all were well within the range typically identified as deviant and features of their offence history (e.g., number of victims, use of force, and intercourse with their victims) also indicated that this was a quite deviant sample. In fact, that is precisely why they were chosen for the study in order to provide the strongest test of the hypothesis that it is unnecessary to directly treat deviant preferences. Treatment for this group did not involve the modification of sexual preferences. Indeed, no mention was made of sexual preferences throughout treatment and, instead, treatment involved all the other components in Marshall's core comprehensive program (see Marshall & Eccles 1995 for a description). This program is, in fact, the one described in this book. No adjunct treatments, such as substance abuse programs, anger management, cognitive skills, and the like, were engaged until the study was complete.

The phallometric results after treatment for these quite deviant offenders indicated marked and statistically significant reductions in deviant arousal with the average index being 0.49, which is well within the normative range. Reductions in deviant arousal were strongly correlated with enhancements in self-esteem ($r = -0.66$) although, unfortunately, no other targets of treatment were evaluated in time to examine the relationship between changes in those targets and deviant arousal. When Marshall (1995) presented these results at a meeting of the Association for the Treatment of Sexual Abusers in New Orleans, the two commentators (Gene Abel and Bill Pithers) both indicated that they had made similar observations. Abel noted that he had observed reductions in deviant arousal among offenders in his program before deviant preferences were addressed, and Pithers reported that a number of his clients showed substantially less deviant arousal after having only received the empathy component of his program.

These admittedly limited set of observations suggest that directly target-ing sexual preferences in the treatment of sexual offenders may be unnecess-ary. If subsequent systematic research confirms these observations, not only will this save therapists a good deal of time, it might suggest that deviant sexual preferences are an epiphenomenon, much as smoke is to fire. If equipping sexual offenders with the attitudes, perceptions, confidence and skills necessary to meet their needs in prosocial ways, indirectly eliminates deviant sexual preferences, as the above findings suggest, then deviant pref-erences can be construed as a way that some inadequate men have of fulfill-ing their needs. Entertaining such fantasies and engaging in deviant behaviours may allow such men to meet their needs for control, power, and sexual release in circumstances where rejection and negative appraisals of their sexual adequacy are absent. In this view, then, teaching these men to meet their whole range of needs in prosocial ways would make it unnecess-ary for them to either fantasize deviant sexual acts or actually engage in such behaviours. These proposals are, at worst, readily empirically testable.

As a final point on this issue of the meaning of deviant sexual acts for the offender, Cortoni, Heil and Marshall (1996) report that sexual offenders use sex as a way of coping with problematic issues to a far greater extent than do other males. They examined various coping strategies and found that the typical response of sexual offenders to stress, emotional difficulties, or other sources of problems, was to seek out sexual contacts in either appropriate or deviant ways. Even removing from the analyses the occasions on which they engaged in deviant acts, sexual offenders still showed a propensity to engage in sex when they were under duress. Thus their initial sexual of-fences may be a response to stress which subsequently becomes entrenched, not because it satisfies deviant desires, but rather because it temporarily reduces personal discomfort. These suggestions are consistent with the find-ings of Proulx and his colleagues (McKibben et al., 1994; Proulx, McKibben & Lusignan, 1996) that sexual offenders respond to distress by increasing their tendency to engage in sexual fantasies of both a deviant and nonde-viant nature.

Chapter 9

RELAPSE PREVENTION

Anthony Eccles and William L. Marshall

> *Forewarned, forearmed; to be prepared is half the victory.*
> Miguel de Cervantes Saavedra, 1547–1616

First employed as an approach to the treatment of addicts, the relapse prevention model was developed by Marlatt and his colleagues in response to the clinical difficulties associated with this challenging population (e.g., Marlatt, 1982). The problem Marlatt attempted to address by the use of relapse strategies was the maintenance of behaviour change. Numerous treatment programs had been demonstrated to produce a cessation of addictive behaviours (W.R. Miller, 1980), but far too many clients relapsed after the withdrawal of treatment. Although George and Marlatt (1989) claimed the same was true for sexual offender treatment, and saw this as the justification for extending the relapse prevention approach to the treatment of these clients, in fact, there is no clear evidence that sexual offenders show dramatic immediate benefits from treatment, only to later relapse. Sexual offending occurs at a far lower frequency than does addictive behaviour, so it is really difficult to distinguish the immediate and delayed behavioural indications of success or failure with sexual offenders. This is particularly true because sexual offender therapists are unable to establish baseline frequencies of the problematic behaviours in any individual other than relying on the rather dubious self-reports of our clients. Indeed, the more we examine the details of sexual offending, the less it appears to be an analogous match for the so-called addictions (Marshall & Marshall, 1998). Although there may, nevertheless, be some sense to applying the relapse prevention model to the treatment of sexual offenders, no one has yet demonstrated that it actually produces a reduction in long-term recidivism relative to cognitive behavioural programs without a relapse prevention component or framework (Marshall & Anderson, 1996).

The first person to adapt Marlatt's relapse prevention approach in order to apply it to sexual offenders was Janice Marques (1982). Shortly after Marques' original outline of how this innovative strategy might be used with sexual offenders, Pithers, Marques, Gibat and Marlatt (1983) provided a detailed description of a comprehensive approach utilizing relapse prevention concepts and procedures. This proved to be instantly popular owing largely to the logical approach of the model and the rather convincing data from its application to addictive behaviours. To date, these remain as the only justification for the continued and very widespread use of relapse prevention with sexual offenders.

The relapse prevention model was readily embraced by the cognitive behavioural researchers and clinicians working with sexual offenders. With its emphasis on the role of cognitive distortions and decision-making processes, the relapse prevention model was clearly compatible with the social learning bases of cognitive behavioural therapy. Also, the stress on improving coping behaviours was readily incorporated into cognitive behavioural treatment programs because these programs emphasized skill development (e.g., Marshall, Earls, Segal & Darke, 1983). The relapse prevention model acted as a useful heuristic, allowing for the identification of problem areas and a ready description of their relationship to the offending behaviour. This also facilitated treatment planning and clarified the relevance of the different elements of treatment in moving toward the ultimate goal of avoiding a reoffence. Finally, the ability of the relapse prevention model to provide a reasonably straightforward way for offenders to conceptualize their difficulties facilitated communication between therapists and clients.

It is probably fair to say that adopting the relapse prevention (RP) model did not markedly change the work of sexual offender therapists in the mid-1980s. However, this model did become extremely important in unifying the various elements within treatment programs by providing a language and a framework. In retrospect, the advantages of the RP model seem to have led to its uncritical acceptance. Certainly, the extent to which the model was adopted was not in response to overwhelming empirical research supporting its central tenets. Indeed, as Ward and his colleagues have noted, there was, and still is, little in the way of systematic research supporting RP's application for sexual offenders (Ward & Hudson, 1996; Ward, Hudson & Siegert, 1995). As we shall see, the results of Ward et al.'s work indicate that at least some elements of the RP model need to be rethought. In this chapter, we will first outline the model as it has been applied to sexual offenders. This will be followed by a review of some of the criticisms that have been levelled against it and the description of an alternative approach proposed by Ward et al. (Ward & Hudson, 1998). Finally, the implications and application of RP to treatment with sexual offenders will be considered.

SEXUAL OFFENDING AND THE RP MODEL

The Marques-Pithers Model

The RP approach, described by Pithers and his colleagues (Pithers, 1990; Pithers, Kashima, Cumming & Beal, 1998), was an evolution of his earlier work. Figure 9.1 describes Pithers' model. While this particular model is not the only RP approach used with sexual offenders, it is the one most widely adopted and cited, and so it will serve to illustrate the way in which RP has been applied to these clients.

Reoffences, or relapses, it is claimed, do not occur in a vacuum. Rather, they are regarded as the culmination of a series of events and situations through which the individual proceeds prior to offending. The model declares that all sexual offenders are likely to slip (i.e., lapse) at some point from a state of complete abstinence. Some will quickly abort their slide along this chain and re-establish abstinence, while others will progress to a reoffence.

The offence process (sometimes called a "cycle" or a "chain") is seen as being initiated by what are called "seemingly unimportant decisions". For example, an offender, previously convicted of peeping in windows at night, may choose to take his dog for a late evening walk, convincing himself that he is only doing so "because the dog needs the exercise and fresh air". Such decisions may seem relatively benign to the casual observer, and these rationalizations will have some validity to the offender himself. Such seemingly unimportant decisions, however, serve to increase the probability of exposure to high-risk situations (e.g., in our example case, seeing partially curtained windows late at night) or high-risk factors (e.g., an erosion of the offender's sense of control over his problem behaviour). Adaptive coping (e.g., calling a support person) at this point can lead to a return to abstinence. A failure to cope, however, will likely lead to further lapses (e.g., engaging in deviant fantasies). At this point, the model proposes that the abstinence violation effect (AVE) becomes a factor. This phenomenon occurs because, as a result of lapsing, the offender sees himself as a failure, and his prior efforts as having failed, and gives up his effort to avoid reoffending. An offender in this position is also said to focus on the immediate rewards and gratification of offending, which, in the language of RP, is referred to as the problem of immediate gratification (PIG). Although, by this stage in his chain, it is becoming increasingly less likely that the offender will do so, it is

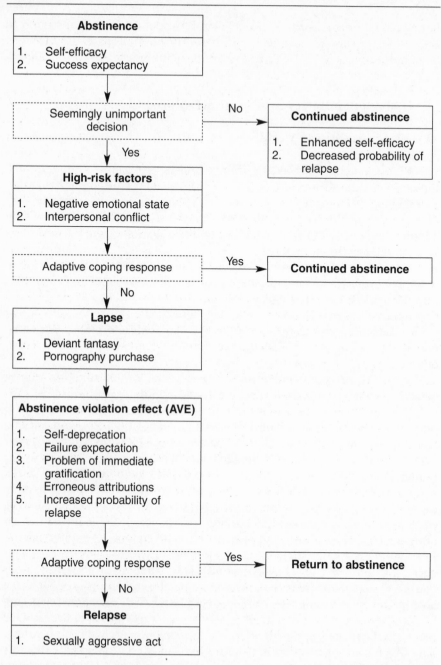

Figure 9.1   Pithers' model of the offence chain. (Reproduced, with permission from H. Barbaree, W.L. Marshall and S. Hudson, *The Juvenile Sex Offender*, Guilford Press, New York, 1993)

nonetheless possible for him to enact adaptive coping at this point and to return to a state of abstinence. He might do this by reframing his lapses as being expected, as not necessarily indicating that he must give up his efforts, and as an indication that their frequency is lower than it was prior to treatment. The offender can in this way put a positive spin on the experience, and he can analyse the lapse to learn more about what puts him at risk. This is an important feature of the RP model as it stresses that there are always alternatives to offending at each stage in the chain, and that the offender can always choose not to continue the chain to its ultimate and disastrous end of offending against an innocent victim. However, a failure to cope successfully will likely lead to a reoffence which, in our example, would involve the offender succumbing to the urge to look in the partially curtained window.

Using this RP model, offenders in treatment are required to examine their past offence(s) in order to define both the characteristic steps in their chain and the high-risk factors or situations to which they are particularly vulnerable. The offence chain, it should be noted, involves not only the behavioural steps leading to an offence, but also the corresponding thoughts and feelings. In addition, deficiencies in the coping skills of the offenders are identified so that skills training can provide them with the capacity to deal with, or avoid, problematic situations in the future. Offenders are assisted in this complex process by clinicians and groups of other offenders (Long, Wuesthoff & Pithers, 1989). This is an important process because neglecting significant factors that predispose an offender to relapse, and incorrectly identifying risk factors, jeopardizes the whole treatment process. For example, if an offender focusses on his alcohol abuse and fails to identify the social anxieties and consequent justifications that lead to his use of alcohol, he is unlikely to develop an effective plan for dealing with his difficulties.

Once a client has identified his own particular risk factors, he must then be prepared to recognize the precursors to them when they arise. Thus, for an individual for whom depression is an important risk factor, negative thinking and a lack of enjoyment in activities that were previously pleasurable might serve as warning signs that his risk to reoffend is increasing. In addition, it is important for an offender to establish warning signs that are potentially observable by others for each of his high-risk factors (Pithers & Gray, 1996). This enables professionals and the offender's support group to determine whether he has lapsed or may be about to engage in high-risk behaviours that could lead to a reoffence. For the offender with depression as a warning sign, a dishevelled and unkempt appearance may signify to others that he is at risk to reoffend. Thus, the support group can render assistance in the event the offender himself is unable, or at that point unwilling, to initiate an adaptive response.

The notion of other individuals in the offender's life assisting in his relapse prevention efforts brings us to one of the most important elements proposed by the RP model. The offence chain identified by the offender should be shared with a support group consisting of family, friends, counsellors and probation or parole offenders. This is designed to both assist in treatment, and in the supervision of the offender after release from formal treatment (Pithers, 1990). The relationship between the offender's support group and his therapist is deemed to be important as offenders are typically unreliable in their self-reports, particularly when they begin to entertain notions of reoffending. Informed supervisors can be even more effective in their supervision if relevant conditions are set by the courts and parole boards (Cumming & Buell, 1996).

Of course, identifying an offence chain and the warning signs associated with it is only half the battle. It is one thing for an offender to know his risk factors and his vulnerabilities; it is quite another for him to know what to do about them. The RP model uses knowledge of the offence chain to direct treatment efforts. With the help of his therapist, an offender is assisted in developing a set of coping skills for dealing with each risk factor in his offence chain. This represents his relapse prevention plan, by which he will attempt to become fully equipped to deal with all potential future problems. A truly comprehensive relapse prevention plan not only provides for a way of avoiding high-risk situations, it also indicates what an offender should do to escape an unavoidable high-risk situation (Steenman, Nelson & Viesti, 1989). Such an approach serves to emphasize that there are always alternatives to offending, right up to the point of the commission of the act.

As we noted, without a great deal of basic research to support it, the RP model has been widely adopted in North America where it is the most commonly used approach for treating sexual offenders (Laws, 1989). Although it was adopted somewhat later in Britain, 43% of programs included in a recent national survey identified relapse prevention as their guiding model (Proctor & Flaxington, 1996).

Critical appraisals of the Marques–Pithers model

Recently, Ward and his colleagues have attempted to both logically and empirically evaluate the RP model (Ward & Hudson, 1996; Ward, Hudson & Siegert, 1995). Their two main criticisms of the model are that: (1) in adapting it from its use with addicts, certain changes were made that have led to conceptual confusion; and (2) certain elements of the model are not supported by the limited available evidence.

In the application of RP to addictions, Marlatt uses the term "lapse" to refer to brief and occasional engagements in the actual problem behaviour itself (e.g., gambling). These lapses provide material for learning more about the high-risk situations to which the person is vulnerable and how to prevent similar lapses in the future. The term relapse is reserved for a complete return to the pre-abstinence level of the problem behaviour. However, such an approach to sexual abuse is unlikely to be palatable to most people. As a consequence, a relapse was redefined as any return or recurrence of the problem behaviour, while a lapse was said to involve high-risk behaviours related to, but exclusive of, actual sexual offending. As Ward and Hudson (1996) point out, a number of implications follow from these decisions.

In moving the lapse further back in the chain, Pithers (1990) has rolled the PIG and AVE together, resulting in a confusing state of affairs where the arousing and positive expectations of the PIG co-occur with the distressing and pessimistic expectations of the AVE. Further, Ward, Hudson and Marshall (1994) point out that this aspect of the model is at variance with data collected in their study which suggest that the AVE is a post-relapse, rather than post-lapse, phenomenon. Ward and Hudson (1996) develop this criticism further to highlight the failure of the model to convincingly describe and explain the relationship among the various constructs. For example, Pithers says that covert processes (i.e., seemingly unimportant decisions) are the only route to high-risk situations. Ward and Hudson, however, point out that while this may be the case when offenders put themselves in situations where victims are available, it is unlikely to apply to other high-risk factors such as negative emotional states. In addition, Ward and Hudson claim that the characteristic application of RP to sexual offenders is overly restrictive and not consistent with available research data. Using a qualitative analysis of the offence descriptions elicited from sexual offenders, Ward, Louden, Hudson and Marshall (1995) established the need for a broader and more flexible approach to describing the sequence of events that precipitate sexual crimes. For example, child molesters who had well-entrenched beliefs that sex between an adult and a child was acceptable and beneficial to both, experienced high levels of positive emotional states during lapses and in high-risk situations.

Aside from the structural problems of the RP model, there are mixed results from treatment outcome studies using the RP approach. In part, this is due to the difficult task of conducting this kind of research. To begin with, as the relapse prevention model was introduced widely only during the mid- and late 1980s, the follow-up times for released offenders are only now becoming sufficiently long to be of real value. Furthermore, while the RP model has a unifying effect on language and treatment procedures, many of the programs described as following the RP model do not seem to meet the requirements of applying RP concepts and treatment procedures (Marshall & Anderson, 1996). Many of these programs describe themselves as RP approaches simply because their aim is to prevent relapses, while others use some of the language of RP but not necessarily all of the procedures.

In their evaluation of treatment outcome, Marshall and Anderson (1996) first note that the results of treatment by more traditional cognitive behavioural programs are, in general, quite good. The so-called RP programs Marshall and Anderson reviewed varied in the degree to which they incorporated the RP model. This allowed Marshall and Anderson to compare programs adhering more strictly to the RP model with those that relied more on traditional cognitive behavioural approaches. Those programs with an extensive after-care component (what Pithers, 1990, called the "external supervisory component") not only did not show more favourable results, they actually seemed to do worse than those with only the "internal management component". Thus, the vigorous and expensive external supervision efforts espoused by Pithers and others may not add value to the basic internal management model that offenders are to use on their own.

However, because relapse prevention is incorporated to varying degrees in cognitive behavioural programs, and because so few outcome studies are available, it is simply not possible to say with any certainty whether the addition of the RP model actually influences recidivism rates, either positively or negatively. In any event, the basic theoretical concepts of the RP model are essentially those of traditional cognitive behavioural therapy (Hanson, 1996). As such, it is unlikely that we will ever get an entirely clear picture of the independent contributions of each. Nonetheless, as Hanson (1996) points out, the RP model has been instrumental in focussing attention on the offenders' long-term risk of recidivism, and this has been an extremely important contribution in its own right.

Ward's model of the offence chain

In response to their criticisms of the RP model, Ward and his colleagues have proposed an alternative that they argue better describes the offence chain (Ward, Louden et al., 1995). In their study, they had a sample of 26 untreated child molesters describe their most recent offence, identifying each discrete event along with the thoughts and feelings that occurred at each of these event times. Using Strauss and Corbin's (1990) grounded theory approach, Ward et al. then broke these descriptions down into meaning units that were sorted into categories. These categories were identified as sequential stages in a rather complex nine-stage model of the offence chain.

In Stage 1 of Ward et al.'s model, the offender's perception of his present circumstances represents the context that provides the background for the development of the offence chain. Stage 1 includes unresolved conflicts from childhood, along with current affective states, and a lack of, or excess of, self-confidence. In Stage 2, the offender begins distal planning which may be overt or covert; in either case, sexual arousal begins at this stage prompting a further escalation to Stage 3. At this point nonsexual contact with a potential victim is initiated, which is followed in Stage 4 by a re-evaluation of the victim in a manner permitting further contact (e.g., "He looks like he needs a friend right now.") In Stage 5, this develops into proximal planning where the cognitive distortions of the offender allow him to believe that the victim is willing and is enjoying the offender's attention. The offence itself occurs in Stage 6, while in Stage 7, the offender goes through an evaluation process subsequent to the offence. While some offenders described experiencing disgust and self-blame at this stage, others evaluated the incident in positive terms. The individual's response in Stage 7 determines the next step in Stages 8 and 9, in which the offender either repeats his offending or attempts to stop.

Criticisms of Ward's offence chain

The model presented by Ward et al. is important in a number of respects. It represents an attempt to develop a model directly from the reports of the offenders themselves rather than from the logical analysis of a theorist. It is flexible to the extent that it can accommodate a number of offences and offender types and, in conjunction with their cognitive deconstructionist interpretation of distortions (Ward, Hudson & Marshall, 1995), it represents an attempt to go beyond simply describing the offence process to explaining it. In addition, Ward et al.'s model moves beyond the offence itself to give consideration to the offender's post-offence cognitions and behaviours which set the stage for either continued offending or an attempt to return to abstinence. Given the relative recency of Ward et al.'s model, it has not yet received independent empirical evaluation. Nonetheless, it is possible to make some observations regarding the framework of the model and its implications for treatment.

Perhaps the most striking feature of the model is in the make-up of the nine stages proposed in the model. By Stage 2, the offender is actually planning, overtly or covertly, to commit an offence. As such, all the childhood factors which may predispose an individual to offend (e.g., neglect, abuse) are rolled into Stage 1, along with all the current relevant issues (e.g., marital and social problems, employment difficulties, and upsetting affect). The four stages that follow detail the unfolding planning and contact with the victim. From a clinical perspective, it would seem injudicious to allocate treatment time to the stages in the same manner in which they are detailed in the model. Of course, it does not follow as a matter of course from Ward et al.'s model that the Stage 1 factors should get relatively little attention. However, Ward et al., by collapsing so many factors into Stage 1, fail to emphasize the importance of each of them, so there is the risk that important predisposing factors will receive only brief consideration in treatment.

Given the manner in which the data were obtained in the Ward, Louden et al. (1995) study, it is perhaps not surprising that there is relatively little emphasis on Stage 1 factors. Quite rightly, Ward and his colleagues acquired the offence scripts from untreated sexual offenders in an effort to avoid contamination. These offenders were asked to describe their most recent or typical offence. Most untreated sexual offenders are oblivious to the role of the more distal influences on their offending. When they are first asked in treatment about their offence, sexual offenders generally focus only on the terminal features of the actual abuse. While the offenders' initial efforts in treatment usually contain some description of the planning and initial contact, these tend to be rather superficial and usually contain little or no emphasis on factors earlier than this. For this reason, perhaps, the offenders in Ward's studies were assisted to construct a satisfactory vignette of their offence. However, this assistance may have contaminated the offenders' responses by imposing the therapists' own construction on the vignettes. The possibility that the offence chains provided by the offenders were rather underdeveloped may have resulted in less complex chains of behaviours and thoughts than was true of their actual offence sequence. On the other hand, being led by the interviewer, the offenders may have reported a more complex sequence of events. In what way either of these two possible influences may have distorted the resulting offence chain is not clear.

A possible response to the criticism that more emphasis should be placed on the features of Stage 1 is that such a requirement itself reflects a biased view of the importance of these factors. Indeed, the goal of the qualitative analysis of the offenders' own scripts is, arguably, to establish empirically what the offence chain really is. In so doing, the eventual result can be taken to be a better reflection of the offence chain because of these empirical roots. However, such a direct method to establish an offence chain is not necessarily going to yield an entirely accurate result. There is no evidence that untreated offenders have a precise understanding of the factors that led to their offending, and this lack of insight is presumably at least one of the reasons why they offended in the first place and why they need the advice and guidance offered in treatment. The events most proximal to the offence, particularly once the decision to offend has been made, are also likely to be those most accessible to the offenders. These factors may well have a significant bearing on the model that such data produces. As such, this model, and the manner in which it was derived, has not conclusively shown that the Stage 1 factors should not be further elaborated.

A second criticism of Ward's model relates to the issue of the abstinence violation effect. Ward et al. (1994) presented data describing the affective responses of offenders to the scripts they compiled during the study that was published later (Ward, Louden et al., 1995). They found that while there was evidence to support the presence of the AVE, it apparently did not occur prior to the offence as Pithers had proposed, but rather *after* the offence had taken place. Not surprisingly, therefore, in the offence chain Ward et al. derived from these data, the AVE occurs after Stage 6 (i.e., after the offence). However, if we examine the data of Ward et al. (1994), we see that in fact 7 of their 26 offenders did report an AVE at the lapse point, just as Pithers had suggested. Thus, while the majority of offenders may well not experience an AVE until an offence has occurred, between a quarter and a third experience it earlier. Placing the AVE post-offence, as Ward et al. do, seems too restrictive in that it will not represent the experience of a number of sexual offenders.

Overall, the distinction between an AVE occurring prior to or after an offence may not be one that has a great deal of validity. It may make most sense clinically to prepare all offenders to deal with such influences as they occur both prior to, and subsequent to, an offence. Teaching offenders to be vigilant for any kind of cognitive distortion and providing them with the ability to challenge these vigorously may well represent the best approach, regardless of the implications of either model.

Covert planning is a feature of Pithers' model and occurs in Stage 2 in Ward's model. Ward and Hudson (1996) delineate some of the difficulties associated with the use of "unconscious desires" (the desires are necessarily unconscious if the decisions that lead to them are "apparently irrelevant" and the planning thereby "covert"). Such phenomena are not easily incorporated into a cognitive behavioural framework and need more explanation than has been provided by the traditional model. Ward, Hudson and Marshall (1995) have attempted to do this using the principles of cognitive deconstruction. A cognitively deconstructed state describes a concrete focus on the steps necessary to meet immediate desires with a corresponding suspension of any abstract considerations such as the harmful, but perhaps delayed, consequences to both victims and the offender. However, it is still assumed, rather than clearly established, that there is such a process as "covert planning".

Much of what is currently construed as covert planning by an offender may simply be his attempt to present himself in a way that absolves him of responsibility for the offence. It certainly suggests that the offence was less calculated and deliberate if the offender had no notion to offend when, for example, he offered to look after the children while his wife went out for an evening with her friends. In recent years, we have been increasingly less likely to accept the notion of covert planning in our clinical work with offenders. In doing so, we have found that pursuing these suggestions by our clients has resulted in many offenders admitting to being fully aware of their planning. There is a danger that models which propose a covert planning option can lead therapists to all too readily accept what offenders say in this regard, or to impose this belief on the offender's presumed offence cycle.

Recently, Ward, Hudson and Keenan (1998) have described a self-regulation model of the offence process. There are two features of this model that are quite important and that represent significant advances over earlier views of how offending unfolds in these men. Ward et al. first note that some child molesters and rapists consider their sexual crimes to be nonoffences, seeing the problem as society's distorted views of sex between adults and children, or about what constitutes rape. They point out that we should, therefore, expect these men to have a positive view of offending and to overtly plan their offences. For these offenders, then, planning would have no covert elements. Ward et al. include in their model both covert and overt planning because they recognize that some sexual offenders will want to resist abusing people, while others will eagerly seek out victims. Subsequent data generated by Hudson, Ward and McCormack (1998) has confirmed the presence in different sexual offenders of approach and avoidance goals concerning offending. Indeed, one-third of their 86 subjects were classified as having an appetitive, positive pathway to offending that involved explicit planning. We believe this model and its supporting data should encourage clinicians to adopt a different approach to construing offence chains, allowing for variability in the explicitness of planning. Perhaps even more importantly, the data generated by Hudson et al. clearly imply that men having different pathways to offending will also have quite different treatment needs.

Ward and his colleagues have continued to challenge researchers and therapists alike to be more specific about the implications of the model they are using and to demand a better empirical basis for it. In this sense, their theorizing and related empirical work will continue to stimulate our thinking and our work.

THE CLINICAL APPLICATION OF RP

The criticisms of the RP model outlined above have implications for its application in treatment. However, before we describe the way in which we utilize the ideas derived from RP theorists, we need to consider the ways in which RP has been used by others. The excellent book edited by Richard Laws (1989) provides detailed descriptions of each aspect of the RP model as it is applied clinically by those who are both experts in, and enthusiastic adherents of, the model. Laws' book is comprehensive but accessible and is ideal reading for those who wish to implement a fully-fledged RP program for sexual offenders. However, not everyone who describes their program as adhering to the RP model enact it in the manner described in Laws' book. Indeed, RP has become such a catch phrase that almost all current treatment packages are described as RP programs, whether or not they really follow the RP model.

Treatment program providers may use the language of RP as a way of describing what they do; they may train their clients in the use of such language (i.e., abstinence violation effect, problem of immediate gratification, seemingly unimportant decisions, high-risk situations); they may construct elaborate offence chains and a series of fail-safe plans to avoid or deal with unavoidable risks; and, they may have extensive post-release supervisory procedures in place. Most program descriptions are sufficiently vague as to make it difficult to infer just what elements of RP they actually utilize. However, both California's project (Marques, Day, Nelson & Miner, 1989) and Vermont's treatment program (Pithers, Martin & Cumming, 1989) contain all of these elements. In that sense, their outcome data can be said to represent an appraisal of the fully-fledged RP model as it is applied to the treatment of sexual offenders. We will consider their outcome data in the appropriate later chapter but suffice to say here that the data are not encouraging.

We believe there are several reasons, independent of the outcome data, for not wanting to implement the full RP package as described by its prime advocates. We will note just two potential problems with this comprehensive package. In the first place, our experience suggests that most, if not all, of our clients would be overwhelmed by having to learn the complex language of RP, by having to detail each feature of their offence chain, and by having to provide a lengthy series of plans to prevent a relapse. When we have attempted to achieve these latter two goals, for instance, our clients have become bored and discouraged. In any event, it seems unlikely to us that our clients would remember all these details once discharged from treatment or released from prison, and we cannot imagine that they would follow instructions to carry their elaborate RP plans with them at all times and refer to them should an unexpected problem arise. Indeed, one of the problems with Ward, Louden et al.'s (1995) complex offence chain is that it tests the limits of therapists' capacities, let alone those of the offenders. We must make our strategies as simple as possible so that our clients are not intimidated by the procedures we suggest to them.

Secondly, making treatment (i.e., that aspect of RP that Pithers, 1990, refers to as the "internal self-management dimension") overly elaborate, and coupling that with extensive post-release supervision, sends a message to our clients that we may not wish them to accept. Such elaborate procedures indicate to our clients that we believe their problems are so extensive as to be all but insurmountable, and that we do not believe they can manage their lives on their own. If, indeed, these are the messages a complete RP approach conveys to clients, then we could expect clients treated in this way to: (1) show no better recidivism rates than a comparable untreated group; and (2) to display a rapid increase in recidivism once external supervision is eventually removed. As we will see in the treatment outcome chapter, these expectations unfortunately seem to be realized. We have, therefore, attempted to utilize the sensible features of the RP model in more circumspect ways than its advocates propose. What follows, then, is our attempt to apply this modified RP approach.

Essentially, there are three features to our application of the RP model: (1) the development of offence chain; (2) the generation of plans to deal with potential future problems; and (3) the delineation of warning signs that serve to indicate to the offender and his supervisor that he is slipping back into problematic ways. We do not use the rest of the detailed language of RP, and we do not routinely describe the abstinence violation effect, the problem of immediate gratification, or any of the other RP concepts, except those noted above.

The offence chain is described to clients as a sequence of events that typically follows the outline provided in Figure 9.2.

We have each offender identify an actual offence from his history and use this as a vehicle for developing an offence chain. This offence chain may or may not reflect the offender's typical modus operandi or initial state that triggers all his offences. Rather, it serves to illustrate the processes that might initiate an unfolding sequence that culminates in an offence. We aim for our offenders to understand the general issues rather than memorize a particular, supposedly prototypical, offence chain. In part this is because most offenders display variability in their offence chain across different occasions of offending. This, of course, is not surprising. When nonoffending males attempt to secure prosocial sexual contacts, they show a versatility that reflects an adaptation to both the circumstances and the perceived characteristics of the potential partner. It would, indeed, be surprising to find that sexual offenders follow rigid strategies.

The background factors, as we call them, refer to any of a number of possible issues that present problems for the offender. He may not have resolved childhood problems such as being physically, sexually, or emotionally abused, and these unresolved issues may have created a vulnerability that makes him responsive to, or seek to create, opportunities to offend. Additional background factors may include relationship difficulties, financial problems, or boredom. All of these, and other troubles, lead offenders to enter a state where they focus on their own inadequacies and feel anger or depression or some other unpleasant mood state. This in turn makes them feel a need to experience some pleasure and gives them a sense of entitlement (e.g., "I am suffering through no fault of my own, so I deserve some pleasure"). This initiates a reduction of awareness of abstract considerations such as the delayed consequences to offending; that is, it initiates the beginnings of a cognitively deconstructed state. At this point, the offender's thinking becomes distorted in a way that facilitates moving into a more deconstructed state (i.e., a more concrete focus on personal desires) which

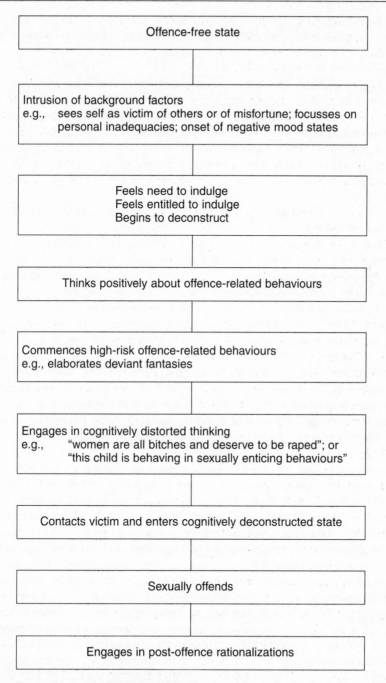

Figure 9.2   Our version of the offence chain

may be enhanced by the unrealistic details of deviant fantasies. More specific victim-focussed distortions follow, which lead to the beginning of the physical steps necessary to secure a victim.

While our offenders are assisted in recognizing all of these intermediate steps, they are only required to write out (or, in the case of an illiterate offender, have a fellow group member write out for them) six or eight particularly relevant factors that reflect the background problems, personal inadequacies, and negative mood states. The identification of these factors is derived, in part, from a previous exercise done early in the program. Early in our program, each offender is required to generate an autobiography (Long et al., 1989) from which he and the therapist can extract features that may be relevant background factors.

We then go through each offender's offence chain making clear the connection between each step and the relationship between thoughts, feelings, and actions at each step on the way to offending. Once again, we emphasize the normality of this unfolding process, making it clear that it is the goal of the process that is unacceptable, while the distorted thinking and self-focussed strategies are to be expected given the inappropriate goal.

As a consequence of developing an offence chain and having identified the risk factors (background, mood, and the typical circumstances within which offending occurs), the offender is then required to provide two or three alternative actions he can take to avoid, or deal with, unavoidable risk factors as they may occur in the future. Of course, most of our offenders did not have the skills necessary to deal with these risk factors when they were referred to us. Their coping skills may have been quite limited. Accordingly, either we train them in appropriate responses, or they are referred to other programs (e.g., cognitive skills, anger management, substance abuse), where they can acquire the requisite skills.

Advocates of the RP model tend to speak of specific skill deficits when they discuss problems in coping (Carey & McGrath, 1989; Steenman et al., 1989). While this is certainly true, it may be an incomplete appraisal of the issue. We (Cortoni & Marshall, 1995, 1996; Marshall, Cripps, Anderson & Cortoni, in press; Marshall, Serran & Cortoni, in press) have shown that sexual offenders also have more generic coping difficulties. For example, child molesters tend to use, as a general coping style, emotionally focussed strategies. In these strategies, the offender directs his attention to the emotional consequences to him of experiencing stress rather than attempting to generate problem-based solutions. Consequently, these offenders tend to wallow in depression, anxiety, and anger, and focus on their inadequacies, all of which we can expect to accelerate their move to offending behaviour. In addition, we found that, compared to other men, sexual offenders are more likely to turn to sex as a way of coping with difficulties (Cortoni, 1998). What is interesting here is that sexual offenders do not simply indulge in their specific deviant acts or fantasies when stressed; they also engage in appropriate sexual activities and entertain other types of deviant fantasies. Table 9.1 describes the findings from our studies concerning the various coping styles and strategies of sexual offenders and comparison groups.

Another aspect to this general inability to deal with problems was revealed in a study where we examined the problem-solving capacities of sexual offenders (Barbaree, Marshall & Connor, 1988). We found that sexual offenders could identify as many potential solutions to the problems presented as did other subjects but, in contrast, they typically chose an inadequate solution. Thus, sexual offenders may have poor general problem-solving skills and may have developed inadequate generic coping styles, rather than simply being deficient in specific skills. Treatment should, therefore, include training in problem-solving and the development of a problem-focussed coping style. Since our institution provides excellent cognitive skills training for all offenders, we do not have to train problem-solving behaviours, but rather, integrate them within each offender's RP plans.

Table 9.1   Coping among sexual offenders

	General coping styles		
	Task-focussed	Emotion-focussed	Avoidance-focussed
Cortoni (1998)			
Child molesters	58.00	54.05[a]	44.27
Rapists	55.76	43.19[b]	47.90
Violent offenders	56.78	40.18[b]	45.87
Marshall, Serran & Cortoni (in press)			
Child molesters	61.20	47.63[a]	47.17
Nonsex offenders	64.67	37.96[b]	47.58
Nonoffenders	60.69	41.34[b]	47.59

	Sex as a coping strategy			
	Any sexual activity	Consenting sex	Rape	Child molestation
Cortoni (1998)				
Child molesters	31.50[a]	15.07[b]	7.50[ab]	7.07[b]
Rapists	28.55[a]	13.14[ab]	8.55[a]	4.55[a]
Offenders	22.27[b]	10.47[a]	6.00[b]	4.00[a]

Note. Read superscripts by column only. Differing superscripts indicate statistically significant differences.

Finally, each offender is required to list behaviours, thoughts, and feelings that might indicate he is on the slippery path back toward offending. He generates two lists of these warning signs: one for himself, and one for an external supervisor. The warning signs for the offender are primarily feelings or thoughts that might not be evident to others, although private behaviours (e.g., surreptitious glances at children) can also be included. The warning signs for others must be clear enough to be evident to others. All of these warning signs are meant to be early steps in the offence chain that lead to an offence and should, therefore, upon detection, provide an opportunity to abort the sequence.

These products (i.e., offence chains, relapse prevention plans, and warning signs) from the offenders are quite varied in their detail and structure, and reflect each offender's own preferences for structure and his capacity to handle information, as well as the complexity of his problems. We aim to keep all offence chains, RP plans, and warning signs, within reasonable limits so that they can be effectively remembered and used by the offender, although some clients can clearly handle a greater information load than others. Our point to each client is not to make these so complicated they will have to continually refer to their products to prevent reoffending. We assume that clients will not avidly read and re-read, day after day, these products. This, we believe, would be an unrealistic objective. Accordingly, we aim for simplicity. We also repeatedly remind our clients that, however extensive their RP plans are, they will never cover all possible future events. They must see them, then, as exemplars guiding a generic problem-solving approach to potential threats to maintaining an offence-free future lifestyle.

The written descriptions of the offender's offence chain, RP plans, and warning signs are copied. One copy remains on his file, one is given to the parole board, one is sent to his external supervisor (usually his parole officer), and one is kept by the offender for future periodic review. Since in Canada parole officers and prison staff are simply different members of an integrated system, the passing of information like this is routine and parole officers expect to receive these details. Feedback from parole officers supervising sexual offenders upon release to the community indicates that this information is valuable in monitoring the behaviour of these men. Post-release supervision ends at the expiry of the offender's full sentence and, for sexual offenders, it is rarely more than 1–2 years post-release. The intensity of supervision typically matches the offender's actuarially determined risk to reoffend, with high-risk offenders being more rigorously supervised in the first 3–6 months of release than the low-risk men. Intense supervision, however, rarely involves more than weekly meetings, occasional unannounced home visits, and, where relevant, random drug-testing. Some released offenders, usually only the high or moderate–high risk offenders, are also required to enter a community-based treatment program, although this rarely involves more than 6 months of once per week treatment.

This, then, is the RP component of our treatment. Clearly, it is more limited in scope and in detail than the literature seems to suggest is necessary. Whether this attempt by us to delimit the extent of the RP component represents a sufficient intervention remains to be seen, but our early data, as we will see in the next chapter, is certainly encouraging.

We have not yet evaluated our specific relapse prevention component, but fortunately other researchers have examined the benefits of their programs. Miner, Day and Nafpaktitis (1989) developed a Situational Competency Test to measure the coping skills of sexual offenders entering and completing treatment in California's Sexual Offender Treatment and Evaluation Project. This measure and two other evaluations (the Test of Basic Relapse Prevention Concepts and an assessment of the clients' ability to produce a cognitive behavioural chain leading to an offence) were administered before and after treatment by Marques, Day, Nelson and Miner (1989). They showed that overall clients improved markedly in their knowledge of RP concepts, in their understanding of the factors (internal and external) that might put them at risk, and in their identified strategies for coping with risk factors.

Beckett, Beech, Fisher and Fordham (1994), in their evaluation of several community-based treatment programs in England, measured a variety of RP skills prior to and after treatment. They reported rather disappointing results. For instance, in the most successful program, only 57% of the clients displayed improved relapse prevention knowledge after treatment, while in three programs the clients evidenced no changes at all. Mann (1996) suggested that these poor results may have been due to the fact that these community programs were all quite brief. Accordingly, she examined the relative benefits from three prison-based extensive programs. One of these programs was a therapeutic community that did not have any cognitive behavioural elements, nor a relapse component. Another was cognitive behavioural, but had no RP component. The third was the standard English prison program, that is, cognitive behavioural and including extensive RP training. The standard program involves approximately 200 hours of treatment, while the therapeutic community program has almost twice as many hours of treatment. In this examination, Mann identified six areas of relevance for assessment: (1) the client's awareness of his thoughts and feelings that led to offending; (2) his willingness to admit planning; (3) his recognition of high-risk situations or factors; (4) his motivation for offending; (5) his strategies to cope with risks; and (6) his ability to indicate how others might know he is at risk. These features were evaluated by a structured interview conducted prior to treatment at several points throughout treatment and at the end of the program.

The findings from Mann's study were quite clear and supported the value of the RP component in achieving its goals. Compared to both the therapeutic community and the cognitive behavioural program without RP training, the standard prison program (i.e., the cognitive behavioural plus RP training) was effective in markedly enhancing RP skills; the two other programs essentially produced no changes. In addition, there were no changes in RP skills among the clients in the standard cognitive behavioural plus RP training program after their initial offence disclosure, nor after the victim empathy component. Enhancements in RP skills occurred only after the RP component was completed.

The presently available data, then, offers encouraging signs that RP training can achieve its goals. However, these studies are limited, and we need to improve the sophistication of our measures and evaluate larger numbers of subjects in order to more convincingly demonstrate the value of RP training. Perhaps more importantly, we need to demonstrate that adding RP training to more traditional cognitive behavioural programs is necessary to produce maximal treatment benefits.

Chapter 10

TREATMENT OUTCOME

I count him braver who overcomes his desires than him who conquers his enemies; for the hardest victory is victory over self.

Aristotle, 384–322 BC

There are several possible ways to evaluate treatment programs for sexual offenders. It is, in the first place, necessary to demonstrate that each of the treatment components (e.g., those targeting cognitive distortions, empathy, social skills, and so on) effectively achieve their goal of enhancing or reducing the targeted behaviors, thoughts or feelings. In the previous chapters, we have reviewed the evidence (or its absence) on the effectiveness of each of our treatment components. For the most part, it appears that these components do, indeed, reach their goals. However, this does not mean that treatment is, therefore, effective, although we would hopefully abandon or modify components that did not achieve their targeted goal. The evaluation of treatment that would satisfy most readers, and that is the focus of concern for the public and those who provide funds to support treatment, concerns whether or not our programs reduce reoffending in the treated sexual offenders.

Actually, most outcome evaluations (as we will call these projects) assess whether or not treatment has eliminated reoffending in more clients than would be expected if we did not treat them. This index of treatment effectiveness involves a reduction in recidivism rates (i.e., in the percentage of clients who subsequently reoffend). We could also examine reductions in the frequency of offending, or the delay from discharge until a reoffence, or a reduction in harmfulness or intrusiveness. Some sexual offenders abuse victims at a high frequency and any reduction in this frequency, or any delay in onset of reoffending, might reflect improvements. Some sexual offenders are viciously abusive and engage in very intrusive behaviours. Reductions in violence or intrusiveness might also be considered an advantage. With almost any other problematic behaviours, these indices would be accepted as legitimate. Not so with sexual offenders, however. The public and policy makers count as a failure a single reoffence, regardless of whether it occurred one day or 10 years after treatment, and whether it was violent or not. Because an initial sexual reoffence can occur up to 20 years after discharge (Hanson, Steffy & Gauthier, 1993; Prentky, Lee, Knight & Cerce, 1997; Soothill & Gibbens, 1978; Thornton, 1998b), there have been suggestions made that an adequate outcome study must follow clients for at least this long (Prentky et al., 1997). This suggestion misses the point that, if we are to compare treated and untreated offenders, the only reason the duration of follow-up is of concern is simply to do with the statistical power necessary to discern differences. From the available data, there is no reason to suppose that the temporal rate of first reoffence is any different between treated and untreated offenders (Hanson et al., 1993; Hanson, Scott & Steffy, 1995), although it is important to note that in these studies, treatment was not demonstrably effective. It may be that effectively treated offenders show different temporal patterns. However, the point here is that we simply have to choose a follow-up period that produces rates of reoffending in the untreated group that are sufficiently high to allow the possibility of demonstrating a treatment effect if any is present (Barbaree, 1997).

Since almost all available studies have limited their focus to recidivism data, we will focus on that index of effectiveness. However, the reader should not be misled by this focus. We consider a simple count of the percentage of clients who reoffend to be a very limited, and insufficiently comprehensive, index of the value of treatment. As we noted, reductions in harm indexed by delays in onset of reoffending and by less violence and intrusiveness, are also important ways to determine the benefits of treatment. Richard Laws (Laws, 1995, 1997) has made this point in a brilliant pair of papers. In addition, a reduction in both the number of victims and the costs resulting from reoffences can also serve as an indication of the value of treating sexual offenders. We will address these two indices of treatment benefits later in this chapter. Similarly, refusal rates and dropouts, if high, seriously reflect on the value of a treatment program.

The debate over the efficacy of treatment of sexual offenders continues, with some authors perceiving encouraging signs from the published data, while others emphatically declare that treatment is not effective. Marshall and his colleagues have persistently read the data optimistically (e.g., Marshall, 1996a or b; Marshall, Jones, Ward, Johnston & Barbaree, 1991; Marshall & Pithers, 1994; Marshall, Ward, Jones, Johnston & Barbaree, 1991), while Quinsey and his colleagues have argued that what evidence is available suggests that treatment produces no benefits (Quinsey, Harris, Rice &

Lalumière, 1993; Quinsey, Khanna & Malcolm, 1998). Furthermore, Quinsey et al. (1993) declared that those studies reporting results favouring treatment over no-treatment cannot make definitive conclusions because the methodology is so flawed that it does not meet appropriate standards of scientific rigour.

This debate would not exist, of course, if all studies of treatment efficacy with sexual offenders were uniformly positive or negative. In an earlier review, Marshall, Jones et al. (1991) considered the value of several treatment outcome studies. They summarized studies (mainly from programs in the United States) conducted before cognitive behavioural therapy was in such widespread use as it is today. The Marshall et al. report indicated variability in the effectiveness of these early programs. When Marshall et al. evaluated more recent programs (i.e., from the mid-70s on), they suggested that the outcome data from both institutional-based and community-based programs generally failed to demonstrate the success of treatment with rapists, but that treatment appeared to be effective with child molesters and exhibitionists. The present review extends Marshall et al.'s examination of the available outcome data, but first we need to consider what would constitute an adequate evaluation.

In a remarkably influential review, Furby, Weinrott and Blackshaw (1989) concluded that "there is no evidence that treatment reduces sex offense recidivism" (p. 25). Furby et al. quite clearly stated that this latter conclusion was based on an absence of evidence, whereas many readers (particularly policy makers) took it to mean that the evidence indicated treatment was ineffective. This latter conclusion could only be true if studies had found that treatment had no effect. It is, however, important to keep in mind that if one study, having adequate methodology, demonstrates that treatment reduces recidivism, then obviously treatment can be effective. Of course, independent replication is necessary to come to firm conclusions, but one well-controlled positive report certainly justifies optimism. What if there are several studies that demonstrate no effects for treatment? Should we then conclude that treatment does not work and therefore give up trying? This, essentially, is the message of Quinsey and his colleagues (Quinsey et al., 1993, 1998). Does this conclusion, however, make sense?

Numerous treatments have been tried with AIDS and so far, none have been effective in curing the disorder. This has not prevented researchers from seeking a cure. Today, it appears possible to slow down the progress of this dreadful disease, and this is surely seen as a valuable intervention, but it would not have happened had researchers given up in the face of repeated failures. So, even if we take a gloomy view of the presently available research on treatment effects with sexual offenders, as Quinsey et al. do, that does not provide a justification for giving up. Indeed, we might wonder why it is that someone would give up so easily in the face of, at best, negligible negative findings. The philosopher, Barrows Dunham, suggests that people who claim that human nature cannot be changed have a hidden purpose: "defense of the existing social arrangements". We will review the available studies and the reader may come to his/her own conclusions, although we do not pretend to be entirely objective in these matters; we are, after all, in the business of treating sexual offenders and have been for a long time.

Quinsey (1998; Quinsey et al., 1993) has made clear what he considers to be the appropriate experimental design for evaluating treatment. He declared that, unless studies meet these rigorous standards, they cannot be said to have demonstrated treatment effectiveness. Essentially, Quinsey's methodological standards seem straightforward and follow from exemplary research that evaluate the effectiveness of interventions in medicine and other psychological problems. Subjects volunteering for treatment should be randomly allocated to treatment or no-treatment, and both groups should be followed for sufficient time after discharge to permit the possibility of discerning differences in outcome.

For several years, one of us (W.L.M.) conducted research on the value of treatment for several disorders, including depression (Taylor & Marshall, 1977), low self-esteem (Marshall & Christie, 1982) and various anxiety disorders (Kleiner, Marshall & Spevack, 1987; Marshall, 1985; Marshall, Parker & Hayes, 1982). In those studies, clients suffering from one of these problems were asked if they would be willing to participate in a controlled study of treatment in which they might be allocated to either no-treatment or a psychological placebo condition. A number of potential subjects refused and demanded appropriate treatment, which was provided. Those who participated were randomly allocated to no treatment or placebo. The suffering of the no-treatment group continued during the treatment phase and for three months thereafter, that being the follow-up period necessary to infer effects. Note that it was the participants, and the participants only, who suffered as a result of our withholding treatment, and that there were no external constraints on their capacity to volunteer for the study.

These two features do not hold true for sexual offenders entering such a controlled study. If sexual offenders are not effectively treated, innocent women and children may suffer at their hands during the relatively long follow-up period (at least five years before we can hope to statistically discern treatment effects, and for many years longer if the purists would have their way). Since it is the potential victims of sexual offenders who may suffer if these men are untreated, then it seems to us that these are the people who should be asked permission to conduct such a study. If we were to conduct such a study, should we ask all Canadian women and children, or only a sample? Whoever we ask must also ensure that they make an informed decision, which would require a formidable effort. In addition, if we were to conduct such an evaluation with sexual offenders incarcerated in

Canadian penitentiaries, we would find numerous external constraints on the ability of these inmates to volunteer. If a sexual offender in a Canadian programs prison does not participate in treatment, he will be removed to another far less attractive institution where he will be more likely to be subjected to harassment. If he does not effectively participate in an approved treatment program, a sexual offender will be denied parole and kept in prison for far longer than he would were he to participate. To conduct a methodologically rigorous study in our settings, therefore, we would not only have to get the offenders' cooperation (and we doubt they would all volunteer, particularly those with the longest sentences and therefore the most dangerous) we would have to convince both the prison administration and the parole board to change their operating rules. Our guess is that, if we were to attempt such a study, we would have volunteers who were not representative of our total population, and we would not secure the cooperation of the authorities, meaning that treated and untreated offenders would be dealt with in radically different ways, thereby confounding treatment effects.

In his response to the Quinsey et al. (1993) demands, Marshall (1993a) noted that there would likely be a public outcry if it became known that treatment for sexual offenders was deliberately withheld in order to release the men to the community to see whether or not they would reoffend. Many people would likely view themselves as unwitting participants in the study, and it is quite possible that such an investigation (and the treatment program that sparked it) would be terminated. Therefore, random allocation to treatment and no-treatment control groups seems neither a feasible, nor an acceptable, approach to the evaluation of treatment with this particular population, unless circumstances beyond the control of researchers provides a fortuitous opportunity. This is what happened in California's treatment and evaluation project (Marques, Day, Nelson & Miner, 1989), where only enough money was provided to treat a small proportion of that state's incarcerated sexual offenders.

Perhaps the most important accepted criterion of treatment evaluations is the demonstration of statistical significance. Ignoring for the moment the number of victims of each sexual offender and the monetary cost of sexual offences to society, it is vital that treatment significantly reduce recidivism beyond any reductions that would have occurred without the intervention. However, in a statistically enlightened article, Barbaree (1997) meticulously demonstrated the fallibility of conclusions drawn from consideration of statistical significance alone. Barbaree pointed out the important effect of the low base rate of recidivism on the sensitivity of hypothesis testing in sexual offender treatment outcome studies. He suggested that treatment effects (i.e., the proportion by which recidivism in the treated group is reduced compared to the untreated group) must also be considered; otherwise, we run the risk of concluding that treatment does not reduce recidivism when it actually does. He noted that when base rates of recidivism are low, large treatment effects are required to detect statistical significance, and treatment effects of the magnitude required to detect significance are not likely to be found in most studies. Therefore, researchers may mistakenly conclude that treatment has not been shown to be effective, and they may conclude, as a consequence, that it would be acceptable to deliberately withhold treatment from sexual offenders in order to conduct further research. In fact, Quinsey et al. (1993) equated "real" reduction in recidivism to "statistically significant" reductions, as if the terms "real" and "statistically significant" were interchangeable. Quinsey et al. went on to state that "statistical significance is a *necessary* criterion for clinical and economic significance" (p. 521; italics appeared in the original article). Clearly, Barbaree's examination of the sensitivity of statistical hypothesis testing in this field indicates that the Quinsey et al. view may be something of an oversimplification.

Barbaree (1997) suggested some ways in which significant treatment effects can be detected. One way is to increase the sample size. However, this would be difficult because it would take several years to generate a sample size large enough in any one institution. This would, in turn, leave the researchers with the problem of ensuring that the same intervention was delivered in the same way over those years, which is unlikely and would be, in any case, difficult to assess. He also suggested that raising the base rate by not relying exclusively on official records would increase the likelihood that significance would be detected. Yet he pointed out that obtaining information that is not part of official records can be labour-intensive and costly. Furthermore, such alternative information may not be accessible to most researchers. However, some support for using information beyond that of conviction or incarceration was found by Prentky et al. (1997). They discovered that relying on conviction or incarceration records alone resulted in an underestimate of approximately 20% of new sexual offences over a 5-year follow-up. Hence, it seems to be worth some effort in obtaining various indicators of recidivism if the base rate can thereby be increased, since this would make the detection of differences between treated and untreated offenders more likely. Not surprisingly, however, very few studies have attempted to do this.

STUDIES EVALUATING TREATMENT EFFECTIVENESS

There are now available a number of studies that report on the effectiveness or otherwise of treatment programs for sexual offenders. Some of these studies report positive benefits for treatment, while others have found no effect for treatment. Unfortunately, a number of these evaluations have not

limitations

provided a satisfactory comparison group of untreated offenders. In our consideration of outcome reports we will ignore studies that do not report comparative untreated base rates. We will begin by describing and evaluating studies that have failed to demonstrate treatment effects, and then we will follow that by a consideration of studies reporting beneficial effects.

Negative outcome studies

There are four reports in the literature where treatment was found not to be effective in reducing recidivism below that of an untreated comparison group.

Quinsey and his colleagues have reported the absence of effectiveness in two treatment programs: one they conducted themselves at Oak Ridge Mental Health Centre, and one they evaluated for Correctional Services of Canada. Many of the residents at Oak Ridge Mental Health Centre are sent there by the courts either because they have been found to be "not guilty by reason of insanity", or because the courts needed an evaluation of their mental fitness to stand trial. Those who enter treatment are the long-term residents, and their offence histories, not surprisingly, place most of them in the category of high risk for recidivism. To illustrate the unusual nature of the history of these sexual offenders, we note observations made by Palmer (1998). He found that, while the same indicators function to allocate both these clients and a large sample of Corrections Canada penitentiary inmates to various levels of risk, the offenders at Oak Ridge in the high-risk category have a better than 80% chance of reoffending, whereas the high-risk offenders in penitentiaries have just over 30% rate of reoffending. Clearly the Oak Ridge inmates are unusually dangerous offenders who are in need of very extensive treatment. Unfortunately, the treatment provided for these offenders seems to have been rather limited.

In their report of this study, Rice, Quinsey and Harris (1991) indicated that 46 of their 50 treated subjects were given aversion therapy aimed at reducing deviant sexual interests, but none were advised on procedures to enhance appropriate interests. The criterion for successful treatment was a reduction in deviant responding at phallometric assessment, but only half the subjects achieved this. In addition to aversion therapy, some of the subjects received sex education and some received heterosexual social skills training, although the authors provided no indication on how effective these treatment components were.

This program would likely be judged by most contemporary treatment providers to be inadequate, or incomplete, for these dangerous offenders, and Rice et al. (1991) admit as much. They note that "the provision of a very brief intervention involving no aftercare or clinical follow-up for serious offenders in the present research may be sufficient to explain the differences in outcome between this and other studies" (p. 386). In addition, however, the treated offenders remained incarcerated at Oak Ridge on wards with other very deviant sexual offenders for several years prior to release, apparently without any further treatment. It seems to us no surprise at all that this treatment program was not effective; however, there are other issues relevant to Quinsey's more general position on the value of treating sexual offenders.

In the first place, the Rice et al. study did not involve the random allocation to treatment or no-treatment that Quinsey (1998; Quinsey et al., 1993) insists is necessary to come to any conclusions about the value of interventions with sexual offenders. In fact, the comparison group was a convenience sample, and the treated subjects were at higher risk for recidivism, had more deviant sexual preferences, and had more severely injured their victims (Rice, Harris & Quinsey, 1993). Nevertheless, Rice et al. (1993) felt justified in concluding that treatment for sexual offenders is demonstrably ineffective. This point of view not only ignores their own dictum that inferences about the value of treatment can only be derived from methodologically sound studies (i.e., random allocation of subjects), but also involves the logical error of generalizing from a single treatment failure to conclude that all treatment programs are ineffective. If Rice et al.'s program had been an ideal intervention for these difficult clients, and if their study had met their own rather idealistic methodological standards, we might be inclined to forgive their cavalier dismissal of the treatment efforts of all other clinicians. Neither their treatment program nor their study, however, met these standards.

Hanson, Steffy and Gauthier (1993) examined recidivism data for 197 child molesters of whom 106 received treatment. All these offenders were released from an Ontario provincial prison between 1958 and 1974. Sexual and violent reconvictions were extracted from official police records. The treatment program was obviously based on early versions of behavioural interventions that attempted to decrease sexual interest in children (by electric aversive therapy) and enhance social competence (by group and individual counselling). The data presented in Table 10.1 collapsed the two control groups described by Hanson et al., but however the data are analysed, the results do not indicate an effect for treatment. From today's perspective, this was a quite limited program and, in that sense, much like Rice et al.'s program, its outcome data serve to confirm the move over the past 20 years to more comprehensive interventions.

In a more recent report, Quinsey et al. (1998) evaluated a program run at the Regional Treatment Centre (Ontario) of Correctional Services of Canada. Because this was a retrospective study, it was not possible to apply the principle of random allocation to treatment and no-treatment; the no-

Table 10.1 Negative and positive treatment outcome from several programs

	Treated	Untreated	
A. *Studies with negative findings*			
Rice et al. (1991)	38*	31	
Hanson et al. (1993)	44	38	
Quinsey et al. (1998)	33	9	(Treatment not required)
		17	(Refused treatment)
		11	(Unsuitable)
Marques (personal communication, March 1998)			
Rapists	11	18	(Untreated volunteers)
		6	(Nonvolunteers)
All Child Molesters	11	13	(Untreated volunteers)
		15	(Nonvolunteers)
Female victims	9	108	(Untreated volunteers)
			(Nonvolunteers)
Male victims	13	18	(Untreated volunteers)
		35	(Nonvolunteers)
B. *Studies with positive findings*			
*Farshall & Barbaree, 1988***			
Child molesters			
female victims	18	43	
male victims	13	43	
Incest offenders	8	22	
*Marshall, Eccles & Barbaree (1991)***			
Exhibitionists			
Study 1	39	57	
Study 2	24		
Looman's et al. (1998) reanalysis of Quinsey et al. (in press)			
Pre-1989 (most serious offenders)	28	52	
Post-1998 (least serious offenders)	7	25	
Nicholaichuk et al. (1998)			
Rapists	14	42	
Child molesters	18	62	
First time offenders			
Rapists	11	32	
Child molesters	9	63	
Repeat offenders			
Rapists	20	52	
Child molesters	32	61	
McGrath, Hoke & Vojtisek (1998)	1	16	(Nonspecialized treatment)
		11	(Refusers)
Bakker et al. (1998)			
Child molesters	8	21	
Proulx et al. (1998)			
Child molesters	6	33	
Rapists	39	71	
Worling & Curwen (1998)			
Adolescents mixed sexual offenders	5	18	

* All figures are sexual offence recidivism rates rounded to the nearest whole number.
** All data for the two Marshall studies are derived from unofficial and official records combined.

treatment group was, therefore, once again a convenience sample. However, in this case the comparison group turned out to be quite inappropriate, although a more appropriate group to sample was available. The comparison groups in Quinsey et al.'s study included: those sexual offenders (n = 183) judged, after thorough assessment, to not require the extensive treatment provided at RTC (Ontario); those who refused the offer of treatment (n = 52); and those (n = 27) deemed unsuited to the RTC (Ontario) program. The latter were judged unsuitable because they either did not speak English or were developmentally handicapped. If the assessments done to determine treatment needs were at all accurate, then clearly the major comparison group (i.e., those who were judged not to need the program) was at lower risk to reoffend than the treated group. Since Quinsey et al. evaluated the whole sample on known risk predictors, they could have determined the differential pretreatment risk of each group, but all they reported was the total sample's risk. In any event, the statistical evaluation of outcome revealed that the treated group had the highest recidivism rate for sexual offences.

Terry Nicholaichuk has access to data on a very considerable group of untreated sexual offenders released from one of Correctional Services of Canada's penitentiaries. Accordingly, he subsequently extracted a sample of these offenders matched on offence histories and demographic variables to Quinsey et al.'s treated subjects. Nicholaichuk and his colleagues (Looman, Abracen & Nicholaichuk, 1998) were able to divide the treated sample into those treated prior to 1989 (the more dangerous group of offenders) and those treated after 1989. Of the early-treated group, 28% reoffended over the follow-up period, during which time 6.8% of the later-treated group had reoffended. Among the comparison groups, 52% of those matched with the pre-1989 treated subjects reoffended, while for those matched with the post-1989 treated group, the recidivism rate was 25%. Evidently, when appropriate comparison groups were provided, the treatment program at RTC (Ontario) was shown to be very effective.

Of course, Quinsey et al.'s evaluation did not meet his own methodological standards (i.e., random allocation of subjects to treatment or no treatment), but this did not prevent him (Quinsey, 1996) from declaring, on the basis of these findings, that treatment for sexual offenders (read *all* sexual offenders) is ineffective. From this conclusion, Quinsey then advocated that Correctional Services of Canada abandon treatment for all but the lowest risk sexual offenders and spend their resources carefully supervising and monitoring the high-risk offenders for at least 10 years after their release from prison. These conclusions were essentially repeated in the published report of these findings (Quinsey et al., 1998), despite Quinsey having the opportunity in the meantime to see Nicholaichuk's reappraisal. In fact, these recommendations are puzzling. First, it is quite clear, as Quinsey well knows, that the base rate recidivism for low-risk sexual offenders is too low to allow treatment to have any demonstrable effect, so why recommend treating these men? Second, there is no evidence at all, however reasonable it may seem, that careful post-release supervision or monitoring has any effect on reducing reoffence rates. For someone who claims the high road on methodological standards (see Quinsey, 1998; Quinsey, Harris, Rice & Lalumière, 1993), these recommendations of Quinsey's seem insecurely based.

While we have pointed to problems, or limitations, to these three reports of negative findings, and in this way perhaps diminished their impact, we should also point out that it is unreasonable to expect all treatment programs, for all sexual offenders, to be effective. This is particularly true given that treatment for sexual offenders is still in the early stages of development. Not only are we still unsure of the full range of problems that beset these men, we still have to determine how to most effectively allocate treatment resources to the different types of offenders and to those at different levels of risk to reoffend. We also have not yet determined how best to individualize the programs that we still tend to provide as a blanket treatment for all offenders. Furthermore, as we suggested in the chapter on therapeutic processes, we can expect different therapist styles and skills to significantly influence treatment outcome. Despite these caveats, however, there are programs that have generated positive outcome data.

Positive outcome studies

We have already discussed Looman et al.'s revised, and positive, comparison of Quinsey et al.'s (1998) examination of RTC (Ontario)'s program. There are, however, at least seven other studies reporting positive outcomes that included well-matched untreated comparison groups. In none of these studies, however, was random allocation of subjects to treatment or no-treatment attempted. In each case, a comparison (or convenience) sample was obtained from the same population of offenders who were dealt with in the same facilities. Matching of these comparison groups with treated subjects was satisfactory in all cases.

Nicholaichuk, Gordon, Andre, Gu and Wong (1998) evaluated the program operated by the Regional Psychiatric Centre (Prairies) of Correctional Services of Canada in Saskatoon. There were 168 rapists and 49 child molesters who received treatment in this program between 1981 and 1996. They were matched with untreated sexual offenders selected from an archive of men held in the Prairie Regional penitentiaries. An appraisal showed that the groups were satisfactorily matched on offence history and demographic variables. Among the treated subjects, 6.1% reoffended over the approximately 6-year follow-up, while 20.5% of the untreated sexual offenders recidivated; these differences are statistically significant. Similar results were evident, examining either first-time offenders or repeat offenders, indicating that the program was, like the RTC (Ontario) program, equally effective in reducing the recidivism rates of both the most and least dangerous offenders.

Steele (1995) reported outcome data for the Minnesota Department of Corrections' program. It is important to note that, at the time of writing, Steele pointed out that Minnesota had the second lowest incarceration rate in the United States, with only one-fifth of all convicted sexual offenders being imprisoned. Thus, the prison-based program is likely to be dealing with the most dangerous sexual offenders. Of the rapists in Steele's report, 14.5% of the treated subjects and 27.3% of the untreated men reoffended during the 1–11 year follow-up period. Among the child molesters, 8.6% of the treated subjects and 20.8% of the untreated offenders recidivated during a similar time period. Unfortunately, Steele did not provide a statistical comparison, but it would be surprising, given the number of subjects, if an analysis failed to reveal significant effects.

We have evaluated our community-based program for both child molesters (Marshall & Barbaree, 1988) and exhibitionists (Marshall, Eccles & Barbaree, 1991). The untreated comparison groups in these two reports were offenders who attended our clinic for evaluation and expressed a desire for treatment, but were unable to participate because they lived too far away to attend regularly. In all cases, we arranged counselling for them in their local community. We were able to access the unofficial records of both the various police precincts in the area we serve and the child protection agencies who have a legal mandate to investigate reports of child molestation. The data extracted from these records, plus that extracted from the official police computer base, revealed recidivism rates between 2.4 and 3 times higher than would have been evident from the official records alone. This provided us with far higher base rates, thereby making it more likely that we could statistically discern a treatment effect if, indeed, there was one. In our examination of the benefits of treatment for nonfamilial child molesters, we found that, for both those who had offended against boys and those who had offended against girls, the treated men had significantly lower rates of reoffending than did the untreated men. The same was true for the incest offenders and the exhibitionists.

In another positive outcome report, McGrath, Hoke and Vojtisek (1998) examined recidivism data for a group of sexual offenders placed on community supervision. Seventy-one offenders completed the specialized sexual offender treatment program, 21 completed a nonspecialized treatment, and 19 refused to participate in treatment. One offender (1.4%) in the specialized treatment group committed a new sexual reoffence during the approximately 5-year follow-up period, whereas 15.6% of the non-specialized treatment group were reconvicted of a sexual reoffence. In the group of offenders who refused treatment, 10.5% committed a sexual reoffence. The authors suggest their results support conclusions that cognitive behavioural and relapse prevention approaches to treatment with sexual offenders are beneficial in reducing the rate of subsequent recidivism.

The comprehensive cognitive behavioural program provided by the New Zealand Prison Services has recently been evaluated, although the follow-up period to date (approximately 2 years) indicates that this report should be considered tentative. Bakker, Hudson, Wales and Riley (1998) followed 238 treated child molesters for 2 years after release, and compared their reoffence rates with a group of 283 untreated offenders who were matched on offence history and demographic variables. Eight percent of the treated men reoffended within the follow-up period, which was a significantly lower recidivism rate than the untreated child molesters (21%). Both comparative raw recidivism rates and survival analyses revealed significant benefits for treatment.

Proulx et al. (1998) examined recidivism among sexual offenders who had either been released from a maximum security psychiatric facility or discharged from a community treatment program in Montreal. Collapsing across the disparate clients from these quite different treatment centres is not ideal, but there is no reason to suppose that this would distort the comparative recidivism of treated and untreated offenders. These researchers compared those offenders who had completed treatment with those who dropped out of the program prior to completion. Both groups were approximately matched on relevant features of their history. Among the 63 child molesters who completed treatment, 5.7% reoffended during the 4-year follow-up, while 33.3% of the 39 noncompleters recidivated. Of the 46 rapists completing treatment, 38.5% reoffended as did 70.8% of the 24 dropouts. A most interesting observation from this evaluation was that among the child molesters, treatment delayed the onset of reoffending: none of the treated subjects reoffended before 2 years after discharge, whereas the untreated clients began reoffending shortly after release and recidivism rates for these subjects approached their maximum levels by the end of the first year at risk.

In a recent evaluation of the sexual offenders program operating at Thistletown Regional Centre for Children and Adolescents, Worling and Curwen (1998) provided convincing data for its effectiveness. They followed 58 treated adolescents and compared them to a group of untreated adolescent sexual offenders. Both groups were matched on various demographic and offence history variables and official recidivism data was examined over a 10-year follow-up period. It is important to note that 66% of the comparison group received some form of treatment outside the Thistletown

Centre, and an additional 30% entered the Thistletown program but dropped out before they had achieved what the authors considered to be satisfactory treatment. Even so, the treated subjects demonstrated significantly lowered recidivism rates for both sexual and nonsexual offences.

Table 10.1 describes the results from all the studies reviewed in this chapter, both the negative and positive findings. It is very important to note that the programs demonstrating treatment effectiveness are all cognitive behavioural in orientation and comprehensive in the targets they address in treatment. Interestingly, none of the positively evaluated programs included much in the way of post-discharge supervision, nor did the prison programs provide more than brief treatment after release from prison settings. To determine whether extensive post-release supervision and treatment is valuable, we need to examine a program that has such a component.

California's treatment and evaluation project (Marques et al., 1989) has extensive post-release supervision and treatment and has generated year-by-year evaluations, the latest of which was kindly provided to us by Marques (March, 1998, personal communication). As we noted in the Relapse Prevention chapter, however, this program also has extensive within-treatment training in relapse prevention, and this may contribute, along with the extensive post-discharge component, to the communication of an unintended message to the clients that they cannot manage alone. This, of course, is rather ironic, given that the aim of relapse prevention programs is to instil self-control in clients. With the best of intentions, therapists can inadvertently take over clients' lives to the detriment of their post-discharge sense of self-direction. The intent of behavioural and cognitive behavioural treatments has always been, and should be, the empowerment of our clients. Any strategies that, even unintentionally, take away from the achievement of this goal will inevitably reduce the effectiveness of treatment. As therapists, we must keep in mind that our approach to treatment can convey many messages, over-and-above the ones we intend to convey.

After release from incarceration, sexual offenders in California's program are very strictly supervised, and are involved in community treatment for at least one year. Our hypothesis is that the extensive and intensive treatment within custody in this program, and the strict post-release supervision and treatment in the community, effectively convey the message to the participants that they are incapable of managing without a therapist or supervisor watching over them. From this hypothesis, two things should follow: (1) treated subjects should do no better than comparable untreated clients; and (2) recidivism rates should reveal among the treated subjects significant increases only after supervision is terminated one year after release from prison. The data provided by Marques confirms both of these predictions. Table 10.1 describes the comparative recidivism data and it can be seen that there are no clear benefits for treatment. However, it is worth noting that the recidivism data for the treated subjects is in every case lower than the data for the untreated offenders. Figure 10.1 describes the survival curves for the treated clients and it is evident that this curve plummets at one year after release just as we expected.

We think Marques' latest findings sound an important note of caution regarding the current enthusiastic extension of both the internal management and external supervisory components of relapse prevention. In particular, the data should strongly encourage treatment providers to do their best to empower the sexual offenders in their programs. This can be achieved in three ways: first, by structuring treatment and supervision in a way that progressively diminishes control by the therapist and supervisor; second, by constantly encouraging independence in the clients; and finally, by providing skills training aimed at enhancing a sense of self-efficacy (e.g., enhancing self-esteem, instilling relationship skills, generating problem-solving and appropriate coping strategies, and otherwise providing the skills and attitudes necessary for competent functioning). These are just the

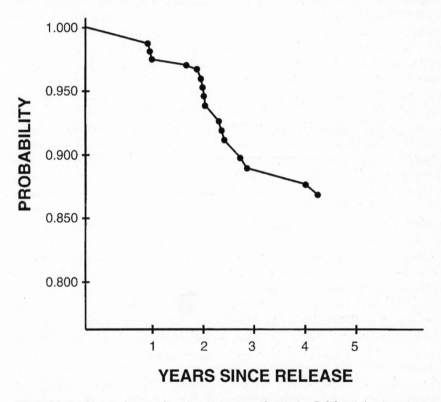

Figure 10.1 Survival rates for treatment completers in California's treatment and evaluation project. Derived from Marques (March, 1998, personal communication).

sorts of structures and processes we engage, and the skills we attempt to instil in our clients. It is also important to note that the internal management element of our relapse prevention component is relatively limited and that the post-release supervision and treatment is brief and nonintensive. Although we have not yet completed an appraisal of our program, our early tentative evaluation (Marshall & Fernandez, 1997) revealed a recidivism rate in the treated offenders of approximately 3%, which is certainly encouraging. Indeed, the components of our program are remarkably similar to the program evaluated by Nicholaichuk et al. (1998), which revealed clearly positive benefits for treatment.

CONCLUSIONS

Our reading of the results listed in Table 10.1 is that they indicate that treatment of sexual offenders can be effective and that the balance of the evidence weighs in favour of a positive treatment outcome. No doubt the sexual offenders treated by Rice et al. (1991) constitute a particularly problematic group, and it may be that no program would effectively reduce their risk. However, just as with Hanson et al.'s (1993) report, the program for these difficult clients was quite limited, and no one would today consider either of these programs to constitute adequate treatment. If we can consider these two evaluations to constitute appraisals of historically outmoded treatment, then we are essentially left with seven reasonably methodologically sound, positive evaluations of current treatment approaches, and one equally sound negative evaluation (Marques' report). This, we believe, should encourage optimism in treatment providers and encourage governments to continue, or begin, to fund treatment programs.

In conclusion, then, we consider the optimistic conclusions we came to several years ago (Marshall, Jones et al., 1991) have been strengthened by the data that have become available in the interim. Despite some negative findings, and the rather gloomy perspective on the value of treatment taken by Quinsey and his colleagues, we believe a reading of the available literature provides grounds for confidence that the treatment for sexual offenders can be effective. This is a conclusion that Hall (1995) came to a few years ago as a result of a meta-analysis of the available evidence. Hall conducted an analysis of 12 studies of treatment with sexual offenders. His results demonstrated a small but robust overall effect size favouring treatment. Hall noted that the overall recidivism rate for treated offenders was 19%, whereas for untreated men it was 27%. He also noted a greater effect size for studies involving outpatient samples than for studies of institutionally based programs. What we have seen in the more recent studies, however, are clear benefits resulting from prison programs.

Finally, cost–benefit analyses (Marshall, 1992; Prentky & Burgess, 1990) have revealed that treatment not only reduces the number of innocent people (primarily women and children) who would otherwise suffer at the hands of untreated sexual offenders, it also saves the taxpayers a very considerable amount of money. However, these cost–benefit analyses did not include the cost of therapy for the victims. Cohen and Miller (1998) derived data relevant to this issue from various American organizations. Based on means for 1991, the total cost of treatment for victims of recent child sexual abuse exceeded $600 million; for victims of historical childhood sexual abuse, the total was over $4 billion; and for adult victims of attempted or completed rape, the cost of their treatment exceeded $800 million. Clearly, the value of treatment with sexual offenders far exceeds the obvious benefits of reduced recidivism. From these types of analyses, it appears that out of every 100 sexual offenders treated, we only have to prevent 3 or 4 who would otherwise have offended from reoffending in order to cover the costs of treatment. Reducing recidivism rates by just 3–4% does not seem a particularly daunting task. Governments often respond to proposals to offer treatment to sexual offenders by claiming they cannot afford to fund such programs. On the contrary, we believe that cost–benefit analyses reveal that governments are, in fact, in the odd position of being unable to afford to not treat sexual offenders.

With the current data at hand, we are optimistic about the future development of sexual offender treatment. We now have available well-researched targets to address in treatment, demonstrably effective procedures for reaching these targets, the beginning of an examination of therapeutic processes, and encouraging, if not methodologically purely based, evidence of the benefits of treatment. We could not imagine a more optimistic note on which to close this book.

BIBLIOGRAPHY

Abel, G.G. (1976). Assessment of sexual deviation in the male. In A.S. Bellack & M. Hersen (Eds.), *Behavioral assessment: A practical handbook* (pp. 437–457). New York: Pergamon Press.

Abel, G.G., Barlow, D.H., Blanchard, E.B., & Guild, D. (1977). The components of rapists' sexual arousal. *Archives of General Psychiatry*, **34**, 895–903.

Abel, G.G., Becker, J.V., Blanchard, E.B., & Flanagan, B. (1981). The behavioral assessment of rapists. In J. Hays, T. Roberts & K. Solway (Eds.), *Violence and the violent individual* (pp. 211–230). Holliswood, NY: Spectrum Publications.

Abel, G.G., Becker, J.V., & Cunningham-Rathner, J. (1984). Complications, consent and cognitions in sex between children and adults. *International Journal of Law and Psychiatry*, **7**, 89–103.

Abel, G.G., Becker, J.V., Cunningham-Rathner, J., Mittelman, M.S., & Rouleau, J.L. (1988). Multiple paraphilic diagnoses among sex offenders. *Bulletin of the American Academy of Psychiatry and the Law*, **16**, 153–168.

Abel, G.G., Becker, J.V., Mittelman, M.S., Cunningham-Rathner, J., Rouleau, J.L., & Murphy, W.D. (1987). Self-reported sex crimes of nonincarcerated paraphiliacs. *Journal of Interpersonal Violence*, **2**, 3–25.

Abel, G.G., Becker, J.V., Murphy, W.D., & Flanagan, B. (1981). Identifying dangerous child molesters. In R. Stuart (Ed.), *Violent behavior: Social learning approaches to prediction, management and treatment* (pp. 116–137). New York: Brunner/Mazel.

Abel, G.G., Becker, J.V., & Skinner, L. (1983). Behavioral approaches to the treatment of the violent person. In L. Roth (Ed.), *Clinical treatment of the violent offender* (pp. 46–63). Washington, DC: NIMH Monograph Series.

Abel, G.G., & Blanchard, E.B. (1974). The role of fantasy in the treatment of sexual deviation. *Archives of General Psychiatry*, **30**, 467–475.

Abel, G.G., Blanchard, E.B., & Becker, J.V. (1978). An integrated treatment program for rapists. In R. Rada (Ed.), *Clinical aspects of the rapist* (pp. 161–214). New York: Grune & Stratton.

Abel, G.G., Gore, D.K., Holland, C.L., Camp, N., Becker, J.V., & Rathner, J. (1989). The measurement of the cognitive distortions of child molesters. *Annals of Sex Research*, **2**, 135–152.

Abel, G.G., Levis, D., & Clancy, J. (1970). Aversion therapy applied to taped sequences of deviant behavior in exhibitionism and other sexual deviations: A preliminary report. *Journal of Behavior Therapy and Experimental Psychiatry*, **1**, 58–66.

Abel, G.G., Osborn, C.A., Anthony, D., & Gardos, P. (1992). Current treatment of paraphiliacs. *Annual Review of Sex Research*, **3**, 255–290.

Abel, G.G., & Rouleau, J.L. (1990). The nature and extent of sexual assault. In W.L. Marshall, D.R. Laws & H.E. Barbaree (Eds.), *Handbook of sexual assault: Issues, theory and treatment of the offender* (pp. 9–21). New York: Plenum Press.

Adams, H.E., & Sturgis, E.T. (1977). Status of behavioral reorientation techniques in the modification of homosexuality: A review. *Psychological Bulletin*, **84**, 1171–1188.

Ageton, S. (1983). *Sexual assault among adolescents*. Lexington, MA: Lexington Books.

Ainsworth, M.D.S, Blehar, M.C., Waters, E., & Walls, S. (1978). *Patterns of attachment: A psychological study of the Strange Situation*. Hillsdale, NJ: Lawrence Erlbaum.

Alexander, J.F., Barton, C., Schiavo, S., & Parsons, B.V. (1976). Systems-behavioral intervention with families of delinquents: Therapist characteristics, family behavior and outcome. *Journal of Consulting and Clinical Psychology*, **44**, 656–664.

Amir, M. (1971). *Patterns of forcible rape*. Chicago: University of Chicago Press.

Annis, H.M., & Chan, D. (1983). The differential treatment model: Empirical evidence from a personality topology of adult offenders. *Criminal Justice and Behavior*, **10**, 159–173.

Ashby, J.D., Ford, D.H., Guerny, B.G., & Guerny, L.F. (1957). Effects on clients of a reflective and leading type of psychotherapy. *Psychological Monographs*, **453**, 71.

Awad, G., Saunders, E., & Levene, J. (1984). A clinical study of male adolescent sex offenders. *International Journal of Offender Therapy and Comparative Criminology*, **28**, 105–115.

Bakker, L., Hudson, S.M., Wales, D., & Riley, D. (1998). An evaluation of the Kia Marama Treatment Programme for Child Molesters. Christchurch, New Zealand: New Zealand Department of Justice.

Bancroft, J.H.J. (1969). Aversion therapy of homosexuality. *British Journal of Psychiatry*, **115**, 1417–1431.

Bancroft, J.H.J. (1971). The application of psychophysiological measures to the assessment and modification of sexual behaviour. *Behaviour Research and Therapy*, **9**, 119–130.

Bancroft, J. (1978). The prevention of sexual offenses. In C.B. Qualls, J.P. Wincze & D.H. Barlow (Eds.), *The prevention of sexual disorders*. New York: Plenum Press.

Bancroft, J.H.J., Jones, H.G., & Pullan, B.R. (1966). A simple device for measuring penile erection. Some comments on its use in the treatment of sexual disorders. *Behaviour Research and Therapy*, **4**, 239–241.

Bancroft, J.H.J., & Marks, I. (1968). Electric aversion therapy of sexual deviations. *Proceedings of the Royal Society of Medicine*, **61**, 796–799.

Bandura, A. (1977). Self-efficacy: Toward a unifying theory of behavior change. *Psychological Review*, **84**, 191–215.

Bandura, A. (1986). *Social foundations of thought and action: A social cognitive theory*. Englewood Cliffs, NJ: Prentice-Hall.

Barbaree, H.E. (1991). Denial and minimization among sex offenders: Assessment and treatment outcome. *Forum on Corrections Research*, **3**, 30–33.

Barbaree, H.E. (1997). Evaluating treatment efficacy with sexual offenders: The insensitivity of recidivism studies to treatment effect. *Sexual Abuse: A Journal of Research and Treatment*, **9**, 111–129.

Barbaree, H.E., Baxter, D.J., & Marshall, W.L. (1989). The reliability of the rape index in a sample of rapists and nonrapists. *Violence and Victims*, **4**, 299–306.

Barbaree, H.E., & Marshall, W.L. (1989). Erectile responses among heterosexual child molesters, father-daughter incest offenders, and matched non-offenders: Five distinct age preference profiles. *Canadian Journal of Behavioral Science*, **21**, 70–82.

Barbaree, H.E., & Marshall, W.L. (1991). The role of male sexual arousal in rape: Six models. *Journal of Consulting and Clinical Psychology*, **59**, 621–630.

Barbaree, H.E., & Marshall, W.L. (1998). Treatment of the sexual offender. In R.M. Wettstein (Ed.), *Treatment of offenders with mental disorders* (pp. 265–328). New York: Guilford Press.

Barbaree, H.E., Marshall, W.L., & Connor, J. (1988). The social problem-solving of child molesters. Unpublished manuscript, Queen's University, Kingston, Ontario, Canada.

Barbaree, H.E., Marshall, W.L., & Lanthier, R.D. (1979). Deviant sexual arousal in rapists. *Behaviour Research and Therapy*, **14**, 215–222.

Barbaree, H.E., Marshall, W.L., Yates, E., & Lightfoot, L.O. (1983). Alcohol intoxication and deviant sexual arousal in male social drinkers. *Behaviour Research and Therapy*, **21**, 365–373.

Barlow, D.H. (1974). The treatment of sexual deviation: Toward a comprehensive behavioral approach. In K.S. Calhoun, H.E. Adams & K.M. Mitchell (Eds.), *Innovative treatment methods in psychopathology* (pp. 121–147). New York: Wiley.

Barlow, D.H., Abel, G.G., Blanchard, E.B., Bristow, A.R., & Young, D.L. (1977). A heterosocial skills behavior checklist for males. *Behavior Therapy*, **8**, 229–239.

Barlow, D.H., & Agras, W.S. (1973). Fading to increase heterosexual responses in homosexuals. *Journal of Applied Behavior Analysis*, **6**, 355–366.

Barlow, D.H., Becker, R., Leitenberg, H., & Agras, W.S. (1970). A mechanical strain gauge for recording penile circumference change. *Journal of Applied Behavioral Analysis*, 3, 72.

Barnard, G.W., Fuller, A.K., Robbins, L., & Shaw, T. (1989). *The child molester: An integrated approach to evaluation and treatment.* New York: Brunner/Mazel.

Bartholomew, K. (1990). Avoidance of intimacy: An attachment perspective. *Journal of Social and Personal Relationships*, **7**, 147–178.

Bartholomew, K. (1993). From childhood to adult relationships: Attachment theory and research. In S. Duck (Ed.), *Learning About Relationships: Understanding Relationship Processes series, Vol. 2.* Newbury Park, CA: Sage.

Bartholomew, K., & Horowitz, L. (1991). Attachment styles among young adults: A test of a four-category model. *Journal of Personality and Social Psychology*, **61**, 226–244.

Bartholomew, K., & Perlman, D. (Eds.) (1994). *Attachment processes in adulthood.* London: Jessica Kingsley.

Batchelor, A. (1988). How clients perceive therapist empathy: A content analysis of "received" empathy. *Psychotherapy*, **25**, 227–240.

Baumeister, R.F. (1991). *Escaping the self.* New York: Basic Books.

Baumeister, R.F. (1993a). *Self-esteem: The puzzle of low self-regard.* New York: Plenum Press.

Baumeister, R.F. (1993b). Understanding the inner nature of low self-esteem: Uncertain, fragile, protective, and conflicted. In R.F. Baumeister (Ed.), *Self-esteem: the puzzle of self-regard* (pp. 201–218). New York: Plenum Press.

Baumeister, R.F., & Leary, M.R. (1995). The need to belong: Desire for interpersonal attachments as a fundamental human motivation. *Psychological Bulletin*, **117**, 497–529.

Baumeister, R.F., Smart, L., & Boden, J.M. (1996). Relation of threatened egotism to violence and aggression: The dark side of high self-esteem. *Psychological Review*, **103**, 5–33.

Baumeister, R.F., & Tice, D.M. (1985). Self-esteem and responses to success and failure: Subsequent performance and intrinsic motivation. *Journal of Personality*, **53**, 450–467.

Baxter, D.J., Barbaree, H.E., & Marshall, W.L. (1986). Sexual responses to consenting and forced sex in a large sample of rapists and nonrapists. *Behaviour Research and Therapy*, **24**, 513–520.

BIBLIOGRAPHY 167

Baxter, D.J., Marshall, W.L., Barbaree, H.E., Davidson, P.R., & Malcolm, P.B. (1984). Deviant sexual behavior: Differentiating sex offenders by criminal and personal history, psychometric measures, and sexual responses. *Criminal Justice and Behavior*, **11**, 477–501.

Beck, A.T. (1967). *Depression: Clinical, experimental and theoretical aspects.* New York: Harper & Row.

Beck, A.T. (1970). Cognitive therapy: Nature and relation to behavior therapy. *Behavior Therapy*, **1**, 184–200.

Becker, J.V., Kaplan, M.S., & Tenke, C.E. (1992). The relationship of abuse history, denial and erectile response: Profiles of adolescent sexual perpetrators. *Behavior Therapy*, **23**, 87–97.

Beckett, R., Beech, A., Fisher, D., & Fordham, A.S. (1994). *Community-based treatment of sex offenders: An evaluation of seven treatment programmes.* Home Office Occasional paper. London: Home Office.

Beech, A., & Fordham, A.S. (1997). Therapeutic climate of sexual offender treatment programs. *Sexual Abuse: A Journal of Research and Treatment*, **9**, 219–237.

Beech, H.R., Watts, F., & Poole, A.D. (1971). Classical conditioning of sexual deviation: A preliminary note. *Behavior Therapy*, **2**, 400–402.

Beitchman, J.H., Zucker, K.J., Hood, J.E., DaCosta, G.A., Akman, D., & Cassavia, E. (1992). A review of the long-term effects of child sexual abuse. *Child Abuse and Neglect*, **16**, 101–118.

Beutler, L.E., Crago, M., & Arizmendi, T.G. (1986). Research on therapist variables in psychotherapy. In S.L. Garfield & A.E. Bergin (Eds.), *Handbook of psychotherapy and behavior change* (pp.). New York: Wiley.

Bijou, S.W., & Orlando, R. (1961). Rapid development of multiple-schedule performances with retarded children. *Journal of Experimental Analysis of Behavior*, **4**, 7–16.

Birchler, G.R., & Webb, L.J. (1977). Discriminating interaction behavior in happy and unhappy marriages. *Journal of Consulting and Clinical Psychology*, **45**, 494–495.

Blader, J.C. (1987). The compatibility in men of sexual arousal and coercion. Unpublished doctoral dissertation, Queen's University, Kingston, Ontario, Canada.

Blader, J.C., & Marshall, W.L. (1989). Is assessment of sexual arousal in rapists worthwhile? A critique of current methods and the developments of a response compatibility approach. *Clinical Psychology Review*, **9**, 569–587.

Blakemore, C.B., Thorpe, J.G., Barker, J.C., Conway, C.G., & Lavin, N.I. (1963). Application of faradic aversion conditioning in a case of transvestism. *Behaviour Research and Therapy*, **1**, 26–35.

Bond, I.K., & Evans, D.R. (1967). Avoidance therapy: Its use in two cases of underwear fetishism. *Canadian Medical Association Journal*, **96**, 1160–1162.

Borduin, C.M., Henggeler, S.W., Blaske, D.M., & Stein, R.J. (1990). Multisystemic treatment of adolescent sexual offenders. *International Journal of Offender Therapy and Comparative Criminology*, **34**, 105–113.

Bowlby, J. (1969). *Attachment and loss: Vol. 1. Attachment.* New York: Basic Books.

Bowlby, J. (1973). *Attachment and loss: Vol. 2. Separation: Anxiety and anger.* New York: Basic Books.

Bowlby, J. (1977). The making and breaking of affectional bonds. *British Journal of Psychiatry*, **130**, 201–210; 421–431.

Bowlby, J. (1979). Psychoanalysis as art and science. *International Review of Psychoanalysis*, **6**, 3–14.

Bradley, G.W. (1978). Self-serving biases in the attribution process: A reexamination of the fact or fiction question. *Journal of Personality and Social Psychology*, **36**, 56–71.

Brake, S.C., & Shannon, D. (1997). Using pretreatment to increase admission in sex offenders. In B.K. Schwartz & H.R. Cellini (Eds.), *The sex offender: New insights, treatment innovations and legal developments* (pp. 5.1–5.16). Kingston, NJ: Civic Research Institute.

Brehm, S.S. (1992). *Intimate relationships* (2nd edn). New York: McGraw-Hill.

Bretherton, I. (1985). Attachment theory: Retrospect and prospect. *Monographs of the Society for Research in Child Development*, **50**, 3–35.

Brunink, S., & Schroeder, H.E. (1979). Verbal therapeutic behavior of expert psychoanalytically oriented, Gestalt and behavior therapists. *Journal of Consulting and Clinical Psychology*, **47**, 567–574.

Buck, R., & Ginsberg, B. (1997) Communicative genes and the evolution of empathy. In W. Ickes (Ed.) *Empathic accuracy* (pp. 17–43). New York: Guilford Press.

Bumby, K. (1994, November). *Cognitive distortions of child molesters and rapists.* Presented at the 13th Annual Research and Treatment Conference of the Association for the Treatment of Sexual Abusers, San Francisco, CA.

Bumby, K.M. (1996). Assessing the cognitive distortions of child molesters and rapists: Development and validation of the MOLEST and RAPE scales. *Sexual Abuse: A Journal of Research and Treatment*, **8**, 37–54.

Bumby, K.M., & Hansen, D.J. (1997). Intimacy deficits, fear of intimacy, and loneliness among sex offenders. *Criminal Justice and Behavior*, **24**, 315–331.

Bumby, K.M., Langton, C.M., & Marshall, W.L. (in press). Shame and guilt, and their relevance for sexual offender treatment. In B.K. Schwartz & H.R. Cellini (Eds.), *The sex offender* (Vol. 3). Kingston, NJ: Civic Research Institute.

Burgess, A.W., Hartman, C.R., & McCormack, A. (1987). Abused to abuser: Antecedents of socially deviant behaviour. *American Journal of Psychiatry*, **144**, 1431–1436.

Burgess, R., Jewitt, R., Sandham, J., & Hudson, B.L. (1980). Working with sex offenders: A social skills training group. *British Journal of Social Work*, **10**, 133–142.

Burke, P.J. (1980). The self: Measurement requirements for an interactionist perspective. *Social Psychology Quarterly*, **43**, 18–29.

Burt, M.R. (1980). Cultural myths and supports for rape. *Journal of Personality and Social Psychology*, **38**, 217–230.

Byrne, D. (1971). *The attraction paradigm.* New York: Academic Press.

Callahan, E.J., & Leitenberg, H. (1973). Aversion therapy for sexual deviation: Contingent shock and covert sensitization. *Journal of Abnormal Psychology*, **81**, 60–73.

Cameron, N.A., & Magaret, A. (1951). *Behavior pathology.* Boston: Houghton Mifflin.

Camp, B.H., & Thyer, B.A. (1993). Treatment of adolescent sex offenders: A review of empirical research. *Journal of Applied Social Science*, **17**, 191–206.

Campbell, J.D., & Lavallee, L.F. (1993). Who am I? The role of self-concept confusion in understanding the behavior of people with low self-esteem. In R.F. Baumeister (Ed.), *Self-esteem: The puzzle of low self-regard* (pp. 3–20). New York: Plenum Press.

Campbell, J.D., & Tesser, A. (1985). Self-evaluation maintenance processes in relationships. In S. Duck & D. Perlman (Eds.), *Understanding personal relationships: An interdisciplinary approach* (Vol. 1) (pp. 107–135). London: Sage Publications.

Carey, C.H., & McGrath, R.J. (1989). Coping with urges and craving. In D.R. Laws (Ed.), *Relapse prevention with sex offenders* (pp. 188–196). New York: Guilford Press.

Cautela, J.R. (1967). Covert sensitization. *Psychological Reports*, **20**, 459–468.

Charcot, J.M., & Magnan, V. (1882). Inversion du sens genital. *Archives of Neurology*, **3**, 53–60.

Check, J.V.P. (1984). *The Hostility Towards Women Scale.* Unpublished doctoral dissertation, University of Manitoba, Canada.

Check, J.V.P., & Malamuth, N.M. (1983). Sex role stereotype and reactions to depictions of stranger versus acquaintance rape. *Journal of Personality and Social Psychology*, **45**, 344–356.

Check, J.V.P., Perlman, D., & Malamuth, N.M. (1985). Loneliness and aggressive behavior. *Journal of Social and Personal Relations*, **2**, 243–252.

Chlopan, B.E., McCain, M.L., Carbonell, J.L., & Hagen, R.L. (1985). Empathy: Review of available measures. *Journal of Personality and Social Psychology*, **44**, 113–126.

Christie, M.M., Marshall, W.L., & Lanthier, R.D. (1979). *A descriptive study of incarcerated rapists and pedophiles.* Report to the Solicitor General of Canada, Ottawa.

Church, R.M. (1963). The varied effects of punishment on behavior. *Psychological Review*, **70**, 369–402.

Ciliska, D. (1990). *Beyond dieting – psychoeducational interventions for chronically obese women: A non-dieting approach.* New York: Brunner/Mazel.

Clark, L., & Lewis, D.J. (1977). *Rape: The price of coercive sexuality.* Toronto: Canadian Women's Educational Press.

Clarke, K.B. (1980). Empathy: A neglected topic in psychological research. *American Psychologist*, **35**, 187–190.

Cohen, F. (1995). Right to treatment. In B.K. Schwartz & H.R. Cellini (Eds.), *The sex offender: Corrections, Treatment and legal practice* (pp. 24.1–24.18). Kingston, NJ: Civic Research Institute.

Cohen, M.A., and Miller T.R. (1998). The cost of mental health care from victims of crime. *Journal of Interpersonal Violence*, **13**, 93–110.

Cohen, M.L., Seghorn, T., & Calmus, W. (1969). Sociometric study of sex offenders. *Journal of Abnormal Psychology*, **74**, 249–255.

Collins, N.L., & Read, S.J. (1990). Adult attachment, working models, and relationship quality in dating couples. *Journal of Personality and Social Psychology*, **58**, 644–663.

Colson, C.E. (1972). Olfactory aversion therapy for homosexual behavior. *Journal of Behavior Therapy and Experimental Psychiatry*, **3**, 185–187.

Committee on Sexual Offenses against Children and Youths (1984). *Report of the Committee on Sexual Offenses against Children and Youths: Vols. 1–11, and summary* (Badgely Report; Cat. No. J2–50/1984/E, Vols. 1–11, H74–13/1984–1E, Summary). Ottawa: Department of Supply and Services.

Conrad, S.R., & Wincze, J.P. (1976). Orgasmic reconditioning: A controlled study of its effects upon the sexual arousal and behavior of adult male homosexuals. *Behavior Therapy*, **7**, 155–166.

Conte, J.R. (1985). Clinical dimensions of adult sexual abuse of children. *Behavioral Sciences and the Law*, **3**, 341–354.

Conte, J.R. (1988). The effects of sexual abuse on children: Results of a research project. *Annals of the New York Academy of Sciences*, **528**, 310–326.

Cooley, C.H. (1902). *Human nature and the social order.* New York: Scribner's.

Coopersmith, S. (1967). *The antecedents of self-esteem.* San Francisco: W.H. Freeman.

Cortoni, F.A. (1998). *The relationship between attachment styles, coping, the use of sex as a coping strategy, and juvenile sexual history in sexual offenders.* Unpublished Doctoral dissertation. Queen's University, Kingston, Ontario, Canada.

Cortoni, F., Heil, P., & Marshall, W.L. (1996, November). *Sex as a coping mechanism and its relationship to loneliness and intimacy deficits in sexual offending.* Paper presented at the 15th Annual Research and Treatment Conference of the Association for the Treatment of Sexual Offenders, Chicago.

Cortoni, F., & Marshall, W.L. (1995, October). *Childhood attachments, juvenile sexual history and adult coping skills in sex offenders.* Paper presented at the 14th Annual Research and Treatment Conference of the Association for the Treatment of Sexual Abusers, New Orleans.

Cortoni, F., & Marshall, W.L. (1996, August). *Juvenile sexual history, sex and coping strategies: A comparison of sexual and violent offenders.* Paper presented at the International Congress of Psychology, Montreal.

Crawford, D.A. (1981). Treatment approaches with pedophiles. In M. Cook & K. Howells (Eds.), *Adult sexual interest in children* (pp. 181–217). London: Academic Press.

Crawford, D.A., & Allen, J.V. (1977). A social skills training programme with sex offenders. Paper presented at the International Conference on Love and Attraction, Swansea, UK. May.

Cross, D.G., & Sharpley, C.F. (1982). Measurement of empathy with the Hogan scale. *Psychological Reports*, **50**, 62.

Cumming, G.F., & Buell, M.M. (1996). Relapse prevention as a supervision strategy for sex offenders. *Sexual Abuse: A Journal of Research and Treatment*, **8**, 231–240.

Cutmore, T.R.H., & Zamble, E. (1988). A Pavlovian procedure for improving sexual performance of noncopulating male rats. *Archives of Sexual Behavior*, **17**, 371–380.

Darke, J.L. (1990). Sexual aggression: Achieving power through humiliation. In W.L. Marshall, D.R. Laws & H.E. Barbaree (Eds.), *Handbook of sexual assault: Issues, theories and treatment of the offender* (pp. 55–72). New York: Plenum Press.

Davidson, P.R., & Malcolm, P.B. (1985). The reliability of the Rape Index: A rapist sample. *Behavioral Assessment*, **7**, 283–292.

Davila, J., Burge, D., & Hammen, C. (1997). Why does attachment style change? *Journal of Personality and Social Psychology*, **73**, 826–838.

Davis, M.H. (1983). Measuring individual differences in empathy: Evidence for a multidimensional approach. *Journal of Personality and Social Psychology*, **44**, 113–125.

Davison, G.C. (1974). *Homosexuality: The ethical challenge*. Presidential address to the 8th Annual Convention of the Association for the Advancement of Behavior Therapy, Chicago.

Deitz, S.R., Blackwell, K.T., Daley, P.C., & Bentley, B.J. (1982). Measurement of empathy toward rape victims and rapists. *Journal of Personality and Social Psychology*, **43**, 372–384.

Deitz, S.R., Littman, M., & Bentley, B.J. (1984). Attribution of responsibility for rape: The influence of observer empathy, victim resistance, and victim attractiveness. *Sex Roles*, **10**, 261–280.

Deutsch, F., & Madle, R.A. (1975). Empathy: Historic and current conceptualizations, measurement and cognitive theoretical perspective. *Human Development*, **18**, 267–287.

De Voge, J.T., & Beck, S. (1978). The therapist–client relationship in behavior therapy. In M. Hersen, R.M. Eisler & P.M. Miller (Eds.), *Progress in behavior modification* (Vol. 4) (pp. 203–249). New York: Academic Press.

Dhawan, S., & Marshall, W.L. (1996). Sexual abuse histories of sexual offenders. *Sexual Abuse: A Journal of Research and Treatment*, **8**, 7–15.

Di Vasto, P.V., Kaufman, L.R., Jackson, R., Christy, J., Pearson, S., & Burgett, T. (1984). The prevalence of sexually stressful events among females in the general population. *Archives of Sexual Behavior*, **13**, 59–67.

Dollard, J., Doob, J., Miller, N.E., Mowrer, O.H., & Sears, R.R. (1939). *Frustration and aggression*. New Haven, CT: Yale University Press.

Dollard, J., & Miller, N.E. (1950). *Personality and psychotherapy: An analysis in terms of learning, thinking and culture*. New York: McGraw-Hill.

Dunham, B. (1947). *Man against myth*. London: Oxford Press.

Dunlap, K. (1932). *Habits, their making and unmaking*. New York: Liveright.

Dwyer, S.M., & Amberson, J.I. (1989) Behavioral patterns and personality characteristics of 56 sex offenders: A preliminary study. *Journal of Psychology and Human Sexuality*, **2**, 105–118.

Dymond, C. (1948). A preliminary investigation of the relation of insight and empathy. *Journal of Consulting Psychology*, **4**, 228–233.

Earls, C.M., & Proulx, J. (1987). The differentiation of francophone rapists and non-rapists using penile circumferential measures. *Criminal Justice and Behavior*, **13**, 419–429.

Edwards, N.B. (1972). Case conference: Assertive training in a case of homosexual pedophilia. *Journal of Behavior Therapy and Experimental Psychiatry*, **3**, 55–63.

Eisenberg, N., & Miller, P.A. (1987). The relation of empathy to prosocial and related behaviours. *Psychological Bulletin*, **101**, 91–119.

Ellis, A. (1962). *Reason and emotion in psychotherapy*. New York: Lyle Stuart.

English, H.B. (1929). Three cases of the "conditioned fear response". *Journal of Abnormal and Social Psychology*, **24**, 221–225.

Esses, V.M. (1989). Mood as a moderator of acceptance of interpersonal feedback. *Journal of Personality and Social Psychology*, **57**, 769–781.

Evans, D.R. (1968). Masturbatory fantasy and sexual deviation. *Behaviour Research and Therapy*, **6**, 17–19.

Evans, D.R. (1970). Subjective variables and treatment effects in aversion therapy. *Behaviour Research and Therapy*, **8**, 147–152.

Eysenck, H.J. (1952). The effects of psychotherapy: An evaluation. *Journal of Consulting Psychology*, **16**, 319–324.

Fagan, J., & Wexler, S. (1988). Explanations of sexual assault among violent delinquents. *Journal of Adolescent Research*, **3**, 363–389.

Farris, H.E. (1967). Classical conditioning of courting behavior in the Japanese quail (*Coturnix coturnix japonica*). *Journal of the Experimental Analysis of Behavior*, **10**, 313–217.

Feeney, J.A., & Noller, P. (1990). Attachment style as a predictor of adult romantic relationships. *Journal of Personality and Social Psychology*, **58**, 281–291.

Feldman, M.P., & MacCulloch, M.J. (1971). *Homosexual behaviour: Therapy and assessment*. Oxford: Pergamon Press.

Fernandez, Y.M., & Marshall, W.L. (1998). *Violence, empathy, social self-esteem and psychopathy in rapists*. Submitted for publication.

Fernandez, Y.M., Marshall, W.L., Lightbody, S., & O'Sullivan, C. (1999). The Child Molester Empathy Measure. *Sexual Abuse: A Journal of Research and Treatment*, **11**, 17–31.

Ferster, C.B., & DeMyer, M.K. (1962). A method for the experimental analysis of the behavior of autistic children. *American Journal of Orthopsychiatry*, **32**, 89–98.

Feshbach, N.D. (1987). Parental empathy and child adjustment/maladjustment. In N. Eisenberg & J. Strayer (Eds.), *Empathy and its development* (pp. 271–291). New York: Cambridge University Press.

Festinger, L. (1957). *A theory of cognitive dissonance*. Evanston, IL: Row Peterson.

Fiedler, F. (1950). The concept of an ideal therapeutic relationship. *Journal of Consulting Psychology*, **14**, 239–245.

Field, H. (1978). Attitudes toward rape: A comparative analysis of police, rapists, crisis counsellors and citizens. *Journal of Personality and Social Psychology*, **36**, 156–179.

Finkelhor, D. (1984). *Child sexual abuse: New theory and research*. New York: Free Press.

Finkelhor, D. (1986). *A sourcebook on child sexual abuse*. Beverly Hills, CA: Sage Publications.

Finkelhor, D., & Browne, A. (1985). The traumatic impact of child sexual abuse: A conceptualization. *American Journal of Orthopsychiatry*, **59**, 238–245.

Finkelhor, D., Hotaling, G., Lewis, I., & Smith, C. (1990). Sexual abuse and its relationship to later sexual satisfaction, marital status, religion and attitudes. *Journal of Interpersonal Violence*, **4**, 379–399.

Firestone, P., Bradford, J.M.W., Greenberg, D.M., Larose, M.R., & Curry, S. (1998). Homicidal and non-homicidal child molesters: Distinguishing psychological, phallometric and criminal features. *Sexual Abuse: A Journal of Research and Treatment*, **10**, 305–324.

Fisher, G. (1969). Psychological needs of heterosexual pedophiliacs. *Diseases of the Nervous System*, **30**, 419–421.

Fisher, G., & Howell, L.M. (1970). Psychological needs of homosexual pedophiles. *Diseases of the Nervous System*, **31**, 623–625.

Fisher, R., & Ury, W. (1981). *Getting to yes: Negotiating agreement without giving in.* Boston: Houghton, Mifflin.

Fleming, J.S., & Courtney, B.E. (1984). The dimensionality of self-esteem: II. Hierarchical facet model for revised measurement scales. *Journal of Personality and Social Psychology*, **46**, 404–421.

Fleming, J.S., & Watts, W.A. (1980). The dimensionality of self-esteem: Some results for a college sample. *Journal of Personality and Social Psychology*, **39**, 921–929.

Fookes, B.H. (1969). Some experiences in the use of aversion therapy in male homosexuality, exhibitionism and fetishism-transvestism. *British Journal of Psychiatry*, **115**, 339–341.

Ford, C.S., & Beach, F.A. (1952). *Patterns of sexual behavior.* London: Methuen.

Frank, J.D. (1971). Therapeutic factors in psychotherapy. *American Journal of Psychotherapy*, **25**, 350–361.

Frank, J.D. (1973). *Persuasion and healing* (2nd edn). Baltimore: Johns Hopkins University Press.

Franks, C.M. (1963). Behavior therapy, the principles of conditioning and the treatment of the alcoholic. *Quarterly Journal of Studies on Alcohol*, **24**, 511–529.

French, T.M. (1933). Interrelations between psychoanalysis and the experimental work of Pavlov. *American Journal of Psychiatry*, **89**, 1165–1203.

Frenzel, R.R., & Lang, R.A. (1989). Identifying sexual preferences in intrafamilial and extrafamilial child sexual abusers. *Annals of Sex Research*, **2**, 255–275.

Freud, S. (1933). *New introductory lectures in psychoanalysis.* (Translation by W.J.H. Sprott). New York: Norton.

Freud, S. (1940). An outline of psychoanalysis. *International Journal of Psychoanalysis*, **21**, 27–84.

Freund, K. (1957). Diagnostika homosexuality u mužů. *Czecholsovakia Psychiatrie*, **53**, 382–393.

Freund, K. (1960). Problems in the treatment of homosexuality. In H.J. Eysenck (Ed.), *Behaviour therapy and the neuroses* (pp. 312–326). Oxford: Pergamon Press.

Freund, K. (1967). Erotic preference in pedophilia. *Behaviour Research and Therapy*, **5**, 339–348.

Freund, K. (1991). Reflections on the development of the phallometric method of assessing sexual preferences. *Annals of Sex Research*, **4**, 221–228.

Freund, K., & Blanchard, R. (1986). The concept of courtship disorder. *Journal of Sex and Marital Therapy*, **12**, 79–92.

Freund, K., & Blanchard, R. (1989). Phallometric diagnosis of pedophilia. *Journal of Consulting and Clinical Psychology*, **57**, 1–6.

Freund, K., Chan, S., & Coulthard, R. (1979). Phallometric diagnoses with "nonadmitters". *Behaviour Research and Therapy*, **17**, 451–457.

Freund, K., Scher, H., Racansky, I.G., Campbell, K., & Heasman, G. (1986). Males disposed to commit rape. *Archives of Sexual Behavior*, **15**, 23–35.

Freund, K., & Watson, R.J. (1991). Assessment of the sensitivity and specificity of a phallometric test: An update of phallometric diagnosis of pedophilia. *Psychological Assessment: A Journal of Consulting and Clinical Psychology*, **3**, 254–260.

Freund, K., Watson, R.J., & Dickey, R. (1991). Sex offenses against female children perpetrated by men who are not pedophiles. *Journal of Sex Research*, **28**, 409–423.

Furby, L., Weinrott, M.R., & Blackshaw, L. (1989). Sex offenders recidivism: A review. *Psychological Bulletin*, **105**, 3–30.

Garland, R.J., & Dougher, M.J. (1991). Motivational intervention in the treatment of sex offenders. In W.R. Miller & S. Rollnick (Eds.), *Motivational interviewing: Preparing people to change addictive behavior* (pp. 303–313). New York: Guilford Press.

Garlick, Y., Marshall, W.L., & Thornton, D. (1996). Intimacy deficits and attribution of blame among sexual offenders. *Legal and Criminological Psychology*, **1**, 251–258.

Gebhard, P.H., Gagnon, J.H., Pomeroy, W.B., & Christenson, C.V. (1965). *Sex offenders: An analysis of types.* New York: Harper Row.

George, W.H., & Marlatt, G.A. (1989). Introduction. In D.R. Laws (Ed.), *Relapse prevention with sex offenders* (pp. 1–31). New York: Guilford Press.

Gilgun, J.F., & Connor, T.M. (1989). How perpetrators view child sexual abuse. *Social Work*, **24**, 249–251.

Glynn, J.D., & Harper, P. (1961). Behaviour therapy in transvestism. *Lancet*, **I**, 619.

Goldberg, S. (1991). Recent developments in attachment theory and research. *Canadian Journal of Psychiatry*, **36**, 393–400.

Goldiamond, I. (1962). The maintenance of ongoing fluent verbal behavior and stuttering. *Journal of Mathetics*, **1**, 57–95.

Gordon, A., Marshall, W.L., Loeber, R., & Barbaree, H.E. (1977). *Toward a definition of social competence in sexual aggressors.* Paper presented at the 1st National Conference of the Evaluation and Treatment of Sexual Aggressives. Memphis.

Gould, S.J. (1983). *Hen's teeth and horse's toes.* New York: W.W. Norton.

Graham, J.M., & Desjardins, C. (1980). Classical conditioning: Induction of luteinizing hormone and testosterone secretion in anticipation of sexual activity. *Science*, **210**, 1039–1041.

Greenwald, A.G., Bellezza, F.S., & Banaji, M.R. (1988). Is self-esteem a central ingredient of the self-concept? *Personality and Social Psychology Bulletin*, **14**, 34–45.

Greenwald, D.P., Kornblith, S.J., Hersen, M., Bellack, A.S., & Himmelhoch, J.M. (1981). Differences between social skills and psychotherapists in treating depression. *Journal of Consulting and Clinical Psychology*, **49**, 757–759.

Griffin, D., & Bartholomew, K. (1994). Models of self and other: Fundamental dimensions underlying adult attachment. *Journal of Personality and Social Psychology*, **67**, 430–445.

Grossman, K.E., & Grossman, K. (1990). The wider concept of attachment in cross-cultural research. *Human Development*, **33**, 31–47.

Groth, A.N. (1979). *Men who rape: The psychology of the offender.* New York: Plenum Press.

Groth, A.N., & Burgess, A.W. (1977a). Rape: A sexual deviation. *American Journal of Orthopsychiatry*, **47**, 400–406.

Groth, A.N., & Burgess, A.W. (1977b). Sexual dysfunction during rape. *New England Journal of Medicine*, **297**, 764–766.

Guthrie, E.R. (1935). *The psychology of learning.* New York: Harper.

Guthrie, E.R. (1959). Association by contiguity. In S. Koch (Ed.), *Psychology: A study of a science. Vol. 1: Conceptual and systematic, Vol. 2: General systematic formulations, learning, and special processes* (pp. 186–189). New York: McGraw-Hill.

Hall, G.C.N. (1989). Sexual arousal and arousability in a sexual offender population. *Journal of Abnormal Psychology*, **98**, 145–149.

Hall, G.C.N. (1995). Sexual offender recidivism revisited: A meta-analysis of recent treatment studies. *Journal of Consulting and Clinical Psychology*, **63**, 802–809.

Hall, G.C.N., & Hirschman, R. (1991). Toward a theory of sexual aggression: A quadripartite model. *Journal of Consulting and Clinical Psychology*, **59**, 662–669.

Hall, E.R., Howard, J.A., & Boezio, S.L. (1986). Tolerance of rape: A sexist or antisocial attitude? *Psychology of Women Quarterly*, **10**, 101–108.

Hanson, R.K. (1996). Evaluating the contribution of relapse prevention theory to the treatment of sexual offenders. *Sexual Abuse: A Journal of Research and Treatment*, **8**, 201–208.

Hanson, K. (in press). Assessing sexual offenders' capacity for empathy. *Psychology, Crime and Law.*

Hanson, R.K., & Bussière, M.T. (1998). Predicting relapse: A meta-analysis of sexual offender recidivism studies. *Journal of Consulting and Clinical Psychology, 66,* 348–362.

Hanson, R.K., Gizzarelli, R., & Scott, H. (1994). The attitudes of incest offenders: Sexual entitlement and acceptance of sex with children. *Criminal Justice and Behavior, 21,* 187–202.

Hanson, R.K., Gray, G.A., McWhinnie, A.J., Forouzan, E., Osweiler, M.C., & Harris, A.J.R. (1997, October). *Dynamic predictors of sexual reoffense project 1997.* Symposium presented at the 16th Annual Conference of the Association for the Treatment of Sexual Abusers, Arlington, VA.

Hanson, K., & Scott, H. (1995). Assessing perspective taking among sexual offenders, nonsexual criminals and nonoffenders. *Sexual Abuse: A Journal of Research and Treatment, 7,* 259–277.

Hanson, R.K. (1997). Invoking sympathy – Assessment and treatment of empathy deficits among sexual offenders. In B.K. Schwartz & H.R. Cellini (Eds.) *The sex offender: New insights, treatment innovations and legal developments* (Vol. II), (pp. 1.1–1.12). Kingston, NJ: Civic Research Institute.

Hanson, R.K., Scott, H., & Steffy, R.A. (1995). A comparison of child molesters and nonsexual criminals: Risk predictors and long-term recidivism. *Journal of Research in Crime and Delinquency, 32,* 325–337.

Hanson, R.K., & Slater, S. (1988). Sexual victimization in the history of sexual abusers: A review. *Annals of Sex Research, 1,* 485–499.

Hanson, R.K., Steffy, R.A., & Gauthier, R. (1993). Long-term recidivism of child molesters. *Journal of Consulting and Clinical Psychology, 61,* 646–652.

Happel, R.M., & Auffrey, J.J. (1995). Sex offender assessment: Interrupting the dance of denial. *American Journal of Forensic Psychology, 13,* 5–22.

Hare, R.D. (1991). *Manual for the Revised Psychopathy Checklist.* Toronto: Multi-Health Systems.

Harris, M.J. (1991). Controversy and culmination: Meta-analysis and research on interpersonal expectancy effects. *Personality and Social Psychology Bulletin, 17,* 316–322.

Harter, S. (1993). Causes and consequences of low self-esteem in children and adolescents. In R.F. Baumeister (Ed.), *Self-esteem: The puzzle of low self-regard* (pp. 87–116). New York: Plenum Press.

Hartley, C.C. (1998). How incest offenders overcome internal inhibitions through the use of cognitions and cognitive distortions. *Journal of Interpersonal Violence, 13,* 25–39.

Hartley, D.E., & Strupp, H.H. (1982). The therapeutic alliance: Its relationship to outcome in brief psychotherapy. In J. Masling (Ed.), *Empirical studies of psychoanalytic theories.* (pp. 1–37). Hillsdale, NJ: Analytic Press.

Hayashino, D.S., Wurtele, S.K., & Klebe, K.J. (1995). Child molesters: An examination of cognitive factors. *Journal of Interpersonal Violence, 10,* 106–116.

Hazan, C., & Shaver, P. (1987). Romantic love conceptualized as an attachment process. *Journal of Personality and Social Psychology, 52,* 511–524.

Hazan, C., & Zeifman, D. (1994). Sex and the psychological tether. *Advances in personal relationships, 5,* 151–177.

Heatherton, T.F., & Polivy, J. (1991). Development and validation of a scale for measuring self-esteem. *Journal of Personality and Social Psychology, 60,* 895–910.

Herman, S.H., Barlow, D.H., & Agras, W.S. (1974). An experimental analysis of classical conditioning as a method of increasing heterosexual arousal in homosexuals. *Behavior Therapy, 5,* 33–47.

Herzberg, A. (1945). *Active psychotherapy*. New York: Grune & Stratton.

Higgins, E.T. (1987). Self-discrepancy: Theory relating self and affect. *Psychological Review*, **94**, 314–340.

Higgins, E.T., Klein, R., & Strauman, T.J. (1985). Self-concept discrepancy theory: A psychological model for distinguishing among different aspects of depression and anxiety. *Social Cognition*, **3**, 51–76.

Higgins, E.T., Klein, R., & Strauman, T.J. (1986). Self-discrepancies and emotional vulnerability: How magnitude, accessibility, and type of discrepancy influence affect. *Journal of Personality and Social Psychology*, **51**, 5–15.

Hildebran, D., & Pithers, W.D. (1989). Enhancing offender empathy for sexual-abuse victims. In D.R. Laws (Ed.), *Relapse Prevention with Sex Offenders* (pp. 236–243). New York: Guilford Press.

Hilton, Z. (1993). Childhood sexual victimization and lack of empathy in child molesters: Explanation or excuse? *International Journal of Offender Therapy and Comparative Criminology*, **37**, 287–296.

Hoffman, M.L. (1977). Empathy: Its development and prosocial implications. In H.E. Howe (Ed.), *1977 Nebraska Symposium on Motivation*, **25**, 169–217.

Hogan, R. (1969). Development of an empathy scale. *Journal of Consulting and Clinical Psychology*, **33**, 307–316.

Holden, R.R., & Fekken, G.C. (1989). Three common social desirability scales: Friends, acquaintances, or strangers? *Journal of Research in Personality*, **23**, 180–191.

Homme, L.E. (1965). Perspectives in psychology: XXIV Control of coverants, the operants of the mind. *Psychological Record*, **15**, 501–511.

Honig, W.K., & Urcuioli, P.J. (1981). The legacy of Guttman and Kalish: Twenty-five years of research on stimulus generalization. *Journal of the Experimental Analysis of Behavior*, **36**, 405–445.

Hoppe, C.M., & Singer, R.D. (1976). Overcontrolled hostility, empathy, and egocentric balance in violent and nonviolent psychiatric offenders. *Psychological Reports*, **39**, 1303–1308.

Horley, J. (1988). Cognitions of child sex abusers. *Journal of Sex Research*, **25**, 542–545.

Howells, K. (1979). Some meanings of children for pedophiles. In M. Cook & G. Wilson (Eds.), *Love and attraction: An international conference* (pp. 519–526). Oxford: Pergamon Press.

Hudson, S.M., Marshall, W.L., Wales, D.S., McDonald, E., Bakker, L.W., & McLean, A. (1993). Emotional recognition skills of sex offenders. *Annals of Sex Research*, **6**, 199–211.

Hudson, S.M., & Ward, T. (1997). Intimacy, loneliness, and attachment style in sex offenders. *Journal of Interpersonal Violence*, **12**, 325–339.

Hudson, S.M., Ward, T., & McCormack, J.C. (1998). *Offense pathways in sexual offenders*. Submitted for publication.

Hull, C.L. (1943). *Principles of behavior: An introduction to behavior theory*. New York: Appleton-Century.

Hunter, J.A., & Goodwin, D.W. (1992). The utility of satiation therapy in the treatment of juvenile sexual offenders: Variations and efficacy. *Annals of Sex Research*, **5**, 71–80.

Hunter, J.A., & Santos, D. (1990). The use of specialized cognitive-behavioral therapies in the treatment of juvenile sexual offenders. *International Journal of Offender Therapy and Comparative Criminology*, **34**, 239–248.

Hutton, D.G. (1991). *Self-esteem and memory for social interaction*. Unpublished doctoral dissertation, Case Western Reserve University, Ohio.

Ingram, R.E., & Kenall, P.C. (1986). Cognitive clinical psychology: Implications for an information processing perspective. In R.E. Ingram (Ed.), *Information processing approaches to clinical psychology* (pp. 3–21). Orlando, FL.: Academic Press.

James, B. (1962). A case of homosexuality treated by aversion therapy. *British Medical Journal*, I, 768–770.

James, W. (1890). *The principles of psychology* (Vol. 1). New York: Henry Holt.

Jamieson, S., & Marshall, W.L. (in press). *Attachment styles and violence in child molesters.*

Johnson, J.A., Cheek, J.M., & Struther, R. (1983). The structure of empathy. *Journal of Personality and Social Psychology*, **45**, 1299–1312.

Johnston, L., & Ward, T. (1996). Social cognition and sexual offending: A theoretical framework. *Sexual Abuse: A Journal of Research and Treatment*, **8**, 55–80.

Johnston, P., Hudson, S.M., & Marshall, W.L. (1992). The effects of masturbatory reconditioning with nonfamilial child molesters. *Behaviour Research and Therapy*, **30**, 559–561.

Jones, M.C. (1924a). The elimination of children's fears. *Journal of Experimental Psychology*, **7**, 382–390.

Jones, M.C. (1924b). A laboratory study of fear: The case of Peter. *Pedagogical Seminary and Journal of Genetic Psychology*, **31**, 308–315.

Katz, D. (in press). Victims of sexual abuse. In A.S. Bellack & M. Hersen (Eds.), *Comprehensive clinical psychology: Vol. 9. Applications in diverse populations* (Vol. Ed., N. Singh). Oxford: Elsevier Science.

Kaufman, K.L., Hilliker, D.R., Lathrop, P., Daleiden, E.L., & Ruby, L. (1996). Sexual offenders' modus operandi: A comparison of structured interviews and questionnaire approaches. *Journal of Interpersonal Violence*, **11**, 19–34.

Kazdin, A.E. (1975). Recent advances in token economy research. In M. Hersen, R.M. Eisler & P.M. Miller (Eds.), *Progress in behavior modification* (Vol. 1) (pp. 233–274). New York: Academic Press.

Kazdin, A.E. (1978). *History of behavior modification: Experimental foundations of contemporary research.* Baltimore: University Park Press.

Kear-Colwell, J., & Pollack, P. (1997). Motivation and confrontation: Which approach to the child sex offender? *Criminal Justice and Behavior*, **24**, 20–33.

Kelley, H.H. (1983). The situational origins of human tendancies: A further reason for the journal analysis of structures. *Personality and Social Psychology Bulletin*, **9**, 8–36.

Kelly, R.J. (1982). Behavioral re-orientation of pedophiliacs: Can it be done? *Clinical Psychology Review*, **2**, 387–408.

Khanna, A., & Marshall, W.L. (1978, November) A comparison of cognitive and behavioural approaches for the treatment of low self-esteem. Paper presented at the 12th Annual Convention of the Association for the Advancement of Behavior Therapy, Chicago, Illinois.

Kinsey, A.C., Pomeroy, W.B., Martin, C.E., & Gebhard, P.H. (1953). *Sexual behavior in the human female.* Philadelphia: Saunders.

Kirkpatrick, L.A., & Hazan, C. (1994). Attachment styles and close relationships: A four-year prospective study. *Personal Relationships*, **3**, 123–142.

Kleiner, L., Marshall, W.L., & Spevack, M. (1987). Training in problem-solving and exposure treatment for agoraphobics with panic attacks. *Journal of Anxiety Disorders*, **1**, 219–238.

Kline, P. (1993). *The handbook of psychological testing.* New York: Routledge.

Knight, R.A., & Prentky, R.A. (1990). Classifying sexual offenders: The development and corroboration of taxonomic models. In W.L. Marshall, D.R. Laws & H.E. Barbaree (Eds.), *Handbook of sexual assault: Issues, theories, and treatment of the offender* (pp. 23–52). New York: Plenum Press.

Knopp, F.H. (1984). *Retraining adult sex offenders: Methods and models.* Syracuse, NY: Safer Society Press.

Knopp, F.H., Freeman-Longo, R.E., & Stevenson, W. (1992). *Nationwide survey of juvenile and adult sex-offender treatment programs.* Orwell, VT: Safer Society Press.

Kobak, R.R., & Hazan, C. (1991). Attachment in marriage: effects of security and accuracy of working models. *Journal of Personality and Social Psychology*, **60**, 861–869.

Kolarsky, A., & Madlafousek, J. (1983). The inverse role of preparatory erotic stimulation in exhibitionists: Phallometric studies. *Archives of Sexual Behavior*, **12**, 123–148.

Kolarsky, A., Madlafousek, J., & Novotna, V. (1978). Stimuli eliciting sexual arousal in males who offend against adult women: An experimental study. *Archives of Sexual Behavior*, **7**, 79–87.

Kolvin, I., Miller, F.J.W., Fletting, M., & Kolvin, P.A. (1988). Social and parenting factors affecting criminal-offence rates. Findings from the Newcastle Thousand Family Study (1947–1980). *British Journal of Psychiatry*, **152**, 80–90.

Koss, M.P., Gidycz, C.A., & Wisniewski, N. (1987). The scope of rape: Incidence and prevalence of sexual aggression and victimization in a national sample of higher education students. *Journal of Consulting and Clinical Psychology*, **55**, 162–170.

Koss, M.P., & Harvey, M.R. (1991). *The rape victim: Clinical and community interventions* (2nd edn). Newbury Park, CA: Sage Publications.

Kremsdorf, R.B., Holman, M.L., & Laws, D.R. (1980). Orgasmic reconditioning without deviant imagery: A case report with a pedophile. *Behavior Research and Therapy*, **18**, 203–207.

Ladouceur, R. (1995). Learning: How experience changes us. In R.A. Baron, B. Earhard & M. Ozier (Eds.), *Psychology: Canadian edition* (pp. 184–223). Scarborough, Ontario: Allyn & Bacon.

Lalumière, M.L., & Quinsey, V.L. (1993). The sensitivity of phallometric measures with rapists. *Annals of Sex Research*, **6**, 123–138.

Lalumière, M.L., & Quinsey, V.L. (1994). The discriminability of rapists from non-sex offenders using phallometric measures: A meta-analysis. *Criminal Justice and Behavior*, **21**, 150–175.

Lamb, M.E., Gaensbauer, T.J., Malkin, C.M., & Schultz, L.A. (1985). The effects of child maltreatment on security of infant-adult attachment. *Infant Behavior and Development*, **8**, 35–45.

Langevin, R., Bain, J., Ben-Aron, M., Coulthard, R., Day, D., Handy, L., Heasman, G., Hucker, S., Purdins, J., Roper, V., Russon, A., Webster, C., & Wortzman, G. (1984). Sexual aggression: Constructing a predictive equation. A controlled pilot study. In R. Langevin (Ed.), *Erotic preference, gender identity, and aggression in men: New research studies* (pp. 39–76). Hillsdale, NJ: Lawrence Erlbaum.

Langevin, R., & Lang, R.A. (1985). Psychological treatment of pedophiles. *Behavioral Sciences and the Law*, **3**, 403–419.

Langevin, R., Paitich, D., Ramsey, G., Anderson, C., Kamrad, J., Pope, S., Geller, G., & Newman, S. (1979). Experimental studies in the etiology of genital exhibitionism. *Archives of Sexual Behavior*, **8**, 307–331.

Langevin, R., Paitich, D., & Russon, A.E. (1985). Are rapists sexually anomalous, aggressive, or both? In R. Langevin (Ed.), *Erotic preference, gender identity, and aggression in men: New research studies* (pp. 13–38). Hillsdale, NJ: Erlbaum.

Langevin, R., Wright, M.A., & Handy, L. (1988). Empathy, assertiveness, aggressiveness, and defensiveness among sex offenders. *Annals of Sex Research*, **1**, 533–547.

Langton, C., & Marshall, W.L. (1998). Cognitive functioning in rapists: Theoretical patterns by typological breakdown. Submitted for publication.

Laws, D.R. (1989). *Relapse prevention with sex offenders.* New York: Guilford Press.

Laws, D.R. (1995, September). *Relapse prevention: The state of the art.* Paper presented at the International Expert Conference on Sex Offenders: Issues, research, and treatment. Utrecht, The Netherlands.

Laws, D.R. (1996). Relapse prevention or harm reduction? *Sexual Abuse: A Journal of Research and Therapy*, **8**, 243–247.

Laws, D.R. (1997, October). Harm reduction. Paper presented at the Annual Research and Treatment Conference of the Association for the Treatment of Sexual Abusers, Arlington, VA.

Laws, D.R., & Marshall, W.L. (1990). A conditioning theory of the etiology and maintenance of deviant sexual preferences and behavior. In W.L. Marshall, D.R. Laws & H.E. Barbaree (Eds.), *Handbook of sexual assault: Issues, theories, and treatment of the offender* (pp. 209–229). New York: Plenum Press.

Laws, D.R., & Marshall, W.L. (1991). Masturbatory reconditioning with sexual deviates: An evaluative review. *Advances in Behaviour Research and Therapy*, **13**, 13–25.

Laws, D.R., Meyer, J., & Holmen, M.L. (1978). Reduction of sadistic arousal by olfactory aversion: A case study. *Behaviour Research and Therapy*, **16**, 281–285.

Laws, D.R., Osborn, C.A., Avery-Clark, C., O'Neil, J.A., & Crawford, D.A. (1987). Masturbatory satiation with sexual deviates. Unpublished manuscript, University of South Florida, Florida Mental Health Institute, Tampa.

Laws, D.R., & Serber, M. (1975). Measurement and evaluation of assertive training with sexual offenders. In R.E. Hosford & C.S. Moss (Eds.), *The crumbling walls: Treatment and counseling of prisoners* (pp. 165–172). Champaign, IL: University of Illinois Press.

Leitenberg, H., & Henning, K. (1995). Sexual fantasy. *Psychological Bulletin*, **117**, 469–496.

Leon, C. (1969). Unusual patterns of crime during La Violencia in Columbia. *American Journal of Psychiatry*, **125**, 1567–1575.

Levy, M.B., & Davis, K.E. (1988). Lovestyles and attachment styles compared: Their relations to each other and to various relationship characteristics. *Journal of Social and Personal Relationships*, **5**, 439–471.

Lieberman, M.A., Yalom, I.D., & Miles, M.B. (1973). *Encounter groups: First facts.* New York: Basic Books.

Lindsley, O.R. (1960). Characteristics of the behavior of chronic psychotics as revealed by free-operant conditioning methods. *Diseases of the Nervous System, Monograph Supplement*, **21**, 66–78.

Lindsley, O.R. (1963). Free-operant conditioning and psychotherapy. *Current Psychiatric Therapies*, **3**, 47–56.

Lipper, M.R., & Greene, D. (1978). *The hidden costs of reward.* Hillsdale, NJ: Lawrence Erlbaum.

Lipton, D.N., McDonel, E.C., & McFall, R.M. (1987). Heterosocial perception in rapists. *Journal of Consulting and Clinical Psychology*, **55**, 17–21.

Lisak, D. (1984). The psychological impact of sexual abuse: Content analysis of interviews with male survivors. *Journal of Traumatic Stress*, **7**, 525–548.

Loeber, R. (1990). Development and risk factors of juvenile antisocial behavior and delinquency. *Clinical Psychology Review*, **10**, 1–41.

Loeber, R., & Dision, T.J. (1983). Early predictors of male delinquency: A review. *Psychological Bulletin*, **94**, 68–99.

Loeber, R., & Stouthamer-Loeber, M. (1986). Family factors as correlates and predictors of juvenile conduct problems and delinquency. *Crime and Justice: An Annual Review of Research*, **7**, 29–149.

Long, J.D., Wuesthoff, A., & Pithers, W.D. (1989). Use of autobiographies in the assessment and treatment of sex offenders. In D.R. Laws (Ed.), *Relapse prevention with sex offenders* (pp. 88–95). New York: Guilford Press.

Looman, J., Abracen, J., & Nicholaichuk, T. (1998). *Recidivism among treated sexual offenders and matched controls: Data from the Regional Treatment Centre (Ontario).* Submitted for publication.

McConaghy, N. (1969). Subjective and penile plethysmograph responses following aversion-relief and apomorphine therapy for homosexual impulses. *British Journal of Psychiatry*, **115**, 723–730.

McConaghy, N. (1970). Penile response conditioning and its relationship to aversion therapy in homosexuals. *Behavior Therapy*, **1**, 213–221.

McConaghy, N. (1975). Aversive and positive conditioning treatments of homosexuality. *Behaviour Research and Therapy*, **13**, 309–319.

McConaghy, N. (1993). *Sexual behavior: Problems and management*. New York: Plenum Press.

McFall, R.M. (1982). A review and reformulation of the concept of social skills. *Behavioral Assessment*, **4**, 1–33.

McFall, R.M. (1990). The enhancement of social skills: An information processing analysis. In W.L. Marshall, D.R. Laws & H.E. Barbaree (Eds.), *Handbook of sexual assault: Issues, theories, and treatment of the offender* (pp. 311–330). New York: Plenum Press.

McGrath, R.J., Hoke, S.E., & Vojtisek, J.E. (1998). Cognitive-behavioral treatment of sex offenders. *Criminal Justice and Behavior*, **25**, 203–225.

McGuire, R.J., Carlisle, J.M., & Young, B.G. (1965). Sexual deviations as conditioned behaviour: A hypothesis. *Behaviour Research and Therapy*, **3**, 185–190.

McGuire, R.J., & Vallance, M. (1964). Aversion therapy by electric shock: A simple technique. *British Medical Journal*, **2**, 594–597.

McIntosh, N.J. (1974). *The psychology of animal learning*. London: Academic Press.

McKibben, A., Proulx, J., & Lusignan, R. (1994). Relationships between conflict, affect and deviant sexual behaviors in rapists and pedophiles. *Behaviour Research and Therapy*, **32**, 571–575.

Magaret, A. (1950). Generalization in successful psychotherapy. *Journal of Consulting Psychology*, **14**, 64–70.

Mahoney, M.J. (1974). *Cognition and behavior modification*. Cambridge, MA: Ballinger.

Mahoney, M.J., & Norcross, J.C. (1993). Relationship styles and therapeutic choices: A commentary. *Psychotherapy*, **30**, 423–426.

Main, M., Kaplan, N., & Cassidy, J. (1985). Security in infancy, childhood, and adulthood: A move to the level of representation. *Monographs of the Society for Research in Child Development*, **50**, 66–104.

Malamuth, N.M. (1981). Rape proclivity among males. *Journal of Social Issues*, **37**, 138–157.

Malamuth, N.M. (1984). Aggression against women: Cultural and individual causes. In N.M. Malamuth & E. Donnerstein (Eds.), *Pornography and sexual aggression* (pp. 19–52). Orlando, FL: Academic Press.

Malamuth, N.M. (1988). A multidimensional approach to sexual aggression: Combining measures of past behaviour and present likelihood. In R.A. Prentky & V.L. Quinsey (Eds.), *Human Sexual Aggression: Current Perspectives* (pp. 123–132). (Annals of the New York Academy of Sciences, Vol. 528).

Malamuth, N.M., & Check, J.V.P. (1980). Sexual arousal to rape and consenting depictions: The importance of the woman's arousal. *Journal of Abnormal Psychology*, **89**, 763–766.

Malamuth, N.M., & Check, J.V.P. (1983). Sexual arousal to rape depictions: Individual differences. *Journal of Abnormal Psychology*, **92**, 55–67.

Malamuth, N.M., Heavey, C.L., & Linz, D. (1993). Predicting men's antisocial behavior against women: The interaction model of sexual aggression. In G.C.N. Hall, R. Hirschman, J.R. Graham & M.S. Zaragoza (Eds.), *Sexual aggression: Issues in the etiology, assessment and treatment* (pp. 63–97). Washington, DC: Taylor & Francis.

Malamuth, N.M., Heim, M., & Feshbach, S. (1980). Sexual responsiveness of college students to rape depictions: Inhibitory and disinhibitory effects. *Journal of Personality and Social Psychology*, **38**, 399–408.

Malcolm, P.B., Davidson, P.R., & Marshall, W.L. (1985). Control of penile tumescence: The effects of arousal level and stimulus content. *Behaviour Research and Therapy*, **23**, 273–280.

Maletzky, B.M. (1974). "Assisted" covert sensitization in the treatment of exhibitionism. *Journal of Consulting and Clinical Psychology*, **42**, 34–40.

Maletzky, B.M. (1980). Assisted covert sensitization. In D.J. Cox & R.J. Daitzman (Eds.), *Exhibition: Description, assessment, and treatment* (pp. 187–251). New York: Garland STPM Press.

Maletzky, B.M. (1991). *Treating the sexual offender*. Newbury Park, CA: Sage Publications.

Maletzky, B.M. (1993). Factors associated with success and failure in the behavior and cognitive treatment of sexual offenders. *Annals of Sex Research*, **6**, 241–258.

Mann, R. (1996, November). *Measuring the effectiveness of relapse prevention intervention with sex offenders*. Paper presented at the 15th Annual Research and Treatment Conference of the Association for the Treatment of Sexual Abusers, Chicago.

Mann, R.E. (1998, October). *Relapse prevention? Is that the bit where they told me all the things I couldn't do anymore?* Paper presented at the 17th Annual Research and Treatment Conference of the Association for the Treatment of Sexual Abusers, Vancouver, BC.

Marks, I.M., & Gelder, M.G. (1967). Transvestism and fetishism: Clinical and psychological changes during faradic aversion. *British Journal of Psychiatry*, **113**, 711–730.

Marks, I.M., Gelder, M.G., & Bancroft, J.H.J. (1970). Sexual deviants two years after electric aversion therapy. *British Journal of Psychiatry*, **117**, 173–185.

Marks, I.M., Rachman, S., & Gelder, M.G. (1965). Methods for assessment of aversion treatment in fetishism with masochism. *Behaviour Research and Therapy*, **3**, 253–258.

Marlatt, G.A. (1982). Relapse prevention: A self-control program for the treatment of addictive behaviours. In R.B. Stuart (Ed.), *Adherence, compliance and generalization in behavioral medicine* (pp. 329–378). New York: Brunner/Mazel.

Marlatt, G.A., & Gordon, J.R. (1985). *Relapse prevention: Maintenance strategies in the treatment of addictive behaviors*. New York: Guilford Press.

Marolla, J., & Scully, D. (1986). Attitudes towards women, violence, and rape: A comparison of convicted rapists and other felons. *Deviant Behavior*, **7**, 337–355.

Marques, J.K. (1982, March). *Relapse prevention: A self-control model for the treatment of sex offenders*. Paper presented at the 7th Annual Forensic Mental Health Conference, Asilomar, CA.

Marques, J.K. (1984). *An innovative treatment program for sex offenders: Report to the Legislature*. Sacramento, CA: California Department of Mental Health.

Marques, J.K., Day, D.M., Nelson, C., & Miner, M.H. (1989). The Sex Offender Treatment and Evaluation Project: California's relapse prevention program. In D.R. Laws (Ed.), *Relapse prevention with sex offenders* (pp. 247–267). New York: Guilford Press.

Marquis, J.N. (1970). Orgasmic reconditioning: Changing sexual object choice through controlling masturbation fantasies. *Journal of Behavior Therapy and Experimental Psychiatry*, **1**, 263–271.

Marshall, W.L. (1971). A combined treatment method for certain sexual deviations. *Behaviour Research and Therapy*, **9**, 292–294.

Marshall, W.L. (1973). The modification of sexual fantasies: A combined treatment approach to the reduction of deviant sexual behavior. *Behaviour Research and Therapy*, **11**, 557–564.

Marshall, W.L. (1974). The classical conditioning of sexual attractiveness: A report of four therapeutic failures. *Behavior Therapy*, **5**, 298–299.

Marshall, W.L. (1979). Satiation therapy: A procedure for reducing deviant sexual arousal. *Journal of Applied Behavioral Analysis*, **12**, 10–22.

Marshall, W.L. (1982). A model of dysfunctional behavior. In A.S. Bellack, M. Hersen & A.E. Kazdin (Eds.), *International handbook of behavior modification and therapy* (pp. 57–78). New York: Plenum Press.

Marshall, W.L. (1984). *Rape as a socio-cultural phenomenon.* J.P.S. Robertson Annual Lecture. Trent University, Peterborough, Ontario.

Marshall, W.L. (1985). The effects of variable exposure in flooding therapy. *Behavior Therapy,* **16**, 117–135.

Marshall, W.L. (1989a). Invited essay: Intimacy, loneliness and sexual offenders. *Behaviour Research and Therapy,* **27**, 491–503.

Marshall, W.L. (1989b). Pornography and sex offenders. In D. Zillmann and J. Bryant Eds.), *Pornography: recent research, interpretations, and policy considerations* (pp. 185–214), Hillsdale, NJ: Lawrence Erlbaum.

Marshall, W.L. (1989c). Intimacy, loneliness, and sexual offenders. *Behavioral Research and Therapy,* **27**, 491–503.

Marshall, W.L. (1992). The social value of treatment for sexual offenders. *Canadian Journal of Human Sexuality,* **1**, 109–114.

Marshall, W.L. (1993a). The treatment of sex offenders: What does the outcome data tell us? A reply to Quinsey et al. *Journal of Interpersonal Violence,* **8**, 524–530.

Marshall, W.L. (1993b). The role of attachment, intimacy, and loneliness in the etiology and maintenance of sexual offending. *Sexual and Marital Therapy,* **8**, 109–121.

Marshall, W.L. (1994a). Pauvreté des liens d'attachement et déficiences dans les rapports intimes chez les agresseurs sexuels. *Criminologie, XXVII,* 55–69.

Marshall, W.L. (1994b). Treatment effects on denial and minimization in incarcerated sex offenders. *Behaviour Research and Therapy,* **32**, 559–564.

Marshall, W.L. (1995). *The sex offender: Monster, victim, or everyman?* Keynote address, 14th Annual Research and Treatment Conference of the Association for the Treatment of Sexual Abusers, New Orleans.

Marshall, W.L. (1996a). The sexual offender: Monster, victim, or everyman. *Sexual Abuse: A Journal of Research and Treatment,* **8**, 317–335.

Marshall, W.L. (1996b). Assessment, treatment, and theorizing about sex offenders: Developments over the past 20 years and future directions. *Criminal Justice and Behavior,* **23**, 162–199.

Marshall, W.L. (1997a). Pedophilia: Psychopathology and theory. In D.R. Laws & W. O'Donohue (Eds.), *Handbook of sexual deviance: Theory and application* (pp. 152–174). New York: Guilford Press.

Marshall, W.L. (1997b). The relationship between self-esteem and deviant sexual arousal in nonfamilial child molesters. *Behavior Modification,* **21**, 86–96.

Marshall, W.L. (in press, a). Sexual preferences: Are they useful in the assessment and treatment of sexual offenders? In D. Fisher, M. Cardgo & B. Print (Ed.), *Sex offenders: Toward improved practice.* London: Whiting & Birch.

Marshall, W.L. (in press, b). Enhancing social skills and relationship skills. In M.S. Carich & S. Mussack (Eds.), *Handbook of sex offender treatment.* Orwell, VT: Safer Society Press.

Marshall, W.L. (in press, c). Diagnosing and treating sexual offenders. In A.K. Hess & J.B. Weiner (Eds.), *The handbook of forensic psychology* (2nd ed.). New York: John Wiley & Sons.

Marshall, W.L., & Anderson, D. (1996). An evaluation of the benefits of relapse prevention programs with sexual offenders. *Sexual Abuse: A Journal of Research and Treatment,* **8**, 209–221.

Marshall, W.L., Anderson, D., & Champagne, F. (1996). Self-esteem and its relationship to sexual offending. *Psychology, Crime & Law,* **3**, 81–106.

Marshall, W.L. & Barbaree, H.E. (1978). The reduction of deviant arousal. *Criminal Justice and Behavior,* **5**, 294–303.

Marshall, W.L., & Barbaree, H.E. (1984). A behavioral view of rape. *International Journal of Law and Psychiatry*, **7**, 51–77.

Marshall, W.L., & Barbaree, H.E. (1988). The long-term evaluation of a behavioral treatment program for child molesters. *Behaviour Research and Therapy*, **26**, 499–511.

Marshall, W.L., & Barbaree, H.E. (1990). An integrated theory of sexual offending. In W.L. Marshall, D.R. Laws & H.E. Barbaree (Eds.), *Handbook of sexual assault: Issues, theories, and treatment of the offender* (pp. 257–275). New York: Plenum Press.

Marshall, W.L., Barbaree, H.E., & Butt, J. (1988). Sexual offenders against male children: Sexual preferences. *Behaviour Research and Therapy*, **26**, 383–391.

Marshall, W.L., Barbaree, H.E., & Christophe, D. (1986). Sexual offenders against female children: Sexual preferences for age of victims and type of behaviour. *Canadian Journal of Behavioural Science*, **18**, 424–439.

Marshall, W.L., Barbaree, H.E., & Eccles, A. (1991). Early onset and deviant sexuality in child molesters. *Journal of Interpersonal Violence*, **6**, 323–336.

Marshall, W.L., Barbaree, H.E., & Fernandez, Y.M. (1995). Some aspects of social competence in sexual offenders. *Sexual Abuse: A Journal of Research and Treatment*, **7**, 113–127.

Marshall, W.L., & Barrett, S. (1990). *Criminal neglect: Why sex offenders go free.* Toronto: Doubleday. (Also reprinted in paperback by Seals/Bantam Books, 1992.)

Marshall, W.L., Bryce, P., Hudson, S.M., Ward, T., & Moth, B. (1996). The enhancement of intimacy and the reduction of loneliness among child molesters. *Journal of Family Violence*, **11**, 219–235.

Marshall, W.L., Champagne, F., Brown, C., & Miller, S. (1997). Empathy, intimacy, loneliness, and self-esteem in nonfamilial child molesters. *Journal of Child Sexual Abuse*, **6**, 87–97.

Marshall, W.L., Champagne, F., Sturgeon, C., & Bryce, P. (1997). Increasing the self-esteem of child molesters. *Sexual Abuse: A Journal of Research and Treatment*, **9**, 321–333.

Marshall, W.L., & Christie, M.M. (1982). The enhancement of social self-esteem. *Canadian Counsellor*, **16**, 82–89.

Marshall, W.L., Christie, M.M., & Lanthier, R.D. (1979). *Social competence, sexual experience and attitudes to sex in incarcerated rapists and pedophiles.* Ottawa: Solicitor General of Canada.

Marshall, W.L., Christie, M.M., Lanthier, R.D., & Cruchley, J. (1982). The nature of the reinforcer in the enhancement of social self-esteem. *Canadian Counsellor*, **16**, 90–96.

Marshall, W.L., Cripps, E., Anderson, D., & Cortoni, F.A. (in press). Self-esteem and coping strategies in child molesters. *Journal of Interpersonal Violence.*

Marshall, W.L., & Darke, J. (1982). Inferring humiliation as motivation in sexual offenses. *Treatment for Sexual Aggressives*, **5**, 1–3.

Marshall, W.L., Earls, C.M., Segal, Z.V., & Darke, J. (1983). A behavioral program for the assessment and treatment of sexual aggressors. In K. Craig and R. McMahon (Eds.), *Advances in clinical behavior therapy* (pp. 148–174). New York: Brunner/Mazel.

Marshall, W.L., & Eccles, A. (1991). Issues in clinical practice with sex offenders. *Journal of Interpersonal Violence*, **6**, 68–93.

Marshall, W.L., & Eccles, A. (1993). Pavlovian conditioning processes in adolescent sex offenders. In H.E. Barbaree, W.L. Marshall, & S.M. Hudson (Eds.), *The juvenile sex offender* (pp. 118–142). New York: Guilford Press.

Marshall, W.L., & Eccles, A. (1995). Cognitive-behavioral treatment of sex offenders. In V.B. Van Hasselt & M. Hersen (Eds.), *Sourcebook of psychobiological treatment manuals for adult disorders* (pp. 295–332). New York: Plenum Press.

Marshall, W.L., Eccles, A., & Barbaree, H.E. (1991). Treatment of exhibitionists: A focus on sexual deviance versus cognitive and relationship features. *Behaviour Research and Therapy*, **29**, 129–135.

Marshall, W.L., & Fernandez, Y.M. (1997). Enfoques cognitivo-conductuales para las parafilias: El tratameinto de la delincuencia sexual. In V.E. Caballo (Ed.), *Manual para el tratamiento cognitivo-conductual de los trastornos psicológicos*, Vol. 1. Trastornos por ansiedad, sexualas, afectivos y psicóticos (pp. 299–331). Madrid: Siglio Veintiuno de España Editores.

Marshall, W.L., & Fernandez, Y.M. (1998). Cognitive-behavioral approaches to the treatment of paraphilias. In V. Caballo (Ed.), *International Handbook of Cognitive Behavioural Treatments of Psychological Disorders* (pp. 281–312). Oxford: Elsevier Science.

Marshall, W.L., & Fernandez, Y.M. (in press). Phallometric testing with sexual offenders: Limits to its value. *Clinical Psychology Review*.

Marshall, W.L., Gauthier, J., & Gordon, A. (1979). The current status of flooding therapy. In M. Hersen, R. Eisler & P. Miller (Eds.), *Progress in behavior modification*, Vol. 7 (pp. 205–275). New York: Academic Press.

Marshall, W.L., & Hambley, L.S. (1996). Intimacy and loneliness, and their relationship to rape myth acceptance and hostility toward women among rapists. *Journal of Interpersonal Violence*, **11**, 586–592.

Marshall, W.L., Hamilton, K., & Fernandez, Y. (1998). *Empathy deficits and cognitive distortions in child molesters*. Submitted for publication.

Marshall, W.L., Hudson, S.M., & Hodkinson, S. (1993). The importance of attachment bonds in the development of juvenile sex offending. In H.E. Barbaree, W.L. Marshall, & S.M. Hudson (Eds.), *The juvenile sex offender* (pp. 164–181). New York: Guilford Press.

Marshall, W.L., Hudson, S.M., Jones, R., & Fernandez, Y.M. (1995). Empathy in sex offenders. *Clinical Psychology Review*, **15**, 99–113.

Marshall, W.L., Jones, R., Ward, T., Johnston, P., & Barbaree, H.E. (1991). Treatment outcome with sex offenders. *Clinical Psychology Review*, **11**, 465–485.

Marshall, W.L., Keltner, A., & Griffiths, E. (1974). An apparatus for the delivery of foul odors: Clinical applications. Unpublished manuscript, Queen's University, Kingston, Ontario, Canada.

Marshall, W.L., & Langton, C.M. (1997). *Cognitive distortions in sexual offenders: Nature and content*. Submitted for publication.

Marshall, W.L., & Lippens, K. (1977). The clinical value of boredom: A procedure for reducing inappropriate sexual interests. *Journal of Nervous and Mental Diseases*, **165**, 283–287.

Marshall, W.L., & McKnight, R.D. (1975) An integrated treatment program for sexual offenders. *Canadian Psychiatric Association Journal*, **20**, 133–138.

Marshall, W.L., & Marshall, L. (1998, October). Sexual addiction and substance abuse in sexual offenders. Paper presented at the 17th Annual Research and Treatment Conference of the Association for the Treatment of Sexual Abusers, Vancouver, Canada.

Marshall, W.L., & Marshall, L.E. (in press). Child sexual molestation. In V.B. van Hasselt & M. Hersen (Eds.), *Aggression and violence: An introductory text*. New York: Allyn & Bacon.

Marshall, W.L., & Mazzucco, A. (1995). Self-esteem and parental attachments in child molesters. *Sexual Abuse: A Journal of Research and Treatment*, **7**, 279–285.

Marshall, W.L., Mulloy, R., & Serran, G. (1998). The identification of treatment-facilitative behaviors enacted by sexual offender therapists. Unpublished manuscript, Queen's University, Kingston, Ontario, Canada.

Marshall, W.L., O'Sullivan, C., & Fernandez, Y.M. (1996). The enhancement of victim empathy among incarcerated child molesters. *Legal and Criminological Psychology*, **1**, 95–102

Marshall, W.L., Parker, L., & Hayes, B. (1982). Treating public speaking problems: A study using flooding and the elements of skills training. *Behavior Modification*, **6**, 147–170.

Marshall, W.L., Payne, K., Barbaree, H.E., & Eccles, A. (1991). Exhibitionists: Sexual preferences for exposing. *Behaviour Research and Therapy*, **29**, 37–40.

Marshall, W.L., & Pithers, W.D. (1994). A reconsideration of treatment outcome with sex offenders. *Criminal Justice and Behavior*, **21**, 10–27.

Marshall, W.L., Serran, G.A., & Cortoni, F.A. (in press). *Childhood attachments and sexual abuse and their relationship to coping in child molesters. Sexual Abuse: A Journal of Research and Treatment.*

Marshall, W.L., Ward, T., Jones, R., Johnston, P., & Barbaree, H.E. (1991). An optimistic evaluation of treatment outcome with sex offenders. *Violence Update*, March, 1–8.

Marshall, W.L., & Williams, S. (1975). A behavioral approach to the modification of rape. *Quarterly Bulletin of the British Association for Behavioural Psychotherapy*, **4**, 78.

Masters, W., & Johnson, V. (1966). *Human sexual response.* Boston: Little, Brown.

Max, L. (1935). Breaking a homosexual fixation by the conditioned reflex technique. *Psychological Bulletin*, **32**, 734.

Mead, G.H. (1934). *Mind, self, and society.* Chicago: University of Chicago Press.

Mehrabian, A., & Epstein, N. (1972). A measure of emotional empathy. *Journal of Personality*, **40**, 525–543.

Meichenbaum, D.H. (1974). *Cognitive behavior modification.* Morristown, NJ: General Learning Press.

Meichenbaum, D. (1977). *Cognitive-behavior modification: An integrative approach.* New York: Plenum Press.

Mendelson, E.F., Quinn, M., Dutton, S., & Seewonarian, K. (1988). A community treatment service for sex offenders: An account at 2 years. *Bulletin of the Royal College of Psychiatrists*, 416–421.

Metts, S., & Cupach, W.R. (1989). The role of communication in human sexuality. In K. McKinney & S. Sprecher (Eds.), *Human sexuality: The societal and interpersonal context* (pp. 139–161). Norwood, NJ: Ablex.

Miller, D.T., & Ross, M. (1975). Self-serving biases in attribution of causality: Fact or fiction? *Psychological Bulletin*, **82**, 213–225.

Miller, G.A., Galanter, E., & Pribram, K.H. (1960). *Plans and the structure of behavior.* New York: Holt, Rinehart & Winston.

Miller, P.A. & Eisenberg, N. (1988). The relationship of empathy to aggressive and externalizing/antisocial behavior. *Psychological Bulletin*, **103**, 324–344.

Miller, R.S. & Lefcourt, H.M. (1982). The assessment of social intimacy. *Journal of Personality Assessment*, **46**, 514–518.

Miller, W.R. (1980). The addictive behaviors. In W.R. Miller (Ed.), *The addictive behaviors: Treatment of alcoholism, drug abuse, smoking and obesity* (pp. 3–10). New York: Plenum Press.

Miller, W.R. (1983). Motivational interviewing with problem drinkers. *Behavioral Psychotherapy*, **1**, 147–172.

Miller, W.R., & Bacca, L.M. (1983). Two-year follow-up of bibliotherapy and therapist-directed controlled drinking training for problem drinkers. *Behavior Therapy*, **14**, 441–448.

Miller, W.R., & Sovereign, R.G. (1989). The Check-up: A model for early intervention in addictive behaviors. In T. Løberg, W.R. Miller, P.E. Nathan, & G.A. Marlatt (Eds.), *Addictive behaviors: Prevention and early intervention* (pp. 219–231). Amsterdam: Swets & Zeitlinger.

Miner, M.H., Day, D.M., & Nafpaktitis, M.K. (1989). Assessment of coping skills: Development of a Situational Competency Test. In D.R. Laws (Ed.), *Relapse prevention with sex offenders* (pp. 127–136). New York: Guilford Press.

Mintz, J., Luborsky, L., & Auerbach, A.H. (1971). Dimensions of psychotherapy: A factor-analytic study of ratings of psychotherapy sessions. *Journal of Consulting and Clinical Psychology*, **36**, 106–120.

Mischel, W. (1968). *Personality and assessment*. New York: John Wiley & Sons.

Mohr, J.W., Turner, R.E., & Jerry, M.B. (1964). *Pedophilia and exhibitionism*. Toronto: University of Toronto Press.

Moll, A. (1911). Die behandlung sexueller perversioner mït versonderer berüchsichtigung der assoziationstherapie. *Zeitschrift Psychotherapie*, **3**, 1–10.

Moore, B.S. (1990). The origins and development of empathy. *Motivation and Emotion*, **14**, 75–79.

Moos, R.H. (1986). *Group environment scale manual* (2nd edn). Palo Alto, CA: Consulting Psychologists' Press.

Morris, R.J., & Suckerman, K.R. (1974). Therapist warmth as a factor in automated systematic desensitization. *Journal of Consulting and Clinical Psychology*, **42**, 244–250.

Mosher, D.L., & Anderson, R. (1986). Macho personality, sexual aggression, and reactions to guided imagery of realistic rape. *Journal of Research in Personality*, **20**, 77–97.

Mosher, D.L., & Sirkin, M. (1984). Measuring a macho personality constellation. *Journal of Research in Personality*, **18**, 150–163.

Mowrer, O.H. (1950). *Learning theory and personality dynamics: Selected papers*. New York: Ronald.

Mullen, P.E., Martin, J.L., Anderson, J.C., Romans, S.E., & Harbison, G.P. (1994). The effect of child sexual abuse on social, interpersonal, and sexual function in adult life. *British Journal of Psychiatry*, **165**, 35–47.

Murphy, W.D. (1990). Assessment and modification of cognitive distortions in sex offenders. In W.L. Marshall, D.R. Laws, & H.E. Barbaree (Eds.), *Handbook of sexual assault: Issues, theories, and treatment of the offender* (pp. 331–342). New York: Plenum Press.

Murphy, W.D. (1997). Exhibitionism: Psychopathology and theory. In D.R. Laws & W. O'Donohue (Eds.), *Sexual deviance: Theory, assessment, and treatment* (pp. 22–39).

Murphy, W.D., Abel, G.G., & Becker, J.V. (1980). Future research issues. In D.J. Cox & R.J. Daitzman (Eds.), *Exhibitionism: Description, assessment, and treatment* (pp. 339–392). New York: Garland STPM Press.

Murphy, W.D., & Barbaree, H.E. (1994). *Assessments of sex offenders by measures of erectile response: Psychometric properties and decision making*. Brandon, VT: The Safer Society Press.

Murphy, W.D., Coleman, E.M., & Haynes, M.R. (1986). Factors related to coercive sexual behavior in a nonclinical sample of males. *Violence and Victims*, **1**, 255–278.

Murphy, W.D., Haynes, M.R., Stalgaitis, S.J., & Flanagan, B. (1986). Differential sexual responding among four groups of sexual offenders against children. *Journal of Psychopathology and Behavioral Assessment*, **8**, 339–353.

Murphy, W.D., Krisak, J., Stalgaitis, S.J., & Anderson, K. (1984). The use of penile tumescence measures with incarcerated rapists: Further validity issues. *Archives of Sexual Behavior*, **13**, 545–554.

Murstein, B.I. (1972). Physical attractiveness and marital choice. *Journal of Personality and Social Psychology*, **22**, 8–12.

Nasby, W., & Kihlstrom, J.F. (1986). Cognitive assessment of personality and psychopathology. In R.E. Ingram (Ed.), *Information processing approaches to clinical psychology* (pp. 217–239). New York: Academic Press.

Neidigh, L., & Krop, H. (1992). Cognitive distortions among child sexual offenders. *Journal of Sex Education and Therapy*, **18**, 208–215.

Nicholaichuk, T., Gordon, A., Andre, G., Gu, D., & Wong, S. (1998). *Outcome of the Clearwater Sex Offender Treatment Program: A matched comparison between treated and untreated offenders*. Submitted for publication.

Nisbett, R.E., & Ross, L. (1980). *Human inference: Strategies and shortcomings of social judgement.* Englewood Cliffs, NJ: Prentice Hall.

Norman, C. (1892). Sexual perversion. In Hack Tuke (Ed.), *Dictionary of psychological medicine* (pp. 220–321). London: Churchill.

O'Dell, J.W., & Bahmer, A.J. (1981). Rogers, Lazarus and Shostrom in content analysis. *Journal of Clinical Psychology, 37,* 507.

O'Donohue, W., Letourneau, E., & Dowling, H. (1997). The measurement of sexual fantasy. *Sexual Abuse: A Journal of Research and Treatment, 9,* 167–178.

O'Donohue, W., & Plaud, J.J. (1994). The conditioning of human sexual arousal. *Archives of Sexual Behavior, 23,* 321–334.

Öhman, A., Erixon, G., & Lofberg, I. (1975). Phobias and preparedness: Phobic versus neutral pictures as conditioned stimuli for human autonomic responses. *Journal of Abnormal Psychology, 84,* 41–45.

O'Reilly, G., Sheridan, A., Carr, A., Cherry, J., O'Donohue, E., McGrath, K., Phelan, S., Tallon, M., & O'Reilly, K. (1998). A descriptive study of adolescent sexual offenders in an Irish community-based treatment programme. *The Irish Journal of Psychology, 19,* 152–167.

Otterbein, K.F. (1979). A cross-cultural study of rape. *Aggressive Behavior, 5,* 425–435.

Overholser, C., & Beck, S. (1986). Multimethod assessment of rapists, child molesters, and three control groups on behavioral and psychological measures. *Journal of Consulting and Clinical Psychology, 54,* 682–687.

Owens, G., Crowell, J.A., Pan, H., Treboux, D., O'Connor, E., & Waters, E. (1995). The prototype hypothesis and the origins of attachment working models: Adult relationships with parents and romantic partners. *Monographs of the Society of Child Development, 60,* 216–233.

Pacht, A.R., & Cowen, J.E. (1974). An exploratory study of five hundred sex offenders. *Criminal Justice and Behavior, 1,* 13–20.

Palmer, W. (1998). Future directions in risk prediction: With illustrations and examples drawn from Warkworth's past. Unpublished report, Warkworth Penitentiary, Campbellford, Ontario, Canada.

Parker, H., & Parker, S. (1986). Father–daughter sexual abuse: An emerging perspective. *American Journal of Orthopsychiatry, 56,* 531–549.

Perkins, D. (1977, June). *Development of a psychological treatment programme for sex offenders in a prison setting.* Paper presented at the Annual Conference of the British Psychological Society, Exeter.

Pithers, W.D. (1990). Relapse prevention with sexual aggressors: A method for maintaining therapeutic change and enhancing external supervision. In W.L. Marshall, D.R. Laws, & H.E. Barbaree (Eds.), *The handbook of sexual assault: Issues, theories and treatment of the offender* (pp. 363–385). New York: Plenum.

Pithers, W.D. (1994). Process evaluation of a group therapy component designed to enhance sex offenders' empathy for sexual abuse survivors. *Behaviour Research and Therapy, 32,* 565–570.

Pithers, W.D., Beal, L.S., Armstrong, J., & Petty, J. (1989). Identification of risk factors through clinical interviews and analysis of records. In D.R. Laws (Ed.), *Relapse prevention with sex offenders* (pp. 77–87). New York: Guilford Press.

Pithers, W.D., Buell, M.M., Kashima, K., Cumming, G., & Beal, L. (1987, May). *Precursors to relapse of sexual offenders.* Paper presented at the 7th Annual Conference of the Association for the Behavioral Treatment of Sexual Abusers, Newport, OR.

Pithers, W.D., & Gray, A.S. (1996). Utility of relapse prevention in treatment of sexual abusers. *Sexual Abuse: A Journal of Research and Treatment, 8,* 171–260.

Pithers, W.D., Kashima, K.M., Cumming, G.F., & Beal, L.S. (1988). Relapse prevention: A method of enhancing maintenance of change in sex offenders. In A.C. Salter

(Ed.), *Treating child sex offenders and victims: A practical guide* (pp. 131–170). Newbury Park, CA: Sage.

Pithers, W.D., & Laws, D.R. (1993). Phallometric assessment. In B.K. Schwartz & H.R. Cellini (Eds.), *The sex offender: Corrections, treatment and legal practice* (pp. 12.1–12.18). Kingston, NJ: Civic Research Institute.

Pithers, W.D., Marques, J.K., Gibat, C.C., & Marlatt, G.A. (1983). Relapse prevention with sexual aggressors: A self-control model of treatment and maintenance of change. In J.G. Greer & I.R. Stuart (Eds.), *The sexual aggressor: Current perspectives on treatment* (pp. 214–239). New York: Van Nostrand Reinhold.

Pithers, W.D., Martin, G.R., & Cumming, G.F. (1989). Vermont Treatment Program for Sexual Aggressors. In D.R. Laws (Ed.), *Relapse prevention with sex offenders* (pp. 292–310). New York: Guilford Press.

Popper, K.R. (1959). *The logic of scientific discovery.* London: Hutchinson.

Prentky, R.A., & Burgess, A.W. (1990). Rehabilitation of child molesters: A cost–benefit analysis. *American Journal of Orthopsychiatry, 60,* 80–117.

Prentky, R.A., Knight, R.A., Sims-Knight, J.E., Strauss, H., Rokous, F., & Cerce, D. (1989). Developmental antecedents of sexual aggression. *Development and Psychopathy, 1,* 153–169.

Prentky, R.A., Lee, A.F.S., Knight, R.A., & Cerce, D. (1997). Recidivism rates among child molesters and rapists: A methodological analysis. *Law and Human Behavior, 21,* 635–659.

Proctor, E., & Flaxington, F. (1996). *Community-based interventions with sex offenders organized by the probation service: A survey of current practice.* London: Association of Chief Probation Officers.

Proctor, E.K., & Rosen, A. (1983). Structure in therapy: A conceptual analysis. *Psychotherapy, 20,* 202–207.

Proulx, J., Aubut, J., McKibben, A., & Coté, M. (1994). Penile responses of rapists and nonrapists to rape stimuli involving physical violence or humiliation. *Archives of Sexual Behavior, 23,* 295–310.

Proulx, J., Coté, G., & Achille, P.A. (1993). Prevention of voluntary control of penile response in a homosexual pedophile during phallometric testing. *Journal of Sex Research, 30,* 140–147.

Proulx, J., McKibben, A., & Lusignan, R. (1996). Relationships between affective components and sexual behaviors in sexual aggressors. *Sexual Abuse: A Journal of Research and Treatment, 8,* 279–289.

Proulx, J., Ouimet, M., Pellerin, B., Paradis, Y., McKibben, A., & Aubut, J. (1998). *Posttreatment recidivism in sexual aggressors.* Submitted for publication.

Proulx, J., Pellerin, B., McKibben, A., Aubut, J., & Ouimet, M. (1998). *Recidivism in sexual aggressors: Static and dynamic predictors of recidivism in sexual aggressors.* Submitted for publication.

Quinn, J.T., Harbison, J., & McAllister, H. (1970). An attempt to shape human penile responses. *Behaviour Research and Therapy, 8,* 27–28.

Quinsey, V.L. (1984). Sexual aggression: Studies of offenders against women. In D. Weisstub (Ed.), *Law and mental health: International perspectives* (Vol. 1, pp. 84–121). New York: Pergamon.

Quinsey, V.L. (1996, August). *A retrospective evaluation of the Regional Treatment Centre Sex Offender Program.* Paper presented at the International Congress of Psychology. Montreal.

Quinsey, V.L. (1998). Comment on Marshall's "Monster, Victim, or Everyman". *Sexual Abuse: A Journal of Research and Treatment, 10,* 65–69.

Quinsey, V.L., Bergersen, S.G., & Steinman, C.M. (1976). Changes in physiological and verbal responses of child molesters during aversion therapy. *Canadian Journal of Behavioral Science, 8,* 202–212.

Quinsey, V.L., & Chaplin, T.C. (1984). Stimulus control of rapists' and non-sex offenders' sexual arousal. *Behavioural Assessment*, **6**, 169–176.

Quinsey, V.L., & Chaplin, T.C. (1988). Penile responses of child molesters and normals to descriptions of encounters with children involving sex and violence. *Journal of Interpersonal Violence*, **3**, 259–274.

Quinsey, V.L., Chaplin, T.C., & Carrigan, W.F. (1979). Sexual preferences among incestuous and nonincestuous child molesters. *Behavior Therapy*, **10**, 562–565.

Quinsey, V.L., Chaplin, T.C., & Carrigan, W.F. (1980). Biofeedback and signalled punishment in the modification of inappropriate sexual age preferences. *Behavior Therapy*, **11**, 567–576.

Quinsey, V.L., Chaplin, T.C., Maguire, A.M., & Upfold, D. (1987). The behavioral treatment of rapists and child molesters. In E.K. Morris & C.J. Braukmann (Eds.), *Behavioral approaches to crime and delinquency: Application, research, and theory* (pp. 363–382). New York: Plenum Press.

Quinsey, V.L., Chaplin, T.C., Varney, G. (1981). A comparison of rapists' and non-sex offenders' sexual preferences for mutually consenting sex, rape, and physical abuse of women. *Behavioral Assessment*, **3**, 127–135.

Quinsey, V.L., & Earls, C.M. (1990). The modification of sexual preferences. In W.L. Marshall, D.R. Laws & H.E. Barbaree (Eds.), *Handbook of sexual assault: Issues, theories, and treatment of the offender* (pp. 279–295). New York: Plenum Press.

Quinsey, V.L., Harris, G.T., Rice, M.E., & Lalumière, M.L. (1993). Assessing treatment efficacy in outcome studies of sex offenders. *Journal of Interpersonal Violence*, **8**, 512–523.

Quinsey, V.L., Khanna, A., & Malcolm, B. (1996, August). *A retrospective evaluation of the RTC Sex Offender Treatment Program*. Paper presented at the World Congress of Psychology, Montreal.

Quinsey, V.L., Khanna, A., & Malcolm, P.B. (1998). A retrospective evaluation of the Regional Treatment Centre Sex Offender Treatment program. *Journal of Interpersonal Violence*, **13**, 621–644.

Quinsey, V.L., Lalumière, M.L., Rice, M.E., & Harris, G.T. (1995). Predicting sexual offenses. In J.C. Campbell (Ed.), *Assessing dangerousness: Violence by sexual offenders, batterers, and child abusers*. Thousand Oaks, CA: Sage Publications.

Quinsey, V.L., & Marshall, W.L. (1983). Procedures for reducing inappropriate sexual arousal: An evaluation review. In J.G. Greer & I.R. Stuart (Eds.), *The sexual aggressor: Current perspectives on treatment* (pp. 267–289). New York: Van Nostrand Reinhold.

Rachman, S. (1966). Sexual fetishism: An experimental analogue. *Psychological Record*, **16**, 293–296.

Rachman, S., & Hodgson, R.J. (1968). Experimentally induced "sexual fetishism": Replication and development. *Psychological Record*, **18**, 25–27.

Rachman, S., & Teasdale, J.D. (1969). Aversion therapy: An appraisal. In C.M. Franks (Ed.), *Behavior therapy: Appraisal and status* (pp. 279–320). New York: McGraw-Hill.

Rada, R.T. (Ed.) (1978). *Clinical aspects of the rapist*. New York: Grune & Stratton.

Raymond, M. (1956). Case of fetishism treated by aversion therapy. *British Medical Journal*, **2**, 854–856.

Reiss, I.L., & Lee, G.R. (1988). *Family systems in America* (4th edn). New York: Holt, Rinehart & Winston.

Rice, M.E., Chaplin, T.E., Harris, G.E., & Coutts, J. (1990). *Empathy for the victim and sexual offender among rapists*. Penetanguishene Mental Health Centre, Research Report No. 7.

Rice, M.E., Chaplin, T.C., Harris, G.T., & Coutts, J. (1994). Empathy for the victim and sexual arousal among rapists and nonrapists. *Journal of Interpersonal Violence*, **9**, 435–449.

Rice, M.E., Harris, G.T., & Quinsey, V.L. (1993). Evaluating treatment programs for child molesters. In J. Hudson & J. Roberts (Eds.), *Evaluating justice: Canadian policies and programs* (pp. 189–203). Toronto: Thompson.

Rice, M.E., Quinsey, V.L., & Harris, G.T. (1991). Sexual recidivism among child molesters released from a maximum security psychiatric institution. *Journal of Consulting and Clinical Psychology*, **59**, 381–386.

Roberts, J.E., & Munroe, S.M. (1994). A multidimensional model for self-esteem in depression. *Clinical Psychology Review*, **14**, 161–181.

Rodin, J., Elias, M., Silberstein, L.R., & Wagner, A. (1988). Combined behavioral and pharmacologic treatment for obesity: Predictors of successful weight maintenance. *Journal of Consulting and Clinical Psychology*, **56**, 399–404.

Rogers, C.R. (1951). *Client-centered therapy.* Boston: Houghton, Mifflin.

Rooth, G. (1973). Exhibitionism, sexual violence and paedophilia. *British Journal of Psychiatry*, **122**, 705–710.

Rosenberg, M. (1965). *Society and the adolescent self-image.* Princeton, NJ: Princeton University Press.

Rowan, E.L. (1988). Pedophilia. *Journal of Social Work and Human Sexuality*, **7**, 91–100.

Russell, D., Peplau, L.A., & Cutrona, C.E. (1980). The Revised UCLA Loneliness Scale, *Journal of Personality and Social Psychology*, **39**, 472–480.

Russell, D.E.H. (1984). *Sexual exploitation: Rape, child sexual abuse and workplace harassment.* Thousand Oaks: Sage Publications.

Russell, D.E.H. (1986). *The secret trauma: Incest in the lives of girls and women.* New York: Basic Books.

Russell, R.J., & Hulson, B. (1991). Physical and psychological abuse of heterosexual partners. *Personality and Individual Differences*, **13**, 457–473.

Salovey, P., & Rodin, J. (1988). Coping with envy and jealousy. *Journal of Social and Clinical Psychology*, **7**, 15–33.

Salovey, P., & Rodin, J. (1991). Provoking jealousy and envy: Domain relevance and self-esteem threat. *Journal of Social and Clinical Psychology*, **10**, 395–413.

Salter, A. (1949). *Conditioned reflex therapy: The direct approach to the reconstruction of personality.* New York: Creative Age Press.

Salter, A. (1995). *Transforming trauma: A guide to understanding and treating adult survivors of child sexual abuse.* Thousand Oaks, CA: Sage Publications.

Samuelson, F. (1981). Struggle for scientific authority: The reception of Watson's behaviorism, 1913–1920. *Journal of the History of the Behavioral Sciences*, **17**, 399–425.

Samuelson, F. (1985). Organizing the kingdom of behavior: Academic battles and organizational policies in the twenties. *Journal of the History of the Behavioral Sciences*, **21**, 33–47.

Sanday, P.R. (1981). *Female power and male dominance.* London: Cambridge University Press.

Sattem, L., Savells, J., & Murray, E. (1984). Sex-role stereotypes and commitment of rape. *Sex Roles*, **11**, 849–860.

Saunders, E., Awad, G.A., & White, G. (1986). Male adolescent sex offenders: The offenders and the offense. *Canadian Journal of Psychiatry*, **31**, 542–549.

Savin-Williams, R.C., & Demo, D.H. (1983). Situational and transituational determinants of adolescent self-feelings. *Journal of Personality and Social Psychology*, **44**, 824–833.

Schaap, C., Bennun, I., Schindler, L., & Hoogduin, K. (1993). *The therapeutic relationship in behavioural psychotherapy.* New York: Wiley.

Scharfe, E., & Bartholomew, K. (1994). Reliability and stability of adult attachment patterns. *Personal Relationships*, **1**, 23–43.

Schewe, P.A., & O'Donohue, W. (1993). Sexual abuse prevention with high-risk males: The roles of victim empathy and rape myths. *Violence and Victims*, **8**, 339–351.

Schindler, L., Revenstorf, D., Hahlweg, K., & Brengelman, J.C. (1983). Therapeuten-verhalten in der verhaltenstherapie: Entwicklung eines instruments zur beur-teilung durch den klienten. *Partnerberatung*, **20**, 149–157.

Schlank, A.M., & Shaw, T. (1996). Treating sex offenders who deny their guilt: A pilot study. *Sexual Abuse: A Journal of Research and Treatment*, **8**, 17–23.

Schrenck-Notzing, A. von (1895). *The use of hypnosis in psychopathia sexualis with special reference to contrary sexual instinct* (translation by C.G. Chaddock, 1956). New York: Julian Press.

Schwartz, B.K. (1995). Decision making with incarcerated sex offenders. In B.K. Schwartz & H.R. Cellini (Eds.), *The sex offender: Corrections, treatment and legal practice* (pp. 8.1–8.18). Kingston, NJ: Civic Research Institute.

Scully, D. (1988). Convicted rapists' perceptions of self and victim: Role taking and emotions. *Gender and Society*, **2**, 200–213.

Sears, R.R. (1943). *Survey of objective studies of psychoanalytic concepts: A report prepared for the Committee on Social Adjustment.* New York: Social Science Research Council.

Sefarbi, R. (1990). Admitters and deniers among adolescent sex offenders and their families: A preliminary study. *American Journal of Orthopsychiatry*, **60**, 460–465.

Segal, Z.V., & Marshall, W.L. (1985). Heterosexual social skills in a population of rapists and child molesters. *Journal of Consulting and Clinical Psychology*, **53**, 55–63.

Segal, Z.V., & Marshall, W.L. (1986). Discrepancies between self-efficacy predictions and actual performance in a population of rapists and child molesters. *Cognitive Therapy and Research*, **10**, 363–376.

Segal, Z.V., & Stermac, L.E. (1984). A measure of rapists' attitudes towards women. *International Journal of Law and Psychiatry*, **7**, 219–222.

Segal, Z.V., & Stermac, L.E. (1990). The role of cognition in sexual assault. In W.L. Marshall, D.R. Laws & H.E. Barbaree (Eds.), *Handbook of sexual assault: Issues, theories, and treatment of the offender* (pp. 161–174). New York: Plenum Press.

Seghorn, T., & Cohen, M. (1980). The psychology of the rape assailant. In W. Cerran, A.L. McGarry & C. Petty (Eds.), *Modern legal medicine, psychiatry, and forensic science* (pp. 533–551). Philadelphia: F.A. Davis.

Seidman, B.T., Marshall, W.L., Hudson, S.M., & Robertson, P.J. (1994). An examination of intimacy and loneliness in sex offenders. *Journal of Interpersonal Violence*, **9**, 518–534.

Seligman, M. (1970). On the generality of the laws of learning. *Psychological Review*, **77**, 406–418.

Senchak, M., & Leonard, K.E. (1992). Attachment styles and marital adjustment among newlywed couples. *Journal of Social and Personal Relationships*, **9**, 51–64.

Serber, M. (1970). Shame aversion therapy. *Journal of Behavior Therapy and Experimental Psychiatry*, **1**, 213–215.

Serber, M. (1972). Shame aversion therapy with and without heterosexual retraining. In R.D. Rubin, J.D. Henderson, H. Fensterheim & L.P. Ullmann (Eds.), *Advances in behavior therapy: Proceedings of the Fourth Conference of the Association for Advancement of Behavior Therapy* (pp.115–119). New York: Academic Press.

Serber, M., & Keith, C.G. (1974). The Atascadero project: Model of a sexual retraining program for incarcerated homosexual pedophiles. *Journal of Homosexuality*, **1**, 87–97.

Seto, M. (1992). *Victim blame, empathy, and disinhibition of sexual arousal to rape in community males and incarcerated rapists.* Unpublished Masters Thesis, Queen's University, Kingston, Ontario.

Shaffer, L.F. (1936). *The psychology of adjustment: An objective approach to mental hygiene.* Boston: Houghton Mifflin.

Shaffer, L.F. (1947). The problem of psychotherapy. *American Psychologist*, **2**, 459–467.

Shapiro, M.B. (1961). The single case in fundamental clinical psychological research. *British Journal of Medical Psychology*, **34**, 255–262.

Shapiro, M.B., & Nelson, E.H. (1955). An investigation of an abnormality of cognitive functioning in a co-operative young psychotic: An example of the application of experimental method to the single case. *Journal of Clinical Psychology*, **11**, 344–351.

Shavelson, R.J., Hubner, J.J., & Stanton, G.C. (1976). Self concept: Validation of construct interpretations. *Review of Educational Research*, **46**, 407–441.

Shaver, P., & Hazan, C. (1987). Being lonely, falling in love: Perspectives from attachment theory. *Journal of Social Behavior and Personality*, **2**, 105–124.

Shaw, T. & Schlank, A.M. (1992, October). Treating sexual offenders who deny their guilt. Paper presented at the Annual Research and Treatment Conference of the Association for the Treatment of Sexual Abusers, Portland, OR.

Shoben, E.J. (1949). Psychotherapy as a problem in learning theory. *Psychological Bulletin*, **46**, 366–392.

Shrauger, J.S. (1975). Responses to evaluation as a function of initial self-perceptions. *Psychological Bulletin*, **82**, 581–596.

Silberstein, L.R., Striegel-Moore, R.H., Timko, C., & Rodin, J. (1988). Behavioral and psychological implications of body dissatisfaction: Do men and women differ? *Sex Roles*, **19**, 219–232.

Simpson, J.A., Rhodes, W.S., & Nelligan, J.S. (1992). Support seeking and support giving within couples in an anxiety-provoking situation: The role of attachment styles. *Journal of Personality and Social Psychology*, **62**, 434–446.

Sizonenko, P.C. (1978). Endocrinology in preadolescents and adolescents. *American Journal of Diseases of Children*, **132**, 704–712.

Skinner, B.F. (1938). *The behavior of organisms: An experimental analysis*. New York: Appleton-Century.

Skinner, B.F. (1953). *Science and human behavior*. New York: Macmillan.

Sloane, R.B., Staples, F.R., Cristol, A.H., Yorkson, N.J., & Whipple, K. (1975). *Psychotherapy versus behavior therapy*. Cambridge, MA: Harvard University Press.

Smallbone, S.W., & Dadds, M.R. (1998). Childhood attachment and adult attachment in incarcerated adult male sex offenders. *Journal of Interpersonal Violence*, **13**, 555–573.

Smallbone, S.W., & Dadds, M.R. (in press). Attachment and coercive sexual behaviour. *Sexual Abuse: A Journal of Research and Treatment*.

Smearson, G., & Byrne, D. (1987). The effects of R-rated violence and erotica, individual differences and victim characteristics on acquaintance of rape proclivity. *Journal of Research in Personality*, **21**, 171–184.

Snowdon, R. (1984). Working with incest offenders: Excuses, excuses, excuses. *Aegis*, **35**, 56–63.

Snyder, M. (1984) When belief creates reality. In L. Berkowitz (Ed.) Advances in experimental social psychology (Vol. 18, pp. 248–306). New York: Academic Press.

Solomon, R.L., & Brush, E.S. (1956). Experimentally derived conceptions of anxiety and aversion. In M.R. Jones (Ed.), *Nebraska Symposium on motivation*, Vol. 4 (pp. 212–305). Lincoln, NE: University of Nebraska Press.

Soothill, K.L., & Gibbens, T.C.N. (1978). Recidivism of sexual offenders: A reappraisal. *British Journal of Criminology*, **18**, 267–276.

Spencer, A. (1998). *Working with sex offenders in prisons and through release to the community: A handbook*. Edinburgh: Scottish Prison Service.

Spencer, S.J., Josephs, R.A., & Steele, C.M. (1993). Low self-esteem: The uphill struggle for self-integrity. In R.F. Baumeister (Ed.), *Self-esteem: The puzzle of low self-regard* (pp. 21–36). New York: Plenum Press.

Stangor, C., & Ford, T.E. (1992). Accuracy and expectancy-confirming processing orientations and the development of stereotypes and prejudice. *European Review of Social Psychology*, **3**, 57–89.

Staples, F.R., Sloane, R.B., Whipple, K., Cristol, A.H., & Yorkson, N.J. (1975). Differences between behavior therapists and psychotherapists. *Archives of General Psychiatry*, **32**, 1517–1522.

Steele, N. (1995). Cost effectiveness of treatment. In B.K. Schwartz & H.R. Cellini (Eds.), *The sex offender: Corrections, treatment and legal practice* (pp. 4.1–4.19). Kingston, NJ: Civic Research Institute.

Steenman, H., Nelson, C., & Viesti, C. (1989). Developing coping strategies for high-risk situations. In D.R. Laws (Ed.), *Relapse prevention with sex offenders* (pp. 178–187). New York: Guilford Press.

Stermac, L.E., & Quinsey, V.L. (1985). Social competence among rapists. *Behavioral Assessment*, **8**, 171–185.

Stermac, L.E., & Segal, Z.V. (1989). Adult sexual contact with children: An examination of cognitive factors. *Behavior Therapy*, **20**, 573–584.

Stermac, L.E., Segal, Z.V., & Gillis, R. (1990). Social and cultural factors in sexual assault. In W.L. Marshall, D.R. Laws & H.E. Barbaree (Eds.), *Handbook of sexual assault: Issues, theories, and treatment of the offender* (pp. 143–159). New York: Plenum Press.

Stevenson, I., & Wolpe, J. (1960). Recovery from sexual deviation through overcoming non-sexual neurotic responses. *American Journal of Psychiatry*, **116**, 737–742.

Stille, R.G., Malamuth, N.M., & Schallow, J.R. (1987, August). *Prediction of rape proclivity by rape myth attitudes, and hostility toward women*. Paper presented at the 95th Annual Meeting of the American Psychological Association, New York.

Storr, A. (1972). *Human destructiveness*. New York: Morrow.

Storr, A. (1980). *The art of psychotherapy* (2nd edn). New York: Routledge.

Stotland, E. (1969). Exploratory investigations in empathy. In L. Berkowitz (Ed.) *Advances in experimental social psychology* (Vol. 4), (pp. 271–314). New York: Academic Press.

Strauman, T.J., & Higgins, E.T. (1988). Self-discrepancies and predictors of vulnerability to distinct syndromes of chronic emotional distress. *Journal of Personality*, **56**, 685–707.

Strauss, A., & Corbin, J. (1990). *Basics of qualitative research: Grounded theory procedures and techniques*. Newbury Park, CA: Sage.

Swan, G.E., & McDonald, M.L. (1978). Behavior therapy in practice: A national survey of behavior therapists. *Behavior Therapy*, **9**, 799–807.

Swann, W.B., Hixon, J.G., & De La Ronde, C. (1991). Embracing the bitter "truth": Negative self-concepts and marital commitment. *Psychological Science*, **3**, 118–121.

Swanson, D.W. (1968). Adult sexual abuse of children. *Diseases of the Nervous System*, **29**, 677–683.

Sweet, A.A. (1984). The therapeutic relationship in behavior therapy. *Clinical Psychology Review*, **4**, 253–272.

Tanay, E. (1969). Psychiatric study of homicide. *American Journal of Psychiatry*, **125**, 1252–1257.

Tarlow, E.M., & Haaga, D.A. (1996). Negative self-concept: Specificity to depressive symptoms and relation to positive and negative affectivity. *Journal of Research in Personality*, **30**, 120–127.

Taylor, F.G., & Marshall, W.L. (1977). Experimental analysis of a cognitive/behavioral therapy for depression. *Cognitive Therapy and Research*, **1**, 59–72.

Tesch, S.A. (1985). The psychosocial intimacy questionnaire: Validation studies and an investigation of sex roles. *Journal of Social and Personal Relationships*, **2**, 471–488.

Thornton, D. (1997, October). *Is relapse prevention really necessary?* Paper presented at the 16th Annual Research and Treatment Conference of the Association for the Treatment of Sexual Abusers. Arlington, VA.

Thornton, D. (1998a). *Sexual reconviction over a sixteen year follow-up in English data.* Unpublished data, Programs Division, English Prison Service, Home Office, London.

Thornton, D. (1998b, October). *Reliability, factor structure and external validity of a standard phallometric protocol.* Paper presented at the 17th Annual Research and Treatment Conference of the Association for the Treatment of Sexual Abusers, Vancouver, BC.

Thorpe, J.G., Schmidt, E., & Castell, D.A. (1963). A comparison of positive and negative (aversive) conditioning in the treatment of homosexuality. *Behaviour Research and Therapy, 1,* 357–362.

Tice, D.M. (1993). The social motivations of people with low self-esteem. In R.F. Baumeister (Ed.), *Self-esteem: The puzzle of low self-regard* (pp. 37–53). New York: Plenum Press.

Tingle, D., Barnard, G.W. Robbins, L., Newman, G., & Hutchinson, D. (1986). Childhood and adolescent characteristics of pedophiles and rapists. *International Journal of Law and Psychiatry, 9,* 103–116.

Tolman, E.C. (1948). Cognitive maps in rats and men. *Psychological Review, 55,* 189–208.

Tolman, E.C. (1952). A cognitive motivation model. *Psychological Review, 59,* 389–400.

Traupmann, J., Hatfield, E., & Wexler, P. (1983). Equity and sexual satisfaction in dating couples. *British Journal of Social Psychology, 22,* 33–40.

Travin, S., & Protter, B. (1993). *Sexual perversion: Integrated treatment approaches for the clinician.* New York: Plenum Press.

Truax, C.B., & Carkuff, R.R. (1967). *Toward effective counseling and psychotherapy.* Chicago: Aldine.

Vallerand, R.J., Pelletier, L.G., & Gagné, F. (1991). On the multidimensional versus unidimensional perspectives on self-esteem: A test using the group-comparison approach. *Social Behavior and Personality, 19,* 121–132.

van Dijk, J.A.M., & Mayhew, P. (1992). *Criminal victimization in the industrial world.* The Hague, Netherlands: Directorate for Crime Prevention.

Ward, T. (in press). Sexual offenders' cognitive distortions as implicit theories. *Aggression and Violent Behavior: A Review Journal.*

Ward, T., Fon, C., Hudson, S.M., & McCormack, J. (1998). A descriptive model of dysfunctional cognitions in child molesters. *Journal of Interpersonal Violence, 13,* 129–155.

Ward, T., & Hudson, S.M. (1996). Relapse prevention: A critical analysis. *Sexual Abuse: A Journal of Research and Treatment, 8,* 177–200.

Ward, T., & Hudson, S.M. (1998). Relapse prevention: Conceptual innovations. Unpublished manuscript, Canterbury University, Christchurch, New Zealand.

Ward, T., Hudson, S.M., & France, K.G. (1993). Self-reported reasons for offending behavior in the child molester. *Annals of Sex Research, 6,* 139–148.

Ward, T., Hudson, S.M., Johnston, L., & Marshall, W.L. (1997). Cognitive distortions in sex offenders: An integrative review. *Clinical Psychology Review, 17,* 479–507.

Ward, T., Hudson, S.M., & Keenan, T. (1998). A self regulation model of the sexual offense process. Unpublished manuscript, Canterbury University, Christchurch, New Zealand.

Ward, T., Hudson, S.M., & McCormack, J. (1997). Attachment style, intimacy deficits, and sexual offending. In B.K. Schwartz & H.R. Cellini (Eds.), *The sex offender: New insights, treatment innovations, and legal developments* (Vol. II) (pp. 2.1–2.14). Kingston, NJ: Civic Research Institute.

Ward, T., Hudson, S.M., & Marshall, W.L. (1994). The abstinence violation effect in child molesters. *Behaviour Research and Therapy, 32,* 431–437.

Ward, T., Hudson, S.M., & Marshall, W.L. (1995). Cognitive distortions and affective deficits in sex offenders: A cognitive deconstructionist interpretation. *Sexual Abuse: A Journal of Research and Treatment*, **7**, 67–83.

Ward, T., Hudson, S.M., & Marshall, W.L. (1996). Attachment style in sex offenders: A preliminary study. *Journal of Sex Research*, **33**, 17–26.

Ward, T., Hudson, S.M., Marshall, W.L., & Siegert, R.J. (1995). Attachment style and intimacy deficits in sex offenders: A theoretical framework. *Sexual Abuse: A Journal of research and Treatment*, **7**, 317–335.

Ward, T., Hudson, S.M., & Siegert, R.J. (1995). A critical comment on Pithers' relapse prevention model. *Sexual Abuse: A Journal of Research and Treatment*, **7**, 167–175.

Ward, T., Louden, K., Hudson, S.M., & Marshall, W.L. (1995). A descriptive model of the offense chain for child molesters. *Journal of Interpersonal Violence*, **10**, 452–472.

Ward, T., McCormack, J., & Hudson, S.M. (1997). Sexual offenders' perceptions of their intimate relationships. *Sexual Abuse: A Journal of Research and Treatment*, **9**, 57–74.

Waring, E.M., & Reddon, J.R. (1983). The measurement of intimacy in marriage. *Journal of Clinical Psychology*, **39**, 53–57.

Watson, J.B. (1913). Psychology as the behaviorist views it. *Psychological Review*, **20**, 158–177.

Watson, J.B. (1914). *An introduction to comparative psychology*. New York: Holt.

Watson, J.B. (1919). *Psychology from the standpoint of a behaviorist*. Philadelphia: Lippincott.

Watson, J.B. (1924). *Behaviorism*. Chicago: The People's Institute.

Weinrott, M.R., & Saylor, M. (1991). Self-report of crimes committed by sex offenders. *Journal of Interpersonal Violence*, **6**, 286–300.

Wells, L.E., & Marwell, G. (1976). *Self-esteem*. Beverly Hills, CA: Sage Publications.

West, M.L., & Sheldon-Keller, A.E. (1994). *Patterns of relating: An adult attachment perspective*. New York: Guilford Press.

White, G.L. (1981). Jealousy and partner's perceived notion for attraction to a rival. *Social Psychology Quarterly*, **49**, 24–30.

Whitman, W.P., & Quinsey, V.L. (1981). Heterosocial skill training for institutionalized rapists and child molesters. *Canadian Journal of Behavioral Science*, **13**, 105–114.

Wickramasekera, I. (1976). Aversive behavior rehearsal for sexual exhibitionism. *Behavior Therapy*, **7**, 167–176.

Wiener, R.L., Wiener, A.T., & Grisso, T. (1989). Empathy and biased assimilation of testimonies in cases of alleged rape. *Law & Human Behaviour*, **13**, 343–355.

Williams, C.A. (1990). Biopsychosocial elements of empathy: A multidimensional model. *Issues in Mental Health Nursing*, **11**, 155–174.

Williams, J.M.G., Watts, F.N., Macleod, C., & Mathews, A. (1997). *Cognitive psychology and emotional disorders* (2nd edn). Chichester: Wiley.

Williams, L.M., & Finkelhor, D. (1990). The characteristics of incestuous fathers: A review of recent studies. In W.L. Marshall, D.R. Laws & H.E. Barbaree (Eds.), *Handbook of sexual assault: Issues, theories, and treatment of the offender* (pp. 231–255). New York: Plenum Press.

Williams, S.M., & Khanna, A. (1990, June). Empathy training for sex offenders. Paper presented at the Third Symposium on Violence and Aggression, Saskatoon, Canada.

Wills, T.A. (1981). Downward comparison principles in social psychology. *Psychological Bulletin*, **90**, 245–271.

Wilson, G.T., & Evans, I.M. (1976). Adult behavior therapy and the therapist–client relationship. In C.M. Franks & G.T. Wilson (Eds.), *Advances in behavior therapy* (pp. 143–162). New York: Brunner/Mazel.

Wilson, R.J., & Langevin, R. (1998). *Emotional congruence in sex offenders against children: A review and empirical validation.* Submitted for publication.

Wittgenstein, L. (1953). *Philosophical investigations* (translation by G.E.M. Anscombe). Oxford: Blackwell.

Wolpe, J. (1958). *Psychotherapy by reciprocal inhibition.* Stanford, CA: Stanford University Press.

Worling, J., & Curwen, T. (1998). *The adolescent sexual offender project: A 10-year follow-up study.* Report on the SAFE-T Program, Thistletown Regional Centre for Children and Adolescents, Toronto: Ontario Ministry of Community and Social Services.

Wormith, J.S. (1986). Assessing deviant sexual arousal: Psychological and cognitive aspects. *Advances in Behaviour Research and Therapy, 8,* 101–137.

Wormith, J.S., Bradford, J.M.W., Pawlak, A., Borzecki, M., & Zohar, A. (1988). The assessment of deviant sexual arousal as a function of intelligence, instructional set and alcohol ingestion. *Canadian Journal of Psychiatry, 33,* 800–808.

Wright, R.C., & Schneider, S.L. (1997). Deviant sexual fantasies as motivated self-deception. In B.K. Schwartz & H.R. Cellini (Eds.), *The sex offender: New insights, treatment innovations and legal developments* (pp. 8.1–8.14). Kingston, NJ: Civic Research Institute.

Yates, A.J. (1958). The application of learning theory to the treatment of tics. *Journal of Abnormal and Social Psychology, 56,* 175–182.

Yates, E., Barbaree, H.E., & Marshall, W.L. (1984). Anger and deviant sexual arousal. *Behavior Therapy, 15,* 287–294.

Zahn-Waxler, C., & Radke-Yarrow, M. (1990). The origins of empathic concern. *Motivation and Emotion, 14,* 107–130.

Zamble, E., Hadad, M., Mitchell, J.B., & Cutmore, T.R.H. (1985). Pavlovian conditioning of sexual arousal: First and second order effects. *Journal of Experimental Psychology: Animal Behavior Processes, 11,* 598–610.

Zamble, E., Mitchell, J.B., & Findlay, H. (1986). Pavlovian conditioning of sexual arousal: Parametric and background manipulations. *Journal of Experimental Psychology: Animal Behavior Processes, 12,* 403–411.

Zilbergeld, B. (1978). *Male sexuality.* Boston: Little, Brown.

Zilboorg, G. (1938). Loneliness. *Atlantic Monthly,* January, 14–19.

Zillman, D. (1989). Effects of prolonged consumption of pornography. In D. Zillman & J. Bryant (Eds.), *Pornography: Research advances and policy considerations* (pp. 127–157). Hillsdale, NJ: Lawrence Erlbaum.

Zuckerman, M. (1979). Attribution of success and failure revisited, or the motivational bias is alive and well in attribution theory. *Journal of Personality, 47,* 245–287.

INDEX

Index compiled by Liz Granger

Related titles of interest...

WILEY

Handbook of Offender Assessment and Treatment
CLIVE HOLLIN
0471 988588   December 1999   650pp   Hardback

Handbook of the Psychology of Interviewing
AMINA MEMON and RAY BULL
0471 974439 February 1999 380pp   Hardback

The Handbook of Forensic Psychology
2nd Edition
ALLEN K. HESS and IRVING B. WEINER
0471 177717 December 1998 832pp   Hardback

Changing Lives of Crime and Drugs
Intervening with Substance-Abusing Offenders
GLENN D. WALTERS
0471 97658X 162pp February 1998 Hardback
0471 978418 162pp February 1998 Paperback

The Psychology of Criminal Conduct
RONALD BLACKBURN
0471 961752 1995 506pp Paperback